From a 'Necessary Evil' to the
Art of Contingency

From a 'Necessary Evil' to the Art of Contingency

Michael Oakeshott's Conception of Political Activity

Suvi Soininen

imprint-academic.com

Published in the UK by Imprint Academic
PO Box 200, Exeter EX5 5YX, UK

Published in the USA by Imprint Academic
Philosophy Documentation Center
PO Box 7147, Charlottesville, VA 22906-7147, USA

ISBN 1-84540-006-2

A CIP catalogue record for this book is available from the
British Library and US Library of Congress

imprint-academic.com/idealists

Contents

Acknowledgements

First of all, I would like to thank Professor Kari Palonen, who served as an invaluable source of inspiration and generosity as the supervisor of my doctoral thesis, of which this book is a revised version. In the same breath I would also like to thank the project "Polity, Contingency and Conceptual Change," led by Kari Palonen and financed by the Academy of Finland, for its support and for providing me with the financial support necessary in order to complete this work.

I would also like to extend my gratitude to Professors Pertti Ahonen and Kyösti Pekonen, who were the first to review this manuscript.

Thanks also to Professor Bruce Haddock, who supervised me during my three-month visit at the University of Wales, Swansea, in 2001.

Steven Gerencser has offered me countless valuable comments and I would also like to thank him for agreeing to act as my opponent when I defended my thesis. I would also like to thank Professor Quentin Skinner, whom I have had the pleasure of meeting on several occasions, for offering me invaluable information on Oakeshott's academic life, Cambridge and the London School of Economics and Politics, as well as for the genuine interest he took in my work.

I would also like to take this opportunity to thank Leena Subra for reading and commenting on my work. I also wish to thank Anitta Kananen, Kia Lindroos and Sari Roman, as well as the other participants of the research seminars organized by the unit of Political Science at the University of Jyväskylä.

The Michael Oakeshott Association and its web pages have been invaluable assets in the completion of this work. Leslie Marsh's efforts in this field are indescribable, and I would also like to thank him for his support of my work.

Efraim Podoksik provided a generous and detailed critique of my manuscript from which this book has greatly benefited.

I would also like to thank my friends for their support, especially Anssi Välimäki for providing me with so much intellectual inspiration and support throughout the process of writing this book.

I also want to thank my family; my sister Sari Soininen, her husband Timo Tuovila and their children, as well as my father, Antti Soininen. My mother Raili Soininen has inspired and guided my interest in reading and studying throughout my life. Thanks also to my mother-in-law, Aili Rehtola.

Last but not least, I would like especially to thank my husband Antti Rehtola, to whom I dedicate this book.

Abbreviations

Works by Oakeshott

EM   Experience and Its Modes (1933)

SP   The Social and Political Doctrines of
      Contemporary Europe (1939)

RP   Rationalism in Politics (1962, new and expanded
      edition 1991)

OHC   On Human Conduct (1975)

OH   On History and Other Essays (1983)

VLL   The Voice of Liberal Learning (1989)

MPME Morality and Politics in Modern Europe (1993)

RPML Religion, Politics and the Moral Life (1993)

PFPS The Politics of Faith and the Politics of Skepticism
      (1996)

WH   What is History? and other essays (2004)

A remark on presenting references in the study

Oakeshott references are usually given with the year of the
first published edition of a given essay or article, its title, the
abbreviation of the essay collection and page number. The
appearance of a question mark in the reference means that the
article/essay in question has been published posthumously
and an approximation of the date it was written is provided
when necessary in order to follow chronological order. Estimated dates of publication are provided by the editors of a
given collection if not otherwise noted. The original publish-
ing forum is also mentioned when necessary. *The Politics of
Faith and the Politics of Skepticism* and *What is History? and other
essays* were published posthumously in their entirety.

CHAPTER I

Introduction: Why Oakeshott?

1: Oakeshott and Politics: The Perspective

It is quite common to speak about Michael Oakeshott's (1901-1990) conception of politics. One famous formula is, of course, Oakeshott's metaphor of politics as a "bottomless and boundless sea; there is neither harbour for shelter nor floor for anchorage, neither starting-place nor appointed destination."[1] As Oakeshott himself anticipated, this characterization of politics has affected many people representing many different genres: for progressivists, it represents the death of ideals, but it also delights *die Schwindelfreien*,[2] who feel no vertigo in the face of it and welcome its anti-foundationality. Equally famously, politics appears as the custody of a manner of living, reflecting Oakeshott's reputation as a conservative. Furthermore, some have characterized his conception of politics as a "politics of conversation," further accentuating its anti-foundational and rhetorical nature. For me, none of these characterizations alone is satisfactory. Yet, each one has its own place in the portrait of Oakeshottian politics that I paint in this book.

My main theme can perhaps best be expressed by presenting two quotations. In 1939, Oakeshott wrote on politics:

> Political action involves mental vulgarity, not merely because it entails the concurrence and support of those who are mentally vulgar, but because of the false simplification of human life implied in even the best of its purposes.[3]

In 1975, politics was characterized instead as calling for:

[1] M. Oakeshott 1951, *Political Education*, RP, p.60.
[2] Ibid.
[3] M. Oakeshott 1939, *The Claims of Politics*, RPML, p. 93. The article was first published as a part of larger symposium in *Scrutiny*, 8, 1939, pp. 146-51.

> ...so exact a focus of attention and so uncommon self-restraint that one is not astonished to find this mode of human relationship to be as rare as it is excellent.[4]

Whereas in Oakeshott's early thought politics was seen as better suited to people who were mentally simple or vulgar, especially in comparison with poets and philosophers, in the later account the ideal type of politics required a specific and high level of political intelligence.[5] Thus, although one need not need take all of Oakeshott's most pointed expressions literally, the differences between the texts from the late 1930s and the mid 1970s, which is also the period examined in this book, are still so great that I find it important to pointedly examine the *development* of his conception of political activity in order to do justice to the flexibility and sensitivity exhibited by his political thought in its contemporary context without compromising any of its originality.

I will argue that it is incorrect to speak about Oakeshott's conception of political activity as such, as it must be dissolved into many different conceptions. It might initially seem as though there are only slight differences in nuance between his texts on politics or political activity, but in the long run I think we can argue that there is a clear shift in Oakeshott's understanding. First, his *attitude* towards political activity shifts from near disdain towards what could be called applauding of politics. Second, the *elements* that Oakeshott attaches to his description of political activity imply an increasing emphasis on politics as a *reflective* activity as opposed to the habitual continuation or preservation of a political tradition.

In short, then, I examine in the following why and how Oakeshott's attitude towards political activity changed. Further, I deal with the question of what *specific aspects* are present in Michael Oakeshott's conception(s) of politics and the related terms in the context of other contemporary ideas and theories. How does Oakeshott's vocabulary change over the course of this period? Are these changes significant? What kind of relevance does Oakeshott have in the contemporary discussions on political theory and thinking? These questions form the main body of the problematic examined in this book.

I will examine Oakeshott's conception of political activity in the British context, mainly within the specific context of post-

[4]   OHC, p.180.
[5]   Ibid.

war political thought. It is important to clarify some of the aspects which contributed to my decision to limit my examination to this primary context. First, in my view there *is* something called "British postwar political thought," which should be distinguished from the broader genre of "Anglophone political thought" that includes the United States. Secondly, I claim that Oakeshott occupies a significant place in the sphere of British postwar political thinking. Thirdly, we must take a specific interest in the relationship between the two. My assertion in this book is that the examination of Oakeshott's vocabulary and its connection to the vocabularies of other contemporary thinkers enables us to uncover innovative ways of conceptualizing the 'political' and 'politics' in relation to some key concepts of British political thought. I also argue that Oakeshott's political thought develops through interaction with his interpretations of 'real' contemporary British politics; Oakeshott's paradigm conception of political activity is inherently British.

The perspective from which I approach Oakeshott's *oeuvre* and the British and Anglo-Saxon debate is that of an "outsider." By this I mean that I retain a certain detachment from the academic discussions and research conventions of Great Britain, which allows me to focus my research on this proximate period. Of course, some problems do arise in relation to this specific period. To use an Oakeshottian term, the postwar discussion surrounding politics is already so "thickly orchestrated" that any attempt to write a kind of overall 'truth' about it would be futile. This, however, is by no means my intention here. Rather, placing a rather limited bulk of texts, i.e. Oakeshott's postwar *oeuvre*, at the centre of my study and examining them in relation to other texts allows me to seriously examine even the fine nuances in the use of concepts. My aim is not to produce any great sweep of political theory, but to contribute to the re-evaluation of Oakeshott's work. Also, I leave Oakeshott's early works largely unexamined, as politics was not his major concern during that time.

Despite a very recent expansion in the field of Oakeshott research,[6] in general, it can be said that Oakeshott remains rather unknown outside the English-speaking academic

---

[6]   See, e.g., S. Gerencser 2000, *The Skeptic's Oakeshott*, A. Farr 1998, *Sartre's Radicalism and Oakeshott's Conservatism*, the five books in *British Idealist Studies: Series 1*, Imprint Academic, 2003-04.

world. This is rather curious considering that he has often been described as the most significant English political philosopher of the 20th century. In part, his being persistently labelled as a High Tory or, to a lesser extent, a Libertarian is certainly a factor in his unfamiliarity. In the "ism" discussions, the general view on Oakeshott is often oversimplified to the extent that his significance may seem to be confined exclusively to them. And it is in this area that my insistence on the recognition of changes in his conception of politics would most likely be rejected. This is, however, not to say that there are no grounds for also discussing Oakeshott in terms of "isms." Especially in his early works, Oakeshott contributed to the tradition of British Idealism. He also published a few 'libertarian' texts (*Contemporary British Politics* 1948, *The Political Economy of Freedom* 1949) and described himself as having a "conservative disposition" in the 1950s.[7] It should also be noted here that for him, the latter meant the propensity to "enjoy what is present and available" and experience changes as deprivation as opposed to the "ignorance" and "apathy" by which those who "notice nothing" and "esteem nothing" react to changes – not as a 'party-ism'.[8] Yet, the fact that many of Oakeshott's contemporaries viewed him as "the ultimate conservative" with a political education that was "a striking contrast to the liberal humanism of Wallas and the stimulus of Laski" cannot be ignored.[9] The Labour MP Richard Crossman's description of Oakeshott's specialities as centring on "deflating and debunking the ideas which have been the motive force of British democracy" may, for example, complicate Oakeshott's own understanding of the separation between theory and practice.[10]

From the perspective of my problematic, the earlier research can be divided into three main categories. To begin with, Oakeshott's early philosophical presuppositions are alleged to have essentially remained intact throughout his work. The chief argument concerning his political thinking is that it either reflects or 'fits' his idealist presumptions. Paul Franco's

---

[7]   M. Oakeshott 1956, *On Being Conserative*, RP, p. 409.
[8]   Ibid.
[9]   R.H.S. Crossman 1958, p. 135.
[10] Ibid.

The Political Philosophy of Michael Oakeshott (1990) is a well-argued example of this view. Franco emphasizes Oakeshott's Hegelian influences and the underlying theory of experience as the key to his interpretation. Franco's book also examines Oakeshott in the context of postwar political thought and thus offers one excellent point of comparison for the present study.

The 'intact' assertion is partly rejected by the second type of interpretation, which identifies three distinct phases in Oakeshott's work, i.e. the early phase, the postwar phase and the late production. It is argued that Oakeshott's postwar texts comprise a departure from his earlier idealism by placing politics at the centre of his sphere of interest and by dropping philosophy from the top of the hierarchy of experience. In his essays in *Rationalism in Politics*, Oakeshott is said to express a rich "dialectical understanding"[11] and to view "philosophy as parasitic upon and as non-contributory to the conversation,"[12] only to return to his even "more extreme idealist claims"[13] of separating philosophy entirely from politics in *On Human Conduct*. In sketching an overall picture of Oakeshott's career I have largely ignored both the 'intact' and 'return' types of interpretation in this book. Both, however, include many thematic insights on various aspects of Oakeshott's work which are also of value to this study and which, as such, are referred to accordingly.

Thus, one point of departure in my reading of Oakeshott's postwar production is to argue in favour of *the thesis of significant changes* in his 'thinking' and vocabulary, the relations of which are by no means transparent. Naturally, continuities exist alongside changes; it is not my intention to argue that there is any sudden reversal of philosophical orientation or any kind of schizophrenic lack of consistency in his works. Continuities can indeed be found in Oakeshott's themes, topics and rhetoric, but not in the sense of writing under a certain system of philosophy, for example.

For a more general account, it is important to note that Oakeshott's overall *oeuvre* escapes any easy categorization. He did not publish an extensive number of major books, but they present such a profound mastery of philosophy, political philosophy and the philosophy of history that he is entitled to be

[11] H. Pitkin 1976, p. 316.
[12] T. Modood 1980, p. 320.
[13] H. Pitkin 1976, p. 316.

referred to as a classic of 20th century thought in all the aforementioned genres.

Oakeshott began his academic career in Cambridge at Gonville and Caius College, where he studied history, acted as a fellow and taught until the year 1949. He was elected to the chair of Political Science at the London School of Economics and Political Science in 1951, from which he retired in 1968.[14] His major publications include the doctoral thesis *Experience and its Modes*, published in 1933, the essay collection *Rationalism in Politics*, published in 1962, *On Human Conduct*, published in 1975 and *On History*, which was published in 1983.

His first philosophical work, *Experience and Its Modes*, was an original contribution to the tradition of British Idealism especially after F.H. Bradley. The book indicated his enduring independence in relation to prevailing academic moods; in this case to logical positivism. Here, Oakeshott defines philosophy as the search for perfect coherence, the totality of experience. Worlds of historical, scientific and practical experience present abstract and defective modes of experience, but only from the standpoint of philosophy.

The conception of philosophy and the presentation of the modes of experience and their inter-relationship remain at the core of the main theoretical disputes concerning Oakeshott's production today. Very generally, it can be said that here Oakeshott kept theory separate from practice; the modes of experience were by definition destined to remain limited worlds resting on unquestioned presuppositions, whereas philosophy was seen as aspiring to transcendence in the absolute coherence of experience.

The essay collection *Rationalism in Politics* is arguably the most famous of his works. The book was first published in 1962 and it soon evoked intense discussion. The two most famous pieces in this collection are the title essay *Rationalism in Politics* (1947) and *Political Education* (1951), both of which were rather heatedly viewed as examples of doctrinaire conservatism. Particularly the latter text had already caused a small storm in a tea-cup when it was delivered as his inaugural

---

[14] For a short biography, see Robert Grant's (1990) presentation in *Thinkers of Our Time: Oakeshott*, pp. 11-23.

lecture at the LSE;[15] the 'conservative skeptic' filling Harold Laski's chair was severely criticized both within the School and academic circles. In these essays, Oakeshott presents his anti-foundational understanding of political activity, although they can also be read as contributions to the discussion and understanding of the teaching of political philosophy or the theory of human knowledge – just to mention a few possibilities. The versatility of Oakeshott's thought is extensive in this respect.

On Human Conduct is composed of three intertwined essays: *On the Understanding of Human Conduct, On the Civil Condition* and *On the Character of a Modern European State*. This book is primarily a refined philosophical undertaking, defining human conduct as conditional and intelligent free action and the civil condition as a mode of association in terms of its rules. The question of whether Oakeshott has modified his original account of the distinction between theory and practice in this book is basically unsolvable, although a stand on the matter will be taken at the end of this book, although acknowledging its partiality. Here, I feel it safe to say that the act of theorizing as an unconditional engagement requires a different kind of understanding than that which is required particularly in engaging in practical conduct.

On History presents a philosophical understanding of history as a mode of enquiry. Oakeshott elaborates the central notions of writing history, such as the notions of past and change. Similarly to the understanding presented in *On Human Conduct*, the central concept of *contingency* refers here to a principle of understanding that is circumstantial in that it is distinguished from something that is necessary or essential.

Oakeshott is famous both for his style of writing, which is admittedly sometimes difficult to grasp but always well-considered and beautiful, and for his avoidance of 'minute' philosophy. He is also notorious for his scarce presentation of references in his work. Yet it is clear that Oakeshott was exceptionally learned in the history of philosophy and political thought and his thought can be examined from the perspective of its relation to many great (and smaller) names of the

[15] For the 'Fabian' history of the School and its 'composition' during Oakeshott's time, see R. Dahrendorf 1995: *LSE. A History of the London School of Economics and Political Science, 1885-1995.*

'canon'.[16] However, Oakeshott also participated in contemporary discussions both in his essays and in his reviews of other authors' works.[17] His activity in *The Journal of Theological Studies* in the 1920s and 1930s indicates the significance of his reflection on religion, however philosophy and politics are also obviously present. In the late 1940s and the early 1950s, Oakeshott was published mainly in the *Cambridge Journal* and, to a lesser extent, in *The English Historical Review*, but his texts also appeared in such forums as *The Times Literary Supplement* and *The Spectator*, making them accessible to a wider audience. The latter was also Oakeshott's main 'public forum' during the 1950s. The later decades were more diffused in this respect. *The Philosophical Quarterly* and *Political Studies* were among the several strictly academic forums in which his work appeared. Additionally, *Crossbow*, which was mostly read by the conservative public, and *The Daily Telegraph* also published Oakeshott's reviews. Yet despite the conservative party bias of some forums, they are more indicative of his continuous intellectual voyage as an historian, a philosopher and a political philosopher than of his possible 'policy-commitments'. And perhaps more than his actual essays, the reviews also reveal him to be a thinker who cannot be described as having lived in an ivory tower in relation to contemporary life and thought.

2: Politics, History and Political Philosophy; Remarks on the Style of Reading and Presentation

At one level *every* political philosopher has concerned himself with what he thinks to be a vital problem of his day... No political thinker concerns himself exclusively with the past any more than he seeks to speak solely to the distant future; the price in both

---

[16] An illuminating example is Wendell John Coats's (2000) book *Oakeshott and His Contemporaries*, in which the 'contemporaries' include such figures as Montaigne, St. Augustine, Hegel, Hobbes, Benjamin Constant, Rousseau and Hume. Aristotle, Bodin and Nietzsche could be added, again just to mention a few.

[17] On Oakeshott's character and influence as a teacher of political thought, see e.g. the symposium on Michael Oakeshott in the *Cambridge Review*, October 1991. Kenneth Minogue's *Michael Oakeshott and the History of Political Thought Seminar* is particularly informative in this respect. As is the case with regard to his character as a teacher, Oakeshott's other academic activities also extend beyond the scope of this study, although it is worth mentioning that he was one of the founders of the *Cambridge Journal* in 1947 (-1952) and acted as a member of the Editorial Board of *Political Theory* from its inception in 1973, for example.

cases would be unintelligibility... At another level, however, many political writings have been intended as something more than *livres de circonstance*; they have been meant as a contribution to the continuing dialogue of Western political philosophy.[18]

Similarly to Sheldon Wolin's aforementioned conception, one can find a version of this 'dual character' of political philosophy, as both actual and enduring, in Oakeshott's thought. In a typically bright sentence he wrote:

Every masterpiece of political philosophy springs from a new vision of the predicament; each is the glimpse of a deliverance or the suggestion of a remedy.[19]

The inspiration of political philosophy that Oakeshott describes here as a human predicament "is a universal appearing everywhere as a particular."[20] And for this reason it is no wonder we can find "an apparently contingent element in the ground and inspiration of a political philosophy, a feeling for the exigencies, the cares, the passions of a particular time, a sensitiveness to the dominant folly of an epoch" in all political philosophy. Whereas Plato and Hobbes are united in their pervading sense of human life as a predicament, the difference between them lies in Plato's thought as animated by "the errors of the Athenian democracy" and Hobbes's thought as coloured by the disputes between those claiming too much "Liberty" or "Authority." In Oakeshott's more recent terms, the examination of Plato's utterances as actions and events in their immediate context and into their links to other contemporary actions in terms of a relationship of contingency represents an inquiry into an '*historical*',[21] i.e. 'dead', past. Instead, if we read Plato as a reflective endeavour of an unhindered impulse with "political experience" as its point of departure, but which is searching for "the permanent character of political activity" on the map of human experience, we approach his thought as philosophy.[22]

---

[18] S. Wolin 1960, p. 25.

[19] Oakeshott 1946, *Introduction to Leviathan*, RP, p. 226.

[20] Ibid.

[21] OH, p. 9

[22] M. Oakeshott 1946-1950, *Political Philosophy*, RPML, pp. 144,151. The essay is estimated to have been written between 1946 and 1950 by Timothy Fuller, the editor of the RPML collection. Later, Oakeshott replaces "political philosophy" with "political theory" and prefers to use "theorizing" for "philosophizing." See M. Oakeshott 1973, *What is Political Theory?*, WH, pp. 391-402; OHC, p. 1. I will only speculate on this change in the concluding chapter, as my chief

However, for Oakeshott, there is also a third way of approaching political philosophy, which is to examine the singularity – not uniqueness – of a given text within the *traditions* of political thought. It is not the fact that Oakeshott distinguishes three distinct traditions of political philosophy that peaks our interest here, but rather the idea that these traditions offer an additional *context* of interpretation for a text of political philosophy. In short, every "masterpiece of political philosophy" has as its context not only the "entire" history of political philosophy as the elucidation of the predicament of mankind, but also "a particular tradition in that history."[23] This is also what rules out the existence of any kind of uniqueness in the case of political philosophies; they always belong to one or another of the main traditions of thought. The singularity that a masterpiece enacts, however, occurs within these traditions since they have the capacity to tolerate and unite internal variety and do not insist upon conformity to a single character.[24] Here, we are one step away from speaking in terms of Pocockian "languages"[25] or Skinnerian "conventions"[26] as being 'appropriate' contexts in which to understand political texts – political philosophy included.

My aim in this book is to find a way to examine Oakeshott's conceptions of politics from all three of these points of view, as I think concentrating on his conception of politics both requires and enables it to a certain degree. I hope to do so without lapsing into irrelevancy, although I must admit that 'combining' a philosophical explanation with an historical one is, for Oakeshott, the equivalent of committing a "'category mistake',"[27] to use Gilbert Ryle's terminology. It is, however, often so notoriously difficult to neatly categorize the two in Oakeshott's own work that I do not see myself as violating his spirit to any great extent in this endeavour. Although Oakeshott wishes to keep the historical mode of understand-

concern lies elsewhere. This also excludes, e.g. examining Oakeshott's 'theory of modality' or his 'theory of plurality'. See T. Nardin 2001, E. Podoksik 2003. Because of the priority of the contemporary context, my work does not focus much attention on Oakeshott's 'Aristotelianism' or 'Hegelianism' etc., also for the simple reason that these aspects have already been examined rather extensively by other scholars. See, e.g., P. Franco 1990b.

[23] Oakeshott 1946, *Introduction to Leviathan*, RP, p. 227.
[24] Ibid.
[25] J. Pocock 1985, p. 19.
[26] Q. Skinner 1972, pp. 154-5.
[27] T. Nardin 2001, p. 42n.

ing separate from philosophy, his main body of production consists of essays, which accommodate both historical and philosophical reflection in a single text.

Today, disputes between textual and contextual methods, normative and 'standpoint-independent' political philosophy, interpretation and over-interpretation, and revisionist and traditional approaches – just to mention a few – definitely leave room for the interpreter of an author's texts to choose her own style of reading. One clear available path would be to faithfully follow the method applied by the author himself. Another option is to carefully report all the significant features and aspects of his works. However, Oakeshott is no methodologist himself. He does not apply any consistent methodology in his work, and, as implied, he moves between different levels of thinking about politics – practical, ideological and philosophical – a bit more liberally than his self-understanding would seem to allow. It is occasionally possible to translate his philosophical conceptions 'back' into the languages of practice or history, as for example the wandering of the metaphor of "conversation" from politics to education and philosophy exemplifies. This operation must, however, be understood as one or another type of *explanation*, not as a prescription. The fact that I also take practical politics into account does not imply that Oakeshott was a covert ideologue, but rather that his thinking is sensitive to the contemporary context. As to the second path, it is not my aim to write a comprehensive study on Oakeshott's entire work, but rather to concentrate on its political aspects, mostly bypassing the level of description.

However, although I do not directly apply any specific method of interpretation in this book, I still utilize some views of conceptual history and the so-called "Cambridge school of history" as well as share some of their commitments, such as treating concepts as Wittgensteinian tools or Weberian instruments in human activities and the understanding of them. In addition, Quentin Skinner's treatment of concepts as "uses in argument" or as "dimensions in linguistic action" is also present in this book.[28] I consider Oakeshott as a conscious contributor to both academic and broader discussions on politics who intends to move his audience and shape the discussions, whether they be contemporary or "eternal," i.e. philosophical, in each individual case.

---

[28] K. Palonen 2003c, p. 17.

As regards the relationship between Oakeshott's conception of politics and the British discussions, my style of reading articles, books reviews and discussions in periodicals and newspapers could be described as a kind of 'dismantling'. I aim at developing a more concentrated view of the understanding of political activity in Great Britain, mainly from the postwar period to the 1970s, than would be possible by merely reflecting on a few 'big names'. I examine Oakeshott's key concepts in relation to both their usage by other writers and their conventions of writing. I end up arguing that Oakeshott's original conception of politics was rather typically 'British' in its emphasis on parliamentary debates and its preference for statesmen over politicians. The shift in this emphasis was completed by 1975, when Oakeshott published his major work, *On Human Conduct.* In this later account of politics, he emphasizes the contingency of human associations and the state, acknowledging more emphatically the role of politics in their arrangements. Oakeshott was by no means merely a detached academic scholar, as is often maintained, but rather intimately involved in contemporary discussions.

Briefly, with regard to my style of reading and presentation in this book: I utilize a consciously one-sided perspective in my reading and interpretation in order to articulate something new and innovative about Oakeshott's political thought, particularly the development of his conception of political activity. My interest is centred more on the discontinuities and conceptual changes in his work than on presenting a kind of great line. After noticing that, especially in terms of the contemporary perspective, some of the most significant changes emphatically take place in his 'smaller' writings, such as book reviews, I ended up emphasizing the inherent inter-textuality that is present in reading Oakeshott's works without representing more summaries of his main texts.[29] As my title suggests, however, the changes in Oakeshott's thought are not treated merely as an internal process, but are also viewed in relation to political events and shifting constellations in politi-

---

[29] I have mainly limited my examination to Oakeshott's published work and some posthumously published texts, as I think my perspective both allows for and perhaps even requires this kind of emphasis. The comprehensive online catalogue of Oakeshott Archives at the Library of the London School of Economics and Political Science, collected in 2001 by Anna Towlson and updated by Efraim Podoksik, has also been an extremely valuable resource both for checking details and gaining an overview of Oakeshott's work.

cal power relationships. Yet, I also limit the overall presentation of the historical events, persons and academic schools of thought that are related to his work by assuming that most of the readers of this volume are already familiar with them.

In a review of R.G. Collingwood's *The Idea of History*, Oakeshott writes: "The task of the historian of ideas, as he saw it, was precisely to understand a writer more profoundly than the writer understood himself,"[30] and the aim of my book is to gain at least a glimpse of this understanding. After all, at the end of the day, all the "flashy technicalities" of methodological reflections are rather irrelevant.[31] The reasons behind the continuing interest in Oakeshott's political philosophy seem to lie in the combination of its vivid awareness of the past, its diagnosis of the contemporary predicament and, above all, its ability to serve as a new touchstone for further thinking. This at least comes close to Oakeshott's own comprehension of a great work of political philosophy, and it certainly corresponds to mine. In the following, I thus hope to present reflections on all three of these aspects in Oakeshott's work on politics.

As to the organization of the book, in Chapter II, I begin by engaging in a closer examination of the earlier interpretations of Oakeshott's thought. In Chapter II.2, which deals with *Liberalism*, I examine Oakeshott's views on politics, individuality and society, particularly in relation to Isaiah Berlin's and Joseph Raz's respective versions of British liberalism. I compare Oakeshott's anti-foundational 'version' of liberalism both to Berlin's conflict-based, individualist "agonistic liberalism" and Raz's more society-based theory. Comparatively, Oakeshott presents a different kind of conception of freedom than that of mainstream liberalism, and he places greater emphasis on the contingent historicity of Western democracies than the aforementioned writers. In these respects, Richard Rorty's "ethnocentric liberalism" offers us a 'natural' point of comparison for Oakeshott's thought, although the American debates surrounding liberalism are otherwise largely neglected in order to retain a contextual closeness to the British discussions. Each version of liberalism as presented by these authors presents a specific understanding of political activity. In Chapter II.3, I examine Oakeshott's persistent legend of conservatism through a contemporary interpreter, Ber-

[30] M. Oakeshott 1947, A Review of R.G. Collingwood, *The Idea of History*, p. 85.
[31] K. R. Minogue 1976, p. 143.

nard Crick, whose own conception of politics surprisingly bears similarities to Oakeshott's. I also focus on Robert Devigne's approximation of Oakeshott to Thatcher's governmental policy – an interpretation in which a 'system' created by a philosopher was 'put into practice' by its exponents. I argue that in the 1940s it would not have been a grave mistake to even liken Oakeshott's views to party conservatism, although the later approximations are usually based on false exaggerations of Oakeshott's conservative disposition. The philosophical "ism" of idealism is examined in Chapter II.4, in which I focus my attention on Steven Gerencser's book *The Skeptic's Oakeshott* (2000), which presents a thorough version of the defence of the thesis of the occurrence of significant shifts in Oakeshott's thinking towards a more skeptical position.

Going through the thesis of the shift in Oakeshott philosophical position helps us to leave philosophical reflection in the background in Chapter III, which focuses on the changes in Oakeshott's use and meaning of the concept of politics, their related vocabulary and their connection to contemporary discussions and ideas on politics. I begin by clarifying the main idea of my examination, which is to assess how Oakeshott's conception of political activity has changed over the years and how this change relates to contemporary discussions on politics, both in terms of affinity and specificity. For this purpose, in the next sections I examine several concepts that are of key importance in terms of understanding Oakeshott's conceptions of politics. As there is an inherent duality in these conceptions – between politics and rationalist politics, the politics of skepticism and faith etc. – which constitutes the continuity of themes in Oakeshott's thinking, it is reflected in the organization of the concepts within the chapters. For example, authority and power are presented as counter, parallel and complementary concepts in Chapter III.2. The treatment of concepts adheres more to a thematic than to a chronological approach, although dates are followed in order to keep track of the changes and shifts in Oakeshott's usage of the vocabulary.

In Chapter III.3, I examine the concepts of ideology and tradition in a similar manner. It is perhaps in this chapter that the change in Oakeshott's conception of political activity becomes most clearly visible. Oakeshott's role in the linguistic turn is also briefly evaluated. It is concluded that he was one of those scholars who were 'ahead' of the mainstream in the social sciences or philosophy in the early 1950s. My view is that Oakeshott's name needs to be added to the list of "exceptions" of 20th century philosophers who have a "lively appreciation of the historicity and mutability of our moral and political concepts."[32] Thus, although my examination is decidedly oriented towards the British and Anglophone discussions mainly from a contemporary perspective, my hope is that it will help to ensure that Oakeshott, along with Martin "Heidegger, R.G. Collingwood, Hannah Arendt and Alasdair MacIntyre," is included amongst the ranks of "Hegel, Kierkekaard and Nietzsche" in this respect.[33] My claim is not that Oakeshott in any sense 'invented' the critical apparatus of, for example, contemporary conceptual history, although I do think that we can justifiably include Oakeshott amongst those thinkers who pioneered the analysis of human conduct in terms of conventions, idioms, languages and practices. He shared their Collingwoodian distrust of perennial questions – the human predicament always changes – and an understanding of the contestability of concepts.[34] Language is treated as constructed and artificial, not referential. As such, one early precept for my study stems from Oakeshott himself:

> It has been the unfortunate illusion of some historians to think that something less than a first-class knowledge of the languages involved in their subject of study will serve their purpose, and to think that a minute and exact attention to the words of a text is unnecessary: they believe themselves to be dealing with things, not words. But the study of a text is a study of its words, and no text will reveal its meaning unless the interpreter goes to it with the questions, 'why this word and not that?', and, 'what precisely, in this literary and historical context, is the connotation of this word?' And the whole answer is never supplied by the text itself.[35]

I hope that, for example, my examination of the concept of tradition, the change in its use and its partial replacement by the concept of practice exemplifies how the choice of words and their specific contexts really does matter in our attempt to

---

[32] T. Ball 1988, p. 4.
[33] Ibid.
[34] T. Ball 2002, p. 25. See W.B. Gallie 1956.
[35] M. Oakeshott 1950/51, A Review of R. H. Barrow: *Introduction to St Augustine. The City of God*, p. 570.

more fully understand the development of Oakeshott's conception of politics.

In Chapter IV, *Rationalism in Politics/Rational Politics*, the earlier discussions are condensed into Oakeshott's different conceptions on politics through his most famous imageries and descriptions of political activity, which are especially distinct in terms of their understanding of contingency. Aspects of agency, anti-foundationalism, contingency and historicity are recalled as central to his view.

In the concluding chapter, *Oakeshott and the Voyage of Theorizing Political Activity*, a re-evaluation of the practice/theory relationship in Oakeshott's thought is presented. I suggest that in his late thought, political activity as a reflective activity is capable of engaging in a dialogue with philosophy on equal terms and, thus, of widening the horizons of political imagination.

CHAPTER II

Platforms of Understanding

1: Introduction: The "Isms" in Discussion

It is not at all clear whether British strains of conservatism and liberalism – the political "isms" often connected to Oakeshott – should be discussed in terms of ideologies, traditions or Pocockian political languages, i.e. as contextual linguistic resources of political action.[1] This distinction is not as clear as it might initially seem, even in Oakeshott's usage, as I hope to show in Chapter III.3, *Ideology/Tradition*. He does not merely treat the "isms" (pejoratively) as ideologies; the issue is more complicated. In this chapter, however, Oakeshott's views are related to political "isms" exclusively from the simpler viewpoint of ideologies, and they are discussed by examining the variations inside both "isms." Liberalism and conservatism are mainly treated as fairly coherent ideologies or doctrines, which were actually acceptable intellectual endeavours for Oakeshott, if one remains aware of their limitations, particularly in comparison with philosophy. In a posthumously published essay, *Political Philosophy*, he wrote:

> From reflection which aims at giving a firm, if narrow, intelligibility to political experience, we may expect a *doctrine*. These are reflective enterprises the work of which lies in an achieved result; and since a conclusion is sought, a term is put to the impetus of reflection.[2]

---

[1]   J. Pocock 1985, p. 19.
[2]   M. Oakeshott 1946-50, *Political Philosophy*, RPML, p. 150. Compare with Quentin Skinner's notion of the "mythology of doctrines." Skinner criticizes the historian who expects each classical writer to enunciate "some doctrine on each of the topics regarded as constitutive of his subject." Q. Skinner 1969, p.32.

Thus, whereas philosophy always remains radically subversive, thinking in terms of doctrines leads one to draw conclusions which tend to be caricatures of the nature of political experience, perhaps rendering politics more understandable.[3]

However, when speaking in terms of "isms," another aspect of the issue often comes to light. Conversely to Oakeshott's view of the matter, ideologies are meant to be treated as foundations or guidelines of political conduct, as is evident in the case of Joseph Raz below. In the case of Isaiah Berlin, whose thinking I also examine in this chapter, treating his work as if it simply belonged to the category of normative, liberal theory would be just as misleading as the inclusion of Oakeshott's work into the same category. Yet, as I see it, neither of them avoids the normative side of political philosophy or theory, and, as such, both have their own aspects to offer to the liberal theory of today. Oakeshott cannot always sustain his insistence on the separation of practice and theory, or philosophy, ideological thinking and practical politics, and he oscillates between what he sees as 'real', non-partisan, descriptive political philosophy and normative theory,[4] although his thought cannot be described as foundationalist as such.

It must be emphasized that my aim here is not to scorn ideological discussions. On the contrary, I view them as fruitful and as an essential part of the British discussions on both political thought and political life. Nor do I wish to belittle Oakeshott's attempt to avoid falling into the trap of a *theoretician*, who intends to replace the everyday experience and knowledge of the cave-dwellers with his own superior, theoretical understanding.[5] Thus, it is noted that although treating Oakeshott as a proponent of (certain sorts of) conservatism or liberalism is a well-justified position from which to read Oakeshott, I also claim that in some important respects "ism" interpretations often neglect the comprehensiveness and fine nuances in Oakeshott's movement within the philosophical field, or even just within his political philosophy.

The same certainly applies to the philosophical "ism" of idealism, which is one possible way of interpreting Oakeshott.

---

[3]   M. Oakeshott 1946-50, *Political Philosophy*, RPML, pp. 148-50.
[4]   An opposite interpretation has recently been presented by Terry Nardin (2001), who explicitly defends Oakeshott as having succeeded in maintaining the theory/practice division. This view will be reviewed in the concluding chapter.
[5]   See OHC, p. 30.

However, I see Oakeshott here as shifting from his original 'open' idealism towards a more skeptical philosophical emphasis, which is especially clear in his political philosophy. My point in this chapter is that one would be doing an injustice, for example, to Oakeshott's own distinct 'language' and vocabulary of philosophy if one were to relate his later production too closely to the tradition of British idealism. The influences of idealism in Oakeshott's thought by no means vanished over the course of his career, although the notion of adhering exclusively to one specific tradition of thought certainly did.

In the following, I make – as Kenneth Minogue once put it – a somewhat blundering assault upon the central ideas of argument put forth by Oakeshott. Thus, his famous "witty and brilliant style" of writing, presented as a smooth, "finished essay in which the surface is smooth at all points," is simplified from the perspective of systemic thinking in terms of "isms."[6] I examine Oakeshott's relationship to the "isms" of liberalism, conservatism and idealism, without which the portrayal of Oakeshott's influence as well as the 'normative' aspect of his political thinking would be difficult.

2: Liberalism

It is no wonder that Oakeshott wrote in the 1970s that what "may now be meant by the word 'liberal' is anyone's guess," as in one sense *everybody* appears to be liberal in British political discussions. [7]It is quite common for a writer to position him/herself as a liberal of *some* sort; either as a socialist liberal, a conservative liberal, or just a liberal in general. Thus, it is perhaps not too much of a stretch to say that, in the broadest sense of the word, nearly all British political philosophers, theorists and politicians share a basis in the liberal tradition in terms of their views on parliamentary institutions and the rights of the individual.[8]

---

[6]   K.R. Minogue 1976, p. 144.
[7]   M. Oakeshott 1975, *Talking Politics*, RP, pp. 439-40.
[8]   This claim is not new, of course. In 1960, referring to a broader Anglophone context, Daniel Bell wrote that "there is today a rough consensus among intellectuals on political issues: the desirability of decentralized power: a system of mixed economy and political pluralism. In that sense, too, the ideological age has ended." Bell 1960, p. 403.

It was Oakeshott's view that it is actually *only* in Great Britain that this tradition has survived the pressures of rationalist politics; in Continental Europe and the United States he sees parliamentary politics as having been more deeply affected by rationalism.[9] Thus, for Oakeshott, especially in Britain, the liberal tradition has grown out of historical contingencies to respect individuality, certain arrangements of property and parliamentary government. Any interpreter of Oakeshott would probably have no difficulty at all placing him under the umbrella of this tradition; all of these aspects are undoubtedly present in his understanding of good politics at some point.

However, speaking in terms of liberal*ism* immediately complicates the issue. As I have already mentioned, from an Oakeshottian perspective, an "ism" is necessarily a simplification of a political experience or tradition. It is the selection of certain features of a tradition, perhaps sharpening them, and placing them into a normative, often systemic political theory.[10] In general, then, Oakeshott's own attitude towards all "isms" – liberalism very much included – was more negative than approving, especially in cases in which an ideology falsely represented itself as a genuine political philosophy. Ideologies are neither explanations nor independent guidelines or sets of principles for political conduct to follow, as they often are portrayed. Instead, they are abridgements of traditions, and as such are subject to "an anatomical study" as opposed to "an oecological study of a tradition of behav-

---

[9]   See, e.g., M. Oakeshott 1947, *Scientific Politics*, RPML, p.102.
[10]   In a recent book, Efraim Podoksik sees Oakeshott primarily as a representative of a "sort of liberalism" as opposed to assigning him the more common label of political conservative. Podoksik 2003a, p. 159. Podoksik argues that the tension in Oakeshott's middle and late thought, often perceived as existing between his conservatism and liberalism, actually reflects a shift in emphasis from the 'Whiggish' to the 'Romantic' element in his liberalism. In addition, one should be able to identify both the "Englishness" and Continental influences in Oakeshott's version of liberalism. From these elements, Podoksik constructs a compelling interpretation of the shift from an 'holistic' view of society towards an emphasized appreciation of individuality in Oakeshott's production. Podoksik's understanding of liberalism is thus broader than mine here. He also connects British liberalism to a wider European intellectual context and presents an alternative way of contextualizing Oakeshott's work.

iour."[11] In short, pretending to lay down *foundations*, ideologies are pseudo-philosophical caricatures of traditions.[12]

Thus, simple, individualist liberalist interpretations of Oakeshott's *oeuvre* can quite easily be dismissed. For example, Anthony Farr's view that in *On Human Conduct* Oakeshott entertains the view of an agent who recalls what may be referred to as 'human nature', or, as Farr puts it, the "real self" as a basis for liberal government, is, in my view, simply an erroneous understanding of his thought. [13]There is no doubt, however, that Oakeshott is undoubtedly a philosopher of *individuality* and, as such, he can be said to belong to the liberal tradition. Yet, it is difficult to concur with David Spitz's argument that the value Oakeshott places on individuality connects him with a great many liberals but distinguishes him from "the entire tradition of political philosophy from Plato and Aristotle through Burke and Mill to theorists (liberal and conservative) alike of our own day," in that "Oakeshott does not believe there is such a thing as society or community; there are only individuals."[14] For Spitz, Oakeshott's individuals in *On Human Conduct* represent the doctrine of abstract individualism, which he sees as false because the "human race is not an individual but a collective thing."[15] Spitz thus argues in terms that Oakeshott himself could never have used. That is, Oakeshott sees all practices and also individuality as necessarily learned, and there is no notion of *unconditional* human community in his theorizing. Human conduct results in a multiplicity of associations, some of which, for example families, may be referred to by other authors as 'communities' but are seen by Oakeshott as associations.[16]

Oakeshott already noted in 1965 that society is perhaps the most ambiguous word in our language.[17] Also, rather similarly to Hannah Arendt's conception,[18] notions of 'social' and 'socialization' mark a hypostatized *understanding* of uncondi-

---

[11] M. Oakeshott 1951, *Political Education*, RP, p. 64
[12] See ibid., pp. 58-69, M. Oakeshott (?), *The Concept of a Philosophy of Politics*, RPML, p. 128.
[13] A. Farr 1998, p. 246.
[14] D. Spitz 1976, p. 344.
[15] Ibid., p. 346.
[16] OHC, p. 88.
[17] M. Oakeshott 1965, A Review of *Philosophy, Politics and Society*, p. 281. Thus, it must be noted that I use "society" for the sake of convenience in this chapter, and that Oakeshott did not approve of the use of the term in his later work.
[18] See H. Pitkin 1998, p. 10-6.

tional and thus unreflective relationships in relation to human 'conduct', which is to be deplored.[19] The word 'social' causes confusion because *human*, intelligent and learned relationships are assimilated to 'processes' or to systems.[20] An unspecified, unconditional interdependence is central to the understanding of a 'social' relationship that the concept of a 'society' denotes.[21] Instead of systems or structures, human conduct subscribes to procedures and different practices, which are inherently multiple:

> Being human is recognizing oneself to be related to others, not as parts of an organism are related, nor as members of a single, all-inclusive 'society', but in virtue of participation in multiple understood relationships and in the enjoyment of understood, historic languages of feelings, sentiments, imaginings, fancies, desires, recognitions, moral and religious beliefs, intellectual and practical enterprises…[22]

Thus, Oakeshott's understanding of human conduct and associations is plural in the sense of different, learned practices. Civility is markedly a collected as opposed to "a 'collective' achievement."[23] As such, the application of any 'permanent', naturalistic terms, such as 'race', is impossible in Oakeshott's thought and vocabulary.

Spitz, however, goes on to treat the ideal types of *universitas*, and especially *societas*, as an ideological way of looking at reality; *societas* appears as the model of a state that is favoured by Oakeshott. I do not object to the possibility of examining *societas* and *universitas* from a utopian perspective, but maintaining the claim that Oakeshott intended for *societas* to refer to a utopian model of a state is "a heap of rubbish," as Oakeshott himself put it in a reply to his critics.[24] For Oakeshott, *universitas*, *societas* and agency are essentially historico-philosophical constructions, not mere abstract 'models' to be imitated in reality.

Questions regarding the relationships between individuality, community and the state are central to discussions sur-

[19] E.g., M. Oakeshott 1972, *Education: The Engagement and Its Frustration*, VLL, pp. 84-5.
[20] M. Oakeshott 1974, *A Place of Learning*, VLL, p. 35, OHC, p. 24.
[21] Ibid., pp. 34-5.
[22] M. Oakeshott 1972, *Education: The Engagement and its Frustration*, VLL, p. 65.
[23] OHC, p.87.
[24] M. Oakeshott 1976, *On Misunderstanding Human Conduct. A Reply To My Critics*, p. 360.

rounding the various present-day versions of liberalism. And it is with regard also to these questions that I see Oakeshott as a possible contributor to the discussion, particularly in terms of his emphasis of the historicity of different understandings of human agency and associations. I thus now turn to an exploration of two rather opposing views on these issues as presented by Raz and Berlin, as well as the more 'Oakeshottian' Rorty, in order to illuminate the complexity of the field.

Raz, Berlin and Oakeshott

It cannot be said that either Raz or Berlin are simple foundationalists in the conventional sense of the term. Both thinkers emphasize the historicity of human associations – as does Oakeshott – but they also present the outline of a normative political philosophy with certain notions that can be read as foundationalist, such as Raz's notions of "personal autonomy" and "collective goods."[25] Both thinkers also have their own ideal images of political activity that are based on their basic assumptions – particularly of individuality and community. Both philosophers can be referred to as distinctively *British* discussants, for although Berlin was born in Riga, his career was markedly Oxfordian. As an almost exact contemporary of Oakeshott's, Berlin (1909-1997) offers a rather natural point of comparison here. He is arguably also the most eminent representative of British liberalism in the 20th century and can thus hardly be bypassed in any examination of the issue. There is no need to present an overview of Berlin's work here, but his views of politics and political philosophy are discussed in the context of the liberal discussion. As to Raz, this philosopher of law is arguably one of the most influential thinkers of political liberalism today. Also as an Oxfordian, his version of liberalism could be described as having a distinctly British or English 'flavour', thus offering a more fruitful point of comparison than, for example, American theoretical models of liberalism in relation to Oakeshott's 'liberalism'.

In his book *The Morality of Freedom* (1986), Joseph Raz sets out to conquer the task of extracting "the political morality of liberalism" from a coherent moral position. He aims at writing a theory of political freedom which includes, for example, a doctrine of justice. Thus, he distinguishes himself from con-

[25] J. Raz 1986.

temporary thinkers, such as John Rawls, by positioning the concept of justice as inferior to the concept of freedom. Raz's explicit aim is to contribute to the discussion of a *doctrine* which he calls the "tradition" of liberalism by offering a liberal foundation for political morality.[26]

In this sense, Raz's aspirations are completely opposite to those of Oakeshott in most of his political thought and philosophy; they consciously aim at a more narrow perspective of a given doctrine in relation to political philosophy. However, as seen, we should not regard this aim as 'illegitimate' from an Oakeshottian perspective; being aware of one's limitations certainly corresponds to Oakeshott's notion of the different levels of political thought.[27] Raz's theorizing attempts to influence the sphere of practice; its reasoning is carried out for the purpose of invoking practical implications through the performances of others.

In a sense, however, Oakeshott does not always even attempt to escape the operation of the 'abridging of a tradition', as is most evident in the essays *The Political Economy of Freedom* (1949) and *Contemporary British Politics* (1948). These essays will be examined in greater detail in their contemporary context later, but I would like here to point out again that Oakeshott's character as a philosopher is in some cases more 'doctrinaire' than he himself might acknowledge. From this perspective, I also find for example Paul Franco's[28] and Wendell John Coats's[29] treatments of civil association as restatements of liberalism quite conceivable and fruitful approaches in their separation of Oakeshott's thinking from materialist, economic or utilitarian versions of liberalism.

Raz can also be seen as deviating from these versions of liberalism. According to him, there is a concept of a "collective good," i.e. an inherent public good, from which certain implications follow.[30] Whereas for economists the public good is mostly contingent and instrumental, for Raz, the "provision of many collective goods is constitutive of the very possibility of

---

[26]   Ibid., p.3.
[27]   See M. Oakeshott 1951, *Political Education*, RP, pp. 43-66; 1991 *Political Discourse*, RP, pp. 70-95.
[28]   P. Franco 1990a, pp. 411-36.
[29]   W. J. Coats 1985, pp. 773-87.
[30]   J. Raz 1986, p. 199.

autonomy."[31] The collective good as the appearance of various opportunities in a society is an essential aspect of the possibility for an individual to have an autonomous life, which lies at the heart of Raz's doctrine.

While acknowledging the inherent danger of anachronisms, one can detect in the concepts of "collective good" and "personal autonomy" one of the basic divisions within Western political philosophy, i.e. the division between the primacy of the individual and the common good or the community. This division has been put forth in numerous ways, although for my purposes here it is quite sufficient to focus on just two of them.

For Terence Ball, Hobbes – often considered to be one of the 'fathers' of liberalism – reconceptualized human agents as "material entities who by their very nature are disconnected social atoms driven by desire and self-interest."[32] Yet he could not purge his notion of agency of "all traces of the older Aristotelian view that all things aim at some end and that human action necessarily involves some view of the good," because human beings are creatures who, for example, communicate and make judgements.[33] If Ball's interpretation is correct, one of the main traits of liberalism would appear to be the replacement of the old conception of the "common good" with the pursuit of an agent's *own* good (interest), although it is impossible to avoid living in the tangled web of social relations.

Conversely, for Tuija Pulkkinen, the division is seen as much more recent; it is a division between "the liberal" and "the Hegelian" traditions of political thought. She interprets Hobbes as having initiated the tradition in which liberty is basically understood as the freedom to act in accordance with one's own will without being obstructed, and in which other human beings are seen as obstacles to free individual motion.[34] In the Hegelian tradition, freedom means autonomy; not only in the negative sense of the word, such as 'freedom from nature', but as the freedom to govern oneself.[35] In addition, for Hegel, the "concept of an individual follows logically only after the concept of community. There is no primary transcen-

---

[31] Ibid., p. 207.
[32] T. Ball 1988, p. 83.
[33] Ibid.
[34] T. Pulkkinen 1996, p. 14.
[35] Ibid., p. 16.

dental individual in the Hegelian political ontology."[36] In Pulkkinen's interpretation, political action in the Hegelian tradition is intentional; it is moral action in the Kantian sense and has the community's best interests at heart, and is not, therefore, conducted out of self-interest.[37] Thus, for Pulkkinen, one distinction between the liberal and Hegelian traditions clearly lies in the primacy of the individual and that of the community. She complicates the issue, however, by noting that J.S. Mill also identifies a positive conception of freedom in the form of the liberty of an individual to develop her/his capacities in all possible directions, which would require a certain kind of society.[38]

In both of these interpretations, the conception of positive liberty is thus not absent from the mainstream version of liberalism, and Joseph Raz's notion of "personal autonomy" simply strengthens this liberal tradition. According to John Gray, Raz's view of the connections between autonomous choice and the good life seems to be genuinely Aristotelian. Autonomous choice is only valuable when it is a component of a life or activity that has intrinsic value.[39] For Raz, negative liberty derives its value from its contribution to positive liberty as autonomy, and he also claims that freedom itself has no distinct value but is instead intimately intertwined with other values.[40] Furthermore, he also rejects the notion of 'rights' as belonging to the moral basis of individuals; thus, for example notions of individuals' right to freedom do not serve as fundamental aspects of liberal democracy. All this is part of his broader programme of displacing individualism from the heart of liberalism, though in the light of the interpretations presented by Ball and Pulkkinen we are entitled to ask whether this aim, based on a widely accepted view regarding the content of the core of liberalism, is in fact a bit misguided. To emphasize this point, in Raz's theory the core of the liberal concern regarding liberty lies in the promotion and protection of personal autonomy, and this concern ties his theory to the 'community' aspect of liberalism.[41] In Raz's vocabulary, a "good is a public good in a certain society if and only if the

[36] Ibid., p. 21.
[37] Ibid., p. 22.
[38] Ibid., 36.
[39] J. Gray 1995, p. 31.
[40] J. Raz 1986, p. 19.
[41] Ibid., p. 203.

distribution of its benefits in that society is not subject to voluntary controlling by anyone other than each potential beneficiary controlling his share of the benefits."[42] Furthermore, he names those *inherent* public goods, the enjoyment of which depends on the non-exclusivity of a society's members, as collective goods. His conception of public goods also acknowledges economic thought – for example access to water can be seen as a *contingent* public good. However, he mainly refers to the 'moral side' of the issue by mentioning, for example, living in a tolerant society as a collective good. He also views living in a society that enables its citizens to make the 'right' choices and thus fosters personal autonomy to be an example of a collective good.

In other words, for Raz, a person is autonomous only if he has a *variety* of available acceptable options from which to choose from.[43] He thus rejects the view of rights theorists that freedom is the mere existence of the capacity to choose. His view of personal autonomy thus demands the inclusion of the concept of "collective goods," i.e. intrinsically valuable social conditions. Therefore, at the very least, "living in a society, which is a collective good, is on this view intrinsically good."[44] Once again we re-encounter a very Aristotelian view of human nature in this liberal theory of politics.

By definition: "A right to autonomy can be had only if the interest of the right-holder justifies holding members of the society at large to be duty-bound to him to provide him with the social environment necessary to give him a chance to have an autonomous life."[45] Furthermore, *rights* have a special force because they are grounds of duties, which are peremptory reasons for action. Importantly, rights also express what is owed to the right-holder in virtue of the respect due to his interest. Raz emphasizes this second point in order to mark the distinctions of his views when compared with those of "moral individualists." In arguments of the latter, rights are seen as a "protective shield against moral demands in the name of the well-being of others" and personal autonomy as a barrier against demands made on the individual in the name of collec-

---

[42] Ibid., p. 198.
[43] Ibid., p. 204.
[44] Ibid., p. 206.
[45] Ibid., p. 247.

tive goals.[46] However, if rights are not bound to the interests of the right-holder, Raz sees them as becoming of 'weak meaning', i.e. they cannot signify matters of special concern because of their importance to the right-holder. Raz thus ends up stressing his earlier point that the notion of an inherent general conflict between individual freedom and the needs of others is illusory. According to him, personal autonomy (although sometimes in conflict with the interests of others) can only be obtained through collective goods, which do not benefit anyone unless they benefit everyone. It is Raz's view that this "fact, rather than any definition, undermines the individualist emphasis on the importance of rights."[47]

In defence of his interdependence thesis regarding rights and collective goods, Raz surveys a few examples which he regards as belonging to the history of liberal practical politics. The right to religious freedom, for example, was initially manifested as the right of conscientious objection, and it thus served as a test of the sincerity between the objector and the community at large. "People enjoyed the right only if they shared the style of life of a known social group. Most commonly they enjoyed it only if they participated in the life of the group. It was unlikely that people would change their whole way of life just in order to avoid service."[48]

Raz continues along similar lines with regard to the right to freedom of contract and the free market, as well as with regard to freedom of speech and an open society. For example, the freedom of the press, which includes privileges not extended to ordinary individuals, still benefits "all who live in that society, for they benefit from the participation of others in the free exchange of information and opinion."[49] According to Raz, the core of freedom of speech is the protection of political speech and the free exchange of information that is of public interest. By public interest he means that it benefits all those who are subject to that political system. Raz does not wish to claim that fundamental rights never compete or conflict with other rights or collective goods. He does, however, intend to point out that rights both depend on and serve collective goods. It follows

---

[46]   Ibid., p. 250.
[47]   Ibid.
[48]   Ibid., p.252.
[49]   Ibid., p. 253.

that in cases of conflict there is no general rule for giving priority to either rights or collective goods.[50]

Rejecting the idea that individual liberty rests primarily on the existence of fundamental moral rights, Raz aspires to assign rights a humbler role in the morality of liberal tradition. He does not deny the significance of rights, but views them as "important ingredients in a mosaic of value-relations whose significance and implications cannot be spelled out except by reference to rights."[51] By definition, the importance of liberal rights is, according to Raz, their service to the public good.

As such, if we read Oakeshott as a liberal thinker, we can identify him with Raz as a thinker who assigns rights a more modest role within the liberal tradition. However, Oakeshott's position in this sense is more radical – he denies that a society necessarily 'needs' rights in any sense. For him, they are a part of political argumentation which one could easily do without. For example, the 1789 Rights of Man in France was a "disclosed, abstracted and abridged" version of the common law rights of Englishmen; originally a habit or tradition, not an idea.[52] This does not in itself constitute any significant contradiction to Raz's thought, but his antifoundational view of how rights are born does. For Oakeshott, a right does not come into existence for the sole purpose of serving some other 'real' good that can be arranged in a hierarchy. Oakeshott uses the example of the legal status of women in order to exemplify this. In his view, women's enfranchisement in Great Britain was the result of the correction of a confusion which existed because women's legal status intimated rights and duties which were not recognized.[53] Oakeshott regards arguments drawn from abstract natural rights as clumsy and irrelevant; the valid argument was to appeal to an incoherence in the legal arrangements of the society pressing for remedy.[54] In a later account, Oakeshott points out that the "language of rights is the language of pretended unconditionals and misdescribes the terms of civil association."[55] The discussion of rights is only appropriate in civil associations, which are associations in terms of rules, when they become determinate as specified in a

[50] Ibid., pp. 253-5.
[51] Ibid., p. 255.
[52] M. Oakeshott 1951, *Political Education*, RP, p. 53.
[53] Ibid., p. 57.
[54] Ibid.
[55] M. Oakeshott 1975, *Talking Politics*, RP, p. 456.

collection of described obligations. Raz also emphasizes rights as linked to duties, but he also claims that the "dynamic aspect of rights" is "their ability to create new duties."[56] Thus, according to Raz, as soon as a right comes into existence it begins to act as a catalyst for the implementation of new arrangements within new situations, whereas Oakeshott denies this kind of (weak) foundationalism altogether. One crucial difference here lies precisely in Raz's basic concept of personal autonomy, to which Oakeshott does not assign nearly as significant a role. Oakeshott undeniably favours individuality, and in a sense 'autonomous' people, the appearance of which he sees as our historical achievement.[57] However, in his scheme of human conduct and civil association the agents are necessarily 'free' regardless of the quality of being substantively 'self-directed', which in a high degree is called 'self-determination' or 'autonomy'.[58] For Oakeshott, an agent is 'free' because his situation is an understood situation and because doing is an intelligent engagement,[59] not because, pace Raz, his choice is free from coercion and manipulation, he is independent or he has adequate options from which to choose from.[60]

Why does Raz regard rights as demanding special constitutional protection? Here, it cannot be that rights would mark the boundary between the private and the public, despite the fact that this view is widely shared among liberal theorists such as Ronald Dworkin and Robert Nozick. For Raz, at least some constitutional rights (freedom of expression, religion, privacy etc.) affording special protection to the individual exist for the purpose of protecting a collective good, which is also an aspect of political culture. The fact that special significance is assigned to these rights guaranteeing the protection of collective goods also implies that "they concern matters which are a legitimate subject of political action."[61] A paradigm example of what governments are actually there for is the protection of public goods, and as such the division cannot be between the private and the public/political when constitutional rights are considered.

---

[56]   J. Raz 1986, p. 171.
[57]   See M. Oakeshott 1961, *The Masses in Representative Democracy*, RP, pp. 363-83.
[58]   OHC, pp. 36-7.
[59]   OHC, p. 37.
[60]   J.Raz 1986, p. 373.
[61]   Ibid., p. 257.

Yet, Raz sets out to defend a different kind of constitutional status accorded to some rights. He defends this particular point at least in part from the institutional angle that provides an alternative to the assumption that the special status of constitutional rights could be explained by their special moral force. Here, constitutional rights are "devices for effecting a division of power between various branches of government."[62] Matters defined as falling under the title of constitutional rights are subjected to the jurisdiction of courts as opposed to ordinary legislative and administrative processes. The judiciary has the right to modify the effect of legislative and governmental actions in these issues. This does not, however, necessitate the existence of a written, entrenched bill of rights. Legal tradition, which comprises such interpretative presumptions as the "presumption that parliament does not intend to derogate from people's civil rights," is equally as powerful a tool in the protection of human rights when in the hands of a judiciary keen to do so. From the institutional point of view, constitutional rights are largely "based" on the actual traditions and practices of the judiciary.[63] As regards this institutional angle towards the constitutional status of some rights, we can see that Raz is in clear agreement with Oakeshott.

However, after presenting the institutional angle, Raz reverts back to using his own vocabulary. He first states that at least some constitutional rights are primarily means of ensuring the institutional protection of collective goods. For him, they exist in cases such as "[where] harming an individual seriously jeopardizes the maintenance of a public good that harm is also a cause of a harm to the community."[64] And this is the argument for including certain "individual" rights under constitutional protection.

Raz then re-examines the question of why constitutional rights should be used as a means of dividing political power between the different organs of government. Very classically put, why should they be used as part of a mechanism of checks and balances?[65] Raz's response is that, used in this way, constitutional rights are an important part of the basic political culture in every country. The basic political culture is separated

---

[62] Ibid.
[63] Ibid., p. 258.
[64] Ibid.
[65] Ibid., p. 259.

from more transient political arrangements, although Raz claims that the distinction is one of degree and as such is not susceptible to precise description. "The distinction is one of stability and importance in the eyes of those who participate in the political process." Constitutional rights are to be understood as protecting the stability of the basic political culture along with a two-chamber legislature or the adoption of entrenched constitutions, for example. Constitutional measures do not exempt issues from political strife, but rather ensure that the courts, which *should* be immune to everyday political pressures, have a greater role. To the extent that the courts succeed in this endeavour, they fulfill "an invaluable function in assuring society of the measure of continuity which is so essential to its well-being."[66]

Raz emphasizes that continuity must not be confused with stagnation; the protection of certain issues does not prevent change as such. A constitution, however, changes "in response to different social processes from those which determine ordinary political change."[67] Yet, if the political acquires a broader meaning (i.e. encompasses all decisions made by authoritative state organs), constitutional issues are subject to change through the political process. In Raz's view, the fact that the constitution affects the existence of the basic political culture (a collective good) serves as a valid reason "for holding it to be a proper subject for political action, even though sometimes the only right political action is to take no action and to leave a certain area free from political interference."[68]

Here, then, we encounter a view of liberalism in which a strong emphasis is conceptually placed on the existence and continuity of a political culture. In addition, in Raz's model political action seems primarily to serve the function of maintaining the community. Politics as such is understood as the actions of state organs. Constitutions exist in the name of the protection of the political culture, and thus the role of rights in the theory of liberalism is certainly humbler than it tends to be in more conventional contexts. I must say that I find this rather ill-suited to Raz's belief in the incommensurability of values, as at least there should, in any given community, be a rather broad consensus regarding the rights to be protected over pol-

---

[66] Ibid., p. 260.
[67] Ibid.
[68] Ibid., p. 261.

itics by a constitution. Thus, Raz's politics becomes predominantly the *protection* of personal freedom as understood in terms of the presupposition of value-pluralism and its expression in personal autonomy – understood very much in the Hegelian sense. According to Raz, fundamental liberal rights deserve special protection because they express values which should play a part in morally worthy political cultures and foster the preservation and gradual development of these aspects of the political culture.[69]

It is of course also Oakeshott's view that a system of laws brings continuity and durability to civil association. However, he emphasizes that there cannot be "an unconditional and unquestionable norm from which all others derive their authority," a 'constitution' which is "not subject to interpretation and immune from inquiry."[70] Oakeshott does not wish to use the language of rights; for him civil authority and civil obligation "are the twin pillars of the civil condition."[71] He strictly denies that a "'general' will," "'social purpose',," "approved moral ideals" or "a common good" and "general interest"[72] could provide any reason for acknowledging the authority of *respublica*, which is the public consideration of *cives*.[73] It is only the acknowledgement of the authority of *respublica* that constitutes civil association, i.e. 'consenting' to the system of law and its jurisdiction. Authority and obligation do not require approval and cannot be explained or justified in terms of the preservation of a worthy political culture. Nor do they protect anyone's interests; politics may begin as a demand of interests, but a rule that is the outcome of a successful political proposal is prescribed by those in authority as a condition to be followed by all in future performances.[74] Civil prescriptions are not devices for procuring the satisfaction of chosen wants and cannot be deduced or inferred from these wants. For example, a "rule obligating *cives* not to kill one another is not a conclusion to be inferred from the theorem that there is a common want (as distinct from organic urge) to remain alive," and "such a rule is not desirable on account of its promoting the satisfaction of this want or frustrating the

---

[69] Ibid., p. 262.
[70] OHC, p. 151.
[71] Ibid., p. 149.
[72] Ibid., p. 152.
[73] Ibid., p. 147.
[74] Ibid., p. 163.

operation of this disposition."[75] With regard to rights, then, Oakeshott and Raz speak entirely different languages.

Raz argues strongly against those liberal views that wish to exclude ideals from politics, in other words the pursuit of some conception of a good life by the government, and in this sense Raz is again in opposition with Oakeshott. He attaches his view of politics as governmental action to Mill's harm principle, i.e. that the only justification for coercively interfering with a person is to prevent him/her from harming others. He uses it, however, in the broader sense of the prevention of causing harm to anyone (him/herself included) as the only justifiable grounds for coercive interference with a person and refers to it as a principle of freedom.[76] So, the government has both a duty to promote the autonomy of the people and the right to use coercion according to the Mill's harm principle in order to stop people from taking actions that would diminish autonomy.[77] The government can also use coercion in order to force people to take actions which are required to improve their options and opportunities. It is here that Raz's ideological thinking becomes perhaps most visible; he recommends a policy of taxation that is derived from these premises. To put it briefly, the government "has an obligation to create an environment providing individuals with an adequate range of options and the opportunities to choose them. The duty arises out of people's interest in having a valuable autonomous life. Its violation will harm those it is meant to benefit."[78] Thus, according to Raz's teaching, a tax that cannot thereby be justified should not be raised. The harm principle indicates the correct way for the state to promote the well-being of its people; *it diminishes politics into the application of the right policy*, although on a very general level.

What options should politics thus make possible? Raz's answer to this question lies in the notion that, for him, autonomy "requires a public culture and is consistent with a tasteful rather than a vulgar and offensive environment."[79] This definition resembles the acknowledgement of the practices or rules of civil association in Oakeshott's vocabulary. According

---

[75]   Ibid., p. 173.
[76]   J.Raz 1986, pp. 412-3.
[77]   Ibid., p. 416.
[78]   Ibid., p. 418.
[79]   Ibid., p. 422.

to Oakeshott, one can speak the vernacular language of civil intercourse either civilly or vulgarly, sometimes even dismissing it altogether. However, the emphasis in Oakeshott's 'liberalism' is on the fact that practices really are *plural*; they are footprints of agents' performances and are thus in a constant state of change. The purpose of rules within a civil association is not to maintain a political culture or to satisfy any specific need – autonomy included. Thus, it seems to me that although Raz stresses his interpretation of value-pluralism as a presupposition of autonomy, his view of politics as the 'government's business' of promoting the good life for its citizens requires the type of consensus view of politics that does not belong to civil association and *societas* but to enterprise association and *universitas*. It seems that Oakeshottian liberalism (if we are referring to his characterization of civil association) allows more room even for the examination of such topics as the current issue of minority cultures in a given society, in that one needs only to acknowledge the authority of the association, not to approve of its purpose or its actions as in enterprise association. Namely, for Raz, "assimilationist policies may well be the only humane course, even if implemented by force of law" if the members of the minority community live an unrewarding life because of being denied the education and opportunities necessary in order to thrive outside the community.[80] Of course, civil association may have rules about for example compulsory education, but these rules are contingent and not mentioned in conjunction with any of the more fundamental principles, as they are in Raz's model of autonomy.

Thus, Raz's politics is based on the promotion of the good life as autonomy, and we might refer to his theory as Aristotelian-Millian. Politics in Razean liberalism is "the art of gradual amelioration," and there is no room for the use of radical political action in order to secure a fundamental change in social conditions, as values are grounded in these social forms.[81] Raz does not endorse 'strong government' as such, but for him it is confined to the maintenance of the framework conditions that are conducive to pluralism and autonomy. Raz's view presupposes some form of government action in the promotion of the good life, which is understood in the sense of positive liberty entailing the fulfilment of human capacity in autonomous life.

[80] Ibid., p. 424.
[81] Ibid., p. 427.

This is a sort of paternalism that is refuted by Oakeshott, for whom "'distributive' justice" has no place in civil association as civil rulers have nothing to distribute.[82] Oakeshott also sharply criticizes the (quasi) theoretical understanding of the state in which 'liberalism' clings to an idea of 'natural rights' as including the enjoyment of certain substantive conditions and views the government as an instrument that provides them.[83]

In terms of the opposition to paternalism, Berlin's liberalism is closer to Oakeshott's views than to Raz's. Where Berlin and Raz do seem to cohere, however, is in their understanding of the role of 'ideas' in relation to political life. That is, both believe that they are constitutive of practical politics, whereas for Oakeshott, at least throughout most of his career, ideas were secondary in politics. As indicated above, Raz derived some general policies from his principles of liberal morality, while for Berlin, the great totalitarian movements of the 20th century "began with ideas in people's heads."[84] For him, such ideas are the substance of ethics, and this conception is in opposition to Oakeshott's famous notion of "practical knowledge," which he sees as being involved in every practical activity, politics very much included.[85]

Technical knowledge can be written in rules, principles and maxims, but this knowledge is not sufficient. Concrete activity always also requires practical knowledge, i.e. knowledge that exists only in practice and can only be imparted and acquired, not taught and learned.[86] Perhaps we might describe it as 'know-how' as opposed to 'know that'[87] in Oakeshott's example that "a pianist acquires artistry as well as technique."[88] Thus, even the Russian Revolution, which for Berlin embodies the manifestation of ideas in politics, is for Oakeshott "not the implementation of an abstract design worked out by Lenin and others in Switzerland: it was a modification of *Russian* circumstances."[89] Thus, we can say that in this sense both Raz and Berlin represent a more foundationalist understanding of

---

[82]   OHC, p. 153 fn.
[83]   Ibid., p. 245 fn.
[84]   I. Berlin 1988, p. 1.
[85]   M. Oakeshott 1947, *Rationalism in Politics*, RP, p. 13.
[86]   Ibid., p. 15.
[87]   A connection between Polanyi's notion of "tacit knowledge," Ryle's "knowing how" and Oakeshott's practical knowledge has often been detected. See, e.g., P. Franco 1990a, p. 110; T. Fuller 1991, p. 331; W. Greenleaf 1968, p. 114.
[88]   M. Oakeshott 1947, *Rationalism in Politics*, RP, p.15.
[89]   M. Oakeshott 1951, *Political Education*, RP, p. 59 fn.

politics in comparison with Oakeshott. As Berlin sees political philosophy as ethics, i.e. as ideas and systems of beliefs regarding the end of life as applied to a society, it becomes clear that the gap between him and Oakeshott continues to grow.[90] For Oakeshott, political philosophy does not rationally seek the pre-established ends of life, and in fact he sees this as an explicitly erroneous way of conceiving it.[91] In his own self-understanding, genuine political philosophy also inevitably inhibits political action,[92] whereas for Berlin and Raz, philosophical ideas may put political activity into motion. Thus, when we return below to Oakeshott's possible contributions to the theory of liberalism, it should be noted that they cannot be found in the form of an alternative set of values or the ends of life.

What also connects Berlin and Raz is their belief in the importance of value-pluralism. Yet, as noted earlier, some doubts may arise as to the thoroughness of that belief in Raz's case, whereas for Berlin, value-pluralism is one of the true cornerstones of his version of liberalism. Of course, the same could also be said of Oakeshott, but his language does not accommodate the common term 'value', and he instead applies the concepts of practice and tradition, which add a different, and once again anti-foundationalist, nuance to his thinking. For him, differing practices and traditions neither exist *a priori* nor are conceptually necessary, but are historically contingent facts of – especially English – political life and Western culture in general.

Berlin's *antimonism,* however, stems from his reading of Machiavelli, in whom he identified the first signs of two incompatible moralities; that which was suitable for the citizens of the Republic and Christian morality.[93] Thus, Berlin's belief in value-pluralism stems from a deviation from his earlier belief in the idea of *philosophia perennis* and his familiarization with Machiavellian dualism.[94] Yet, in my view, although there is an inherent historicity in his insight of differing cultures and times with differing values, Berlin still says that what makes it possible for us to understand the "Ancient

---

[90] I. Berlin 1988, p.1.
[91] M. Oakeshott (?), *The Concept of a Philosophy of Politics*, RPML, pp. 120-5; c. 1946-50, *Political Philosophy*, RPML, pp. 153-4.
[92] M. Oakeshott (?), The Concept of a Philosophy of Politics, RPML, p. 124.
[93] I. Berlin 1988, pp. 6-7.
[94] Ibid., p. 7. R. Jahanbegloo 1992, p. 54.

Greeks" is that "what makes men human is common to them, and acts as a bridge between them."[95]

According to Berlin, there is a certain "humanness" amongst men which deserves to be examined in its own light. For Berlin, the *scope* of values must move "within the human horizon," and thus although I think he is referring to the same kind of historicity of human beings to which Oakeshott refers, Oakeshott's vocabulary seems more 'precise'. It cannot be stressed enough that there is no room in Oakeshott's philosophy for the notion of 'human nature'. In his view, a "human being is a 'history' and he makes this 'history' for himself out of his responses to the vicissitudes he encounters."[96] A human being is as contingent as his or her culture; there is no 'bridge' between us and the Ancient Greeks; a person needs to use his skills as an historian (or a common reader, albeit with a different result) and interpret the survivals of the past in order to understand this or other distant cultures. There may of course be some 'living' practices or traditions present which may help us to understand e.g. the Renaissance man, but this does not imply any notion of a common human nature.

Berlin emphasizes the incommensurablity or incompatibility of values which compose the essence of "what they are and what we are."[97] Thus, for Berlin, the colliding values are in our 'nature' – this 'historico-ontological' claim thus lies at the very heart of his liberalism. For Oakeshott, the human being's capability and *willingness* to make choices arose out of a break with communal ties in thirteenth century Italy and was only firmly established in Europe around the middle of the sixteenth century.[98] In Oakeshott's words: "Human individuality is an historical emergence, as 'artificial' and as 'natural' as the landscape."[99] Therefore, for Oakeshott, the emergence of an Orwellian world without *any* Winstons would be more feasible than in Berlin's understanding, and in this sense Oakeshott's thought seems to leave room even for 'utopian' (or 'dystopian') thinking – if we apply the term 'utopia' in the sense of its being the vision of a possible world. In Berlin's view, total solutions are not only impracticable but also inco-

[95] I. Berlin 1988, p. 9.
[96] M. Oakeshott 1975, *A Place of Learning*, VLL, p. 9.
[97] I. Berlin 1988, p. 11.
[98] Oakeshott 1961, *The Masses in Representative Democracy*, RP, pp. 365-6.
[99] Ibid., p. 370.

herent and thus illusory.[100] A final solution would imply the repression of a basic human nature as representing itself in the form of colliding values and an inherent willingness, as well as in the capacity to make choices.

In *On Human Conduct*, Oakeshott's reference to agency implies the theorization of *conduct*. Here, freedom only implies the recognition of 'doing' as an intelligent engagement; it is action that is linked with a learned and understood belief and is "distinguished from a genetic, a psychological, or a social process or from a consequence of causal conditions."[101] Freedom is *inherent* in agency as the "independence enjoyed by the agent in respect of being a reflective consciousness," and "recognitions of himself and of the world of *pragmata* he inhabits, which he has turned into wishes, and wishes he has specified in choices of actions and utterances."[102] It must be emphasized that Oakeshott's account of human freedom is not that of (ontological, individualist) liberalism: this understanding neither excludes "the obedient service to the master" nor implies the necessity of certain conditions, such as the private sphere.[103] It does not require that the agent possess a 'subjective will' or any kind of substantive self-sufficiency. Agency and choice are always intertwined with acknowledging practices, and the nature of these practices is always undetermined. As such, what we might refer to as Oakeshott's 'liberalism', i.e. for example his understanding and occasional praise of civil association is not based on his understanding of some basic nature possessed by all human beings that would best flourish under such conditions. Instead, it is based on the contingent fact that it is the best human relationship in terms of our obligation to our current, historically transformed human disposition of individuality.[104]

What about Berlin's view of politics then? Berlin's discussion regarding the coexistence of a minimally *decent* society and the conception of human nature seems to indicate the need for some consensus in his view of politics. However, the importance he places on consensus is really limited to this conception of a 'minimally' decent society – whatever that might

[100] I. Berlin 1988, p. 12.
[101] OHC, p. 41.
[102] Ibid., p. 40.
[103] Ibid., p. 41.
[104] See M. Oakeshott 1975, *Talking Politics*, RP, pp. 459-60.

entail at any given time. His politics, conversely, is a politics of conflicts. When ends are agreed upon, politics is diminished into technology, a mere discussion of the right means, as in Engels's (imitating Saint-Simon) phrase "replacing the government of persons by the administration of things."[105]

His conception of politics is closely intertwined with his views of negative and positive liberty. We saw above how Raz both utilizes this distinction between different conceptions of liberty and positions himself in support of the view of positive liberty as a fundamental aspect of a worthwhile human life and liberal politics. Berlin, instead, is famous for his vigorous support of the primacy and utmost importance of negative liberty in a free society. This is his Hobbesian view of man as 'naturally free', as someone who must violate his own essence when giving up one liberty in order to preserve the rest. That is, one of Berlin's basic questions of politics is how to reconcile and judge the standards between authority and liberty as defined as an area free of coercion. In Berlin's reading of the human condition, *authority* and *law* are always restrictive of a man's action, and he thus sees liberty/freedom (he uses these terms synonymously) as lying primarily in the *private* sphere.[106]

Like Raz, Berlin certainly believes in the importance of human rights and, similarly, he does not believe in *a priori* lists of such rights. Rather, for him, the basis of liberal morality is found in justice in its simplest and most universal sense:

> Equality of liberty; not to treat others as I should not wish them to treat me; repayment of my debt to those who alone have made possible my liberty or prosperity or enlightenment.[107]

As such, we return to the problem of the reconciliation of authority and liberty. Importantly, in Berlinian liberalism authority is by definition bad, simply because it necessarily conflicts with liberty.

For him, two basic and logically distinct questions concerning authority in relation to the two concepts of liberty are "'Who governs me?'" and "'How far does government interfere with me?'"[108] The latter question indicates the need for a "sacred frontier" of privacy, which Berlin sees as necessary if a

[105] Cited in I. Berlin 1958, p. 191.
[106] I. Berlin 1958, pp. 191-200.
[107] Ibid., p. 197.
[108] Ibid., p. 202.

society is to remain liberal; thus, the private needs to be *saved* from the public and the political. The former question, on the other hand, is connected to the concept of positive liberty in terms of one being one's own master. Anyone who claims that rationality is a common trait possessed by all men can also claim authority; there is no grave difference between 'democratic sovereignty' and benevolent despot in this sense. The only question that matters for Berlin is that of how *much* authority is given to a specific quarter, not *who* possesses it. In his view, no one should be given enough authority so as to violate the absolute right to refuse to behave inhumanely. This definition outlines the basic argument behind Berlin's liberalism; there must be a society in which there are frontiers of freedom that nobody should be permitted to cross.[109] Importantly, according to Berlin, those who advocate the extreme importance of negative liberalism wish to decrease authority as such to certain limits, whereas the supporters of positive liberty wish to place it in their own hands.[110] Additionally, in Berlin's use, the terms authority, power and coercion are applied almost synonymously, as they often are in British political thought. Oakeshott represents an important exception in this sense, as will be argued later in the section on *Talking Politics*. For him, the existence of an office of authority and vehicles of power are two conceptually distinct things, and authority as such does not represent anything negative, nor is it seen as a restraint of liberty. For Oakeshott, *political freedom presupposes authority*. Yet, it must be noted that in the late 1940s and 1950s, when Oakeshott did not yet clearly distinguish between authority and power, he was also concerned about great monopolies of power.[111] In addition, in the posthumously published *The Politics of Faith and The Politics of Skepticism* (1996), Oakeshott condemns the authorization of an "'omnipotent' government" – so in this sense, Oakeshott's views are not always that far removed from Berlin's.[112]

Berlin is not entirely *against* positive liberty, however. He sees it as essential in the achievement of a decent existence.[113] He claims to have been more cautious about using this concept

---

[109] Ibid., p. 235.
[110] Ibid., p. 237.
[111] See, e.g., Oakeshott 1948, *Contemporary British Politics*, p. 486.
[112] PFPS, p. 27.
[113] R. Jahanbegloo 1992, p. 41.

merely because this positive sense of liberty is more easily perverted into tyranny. Although Berlin's conception of politics is that it arises out of conflicting, incommensurable ends, it also includes the traditional liberal view of authority as a mitigator of these conflicts and must also be able to ensure that pluralism prevails. According to Berlin, politics must necessarily include compromises if "destructive conflict" is to be avoided, and it thus also requires a minimum degree of toleration.[114] In my view, we may refer to Berlinian politics as a 'politics of conflicts and toleration', although it must be noted that the Berlinian conflict view does not refer to politics as an activity that constitutes ends, but instead his conflict is more a question of a relationship between given ends.

Oakeshott and Rorty's Postmodern Bourgeois Society

Berlin famously ended his essay *Two Concepts of Liberty* with a quotation by Joseph Schumpeter:

> To realise the relative validity of one's convictions and yet stand for them unflinchingly, is what distinguishes a civilized man from a barbarian.[115]

Although ultimate values are universal and objective for Berlin, they can also change – and have changed – over the course of history. In this sense, we can also view Berlin's liberalism as historical and contingent, although his view of human nature bears some ontological assumptions despite its claimed historicity.[116] It is in the former sense, however, that Richard Rorty interprets Berlin in his *Contingency, Irony and Solidarity* (1989), in which he outlines his understanding of contemporary liberalism. He thus disassociates himself from two popular interpretations of Berlin, that of romantic anti-rationalism, or agonistic liberalism, as well as that of benign rationalism, and attaches his label of "liberal irony" to Berlin's thought. Rorty lists Berlin among those liberals – including some of his other "heroes," such as Dewey, William James, Proust and Wittgenstein – for whom the only justification for liberal democracy is the historical contingency of its existence and

---

[114] Ibid., 44.
[115] I. Berlin 1958, p. 242.
[116] A similar observation is made by Robert A. Kocis, who says that there is a logical flaw between Berlin's incommensurablity thesis and the endorsement of individual liberty as "a truer and more humane ideal" than positive liberty. R. A. Kocis 1980, p. 39.

each human's conviction of its superiority in comparison with other cultures while still acknowledging the relative validity of his or her own beliefs.[117]

It is primarily because of this interpretation that Oakeshott has also become known as a liberal ironist and as someone associated with the Berlinian version of liberalism: a connection which is perhaps best summarized by Oakeshott himself:

> … liberalism is not an abstract idea or a rationalist plan for a society, but an attitude to social and personal life, coeval with our civilization.[118]

Yet, as I mentioned above, there are other compelling interpretations of Berlin that refute Rorty's comprehension. First, Robert A. Kocis associates Berlin with Oakeshott as a critic of *rationalism*; both are opposed to the conception of political questions as automatically answerable by reference to a rationalist structure of some kind.[119] Yet he emphasizes that neither falls into the category of the irrationalist view of politics; they both view politics as civil interaction and are concerned with politics as the public deliberation of the arrangements of a society. Politics is neither the drawing of implications from some axiomatic assumptions nor "so emotive as to be based on an irrational cohesion of persons."[120] For both Oakeshott and Berlin, politics is not only the question of "'How should I vote?'" but also of "'How shall I live?'" According to Kocis, the common features between Berlin and Oakeshott are the preservation of civility as the main task of politics and the sharing of opposing teleological approaches to politics, because of their opposition to paternalistic politics. Yet Kocis, along with Jonathan Riley, argues that Berlin's thought includes a certain kind of rationalism in the form of the belief in the fundamental value of negative liberty as setting the common moral horizon for human beings, whereas this horizon is absent from Oakeshott's work. Thus, Gray's dictum of agonistic pluralism and the importance of the existence of a *radical* choice between conflicting ends in politics[121] is moderated by Kocis[122] and

---

[117] R. Rorty 1989, p. 46.
[118] M. Oakeshott 1947, A Review of William Aylott Orton: *The Liberal Tradition*, p. 262.
[119] R. A. Kocis 1980, p. 50.
[120] Ibid.
[121] J. Gray 1995.
[122] R. A. Kocis 1980, p. 51.

Riley[123] by setting the limitation of choice according to this common moral horizon of humankind to Berlin's view. This limitation also weakens Rorty's description of Berlin as a liberal ironist in favour of Riley's characterization of him – along with Berlin's understanding of himself – as a liberal rationalist. Berlin justifies his preference of liberal cultures over illiberal ones with this common moral horizon, which requires the existence of a core minimum of human rights in order to exist. Although his thought, with its preference for value pluralism and the inevitability of conflicts, is necessarily anti-utopian, a 'weaker' version of reason remains at the heart of his liberalism. As Riley puts it:

> Yet, although reason is weaker than its mainstream promoters would have us believe, it remains for Berlin the ultimate guide in ethical and political life. It apparently justifies a common moral horizon that is minimally liberal in content... The radical freedom to create and pick among plural and incomparable ideals, so prized by the romantics, is thus kept within reasonable liberal limits.[124]

Noel Annan also characterizes the distinction between Berlin and Oakeshott as between a "moderate rationalist" and a "relativist." In his interpretation, Berlin is opposed to Oakeshott because the former believes that reason can be applied to any number of social problems and produce results.[125] "Reason may diminish the bruising conflicts between good ends" and is "needed to sort out the conflicting aims of justice, privation and personal freedom."[126] As has already become evident, I tend to agree with these interpretations of Berlin as a supporter of a "benign" view of liberalism in which the rational comparison of conflicting values is, to a certain extent, permitted.[127]

　　In comparison to e.g. Raz, Oakeshott's irony becomes visible even, for instance, in his habit of putting terms like 'justice' and 'injustice' in quotation marks, whereas Raz takes these concepts more 'seriously'.[128] If it is correct, however, to characterize Oakeshott as a liberal ironist, for whom there are no metaphysical foundations for liberal cultures, does this imply

[123] J. Riley 2001, p. 285.
[124] Ibid., p. 295.
[125] N. Annan 1998, p. xiii.
[126] Ibid., pp. xiii-xiv.
[127] J. Riley 2001, p. 283.
[128] See, e.g., M. Oakeshott 1991, *Political Discourse*, RP, p. 83.

that it is equally permissible to refer to him as a relativist? Answering this question requires focussing on the examination of Oakeshott's relationship to rationalism, his view of politics and the scope and 'objectives' of state action, all of which are central to both Berlin's and Raz's thought. In addition, these factors must be considered in terms of their relationship to Rorty's view of a "postmodern bourgeois society."[129]

It is common to contrast a *rational* or even rational*ist* view of human beings and life with either an irrational or a relativist view of life. The former notion's potential illumination of Oakeshott's view of a choosing agent is undeniable, although I generally agree with Paul Franco that his modification of the notion of the agent purges his notion from the conceptual realm of "abstract individualism" and the "notion of consent" in political theory. [130]According to Franco, Oakeshott's notion of agency consists of the "thoroughly Hegelian conception of the relationship between freedom or will and a moral practice that overcomes the opposition between individual and government, will and law, and freedom and authority."[131] Although I tend not to read Oakeshott in quite as Hegelian a way as Franco, this interpretation does make a lot of sense. For Oakeshott, an agent is a "fugitive; not a generic unity but a dramatic identity without benefit of a model of self-perfection."[132] However, although there is no abstract individualism or notion of a closed identity in this agency, there is something thoroughly Hobbesian about Oakeshott's characterization of the transactions between mortal agents:

> … its outcome not merely uncertain but fragile and soon dissipated. Every satisfaction is casual and late or soon a casualty. Where conduct is the choice and pursuit of substantive conditions of things every achievement is evanescent, and (as Augustine says) he who thinks otherwise 'understands neither what he seeks nor what he is who seeks it'. And no projected future can be any different from the present in this respect.[133]

---

[129] R. Rorty 1983, p. 583.

[130] P. Franco 1990b, p. 423.

[131] Ibid.

[132] OHC, p. 84. On Jean-Paul Sartre's conception of agency, which has certain similarities to Oakeshott's view, see L. Subra 1997, pp. 102-17; 200-9. Additionally, Leena Subra's reading of the inescapable political dimension of conflict, contingency and choosing in the human situation offers a fruitful and profound basis for further comparisons of Oakeshott's and Sartre's views. See ibid., pp. 215-6.

[133] OHC, p. 84.

This is reminiscent of Hobbes in its characterization of the temporary nature of all achievements:

> ... the Felicity of this life, consisteth not in the repose of a mind satisfied. For there is no such *finis ultimus* (utmost aim) nor *summum bonum* (greatest good) as is spoken of in the Books of the old Moral Philosophy.... Felicity is a continual progress of the desire, from one object to another; the attaining of the former, being still but the way to the later. The cause whereof is, that the object of man's desire is not to enjoy once only, and for one instant of time; but to assure forever, the way of his future desire.[134]

In Gray's interpretation, for Hobbes, the human good in life is a life that is in perpetual motion, while the greatest evil can thus only be immobility or death as the cessation of all movement and all desire.[135] Oakeshott's greatest evil would be to hinder a human being from choosing, because agency necessarily consists of choosing, a human being would loose his/ her agency by being deprived of the possibility to choose. By definition, for Oakeshott, an agent is a reflective intelligent being who is both capable of choosing within changing situations and inherently alterable; he/she is a fugitive caught between a performance and a practice.

Oakeshott's notion of agency in *On Human Conduct* is not, however, political, but theoretical. In my reading, an agent is not, in this basic sense, less free even when living in a totalitarian society. However, within the framework of civil association, Oakeshott's citizen coheres with Rorty's characterization of a liberal ironist when one recognizes his political (or civil) freedom as contingent. This type of liberal ironist is aware of his or her own inescapable *historicity* in being unable to rise above the contingency of situation and language.[136] This type of citizen would be an ideal member of Rorty's liberal utopia – a citizen among people who "had a sense of the contingency of their language of moral deliberation, and thus of their consciences, and thus of their community."[137] Conversely to Berlin's agent, neither Rorty's nor Oakeshott's agents hold any

---

[134] T. Hobbes, *Leviathan*, cited in J. Gray 1993, p. 5. I chose to use Gray's citation in order to also do justice to his remark that in Oakeshott's interpretation human fulfilment is found in Felicity as a transitory perfection, having no finality for Hobbes. Ibid., p. 5. There is certainly a connection between this interpretation and Oakeshott's own notion of human agency.

[135] Ibid.

[136] R. Rorty 1989, pp. 46-50.

[137] Ibid., p. 61.

external standpoints in terms of a moral horizon, but instead relinquish their yearning to identify the philosophical foundations of their being. In my view, however, one significant aspect of Oakeshott's work is that it does contain a conception of *rationality* – and morality, as Rorty suggests – which saves him from falling into the abyss of (at least extreme) relativism.

In a letter to Karl Popper, Oakeshott says that there is *nothing* common to all men – rationality and reason included. He writes that what unites men much more forcefully than reason is e.g. "a common civilisation (where it exists), common habits of behaviours (where they exist) neither of which are rational, dependent upon argument common to *all men*."[138] As such, Oakeshott clearly confirms the existence of a form of *cultural* 'relativism', or better yet, relationalism. Schumpeter's notion of being aware of the relativity of one's own convictions while unflinchingly sticking to them applies when we refer to just some of the individualist aspects of Western culture examined and endorsed by Oakeshott in his writings.[139] As such, we can also confirm Rorty's understanding of Oakeshott as coinciding with Wilfrid Sellar's thesis that "morality is a matter of what he calls 'we intentions,' i.e. that the core meaning of 'immoral action' is 'the sort of thing *we* don't do."[140] In place of a common conception of rationality as aspiring to premeditated ends by available means, Oakeshott suggests his own view:

> …the only significant way of using the word 'rational' in relation to conduct is when we mean to indicate a quality or characteristic (and perhaps a desirable quality or characteristic) of the activity itself, then it would appear that the quality concerned is not mere 'intelligence', but faithfulness to the knowledge we have of how to conduct the specific activity we are engaged in. 'Rational' conduct is acting in such a way that the coherence of the idiom of activity to which the conduct belongs is preserved and possibly changed. This, of course, is something different from faithfulness to the principles or rules… [they, SS] are mere abridgements of the coherence of the activity and we may be faithful to them while losing touch with the activity itself.[141]

---

[138] M. Oakeshott 1948, *A Letter to Karl Popper*.

[139] Yet, this does not mean 'insularism' in the sense of our being unable to try to understand other cultures (or history), as is evident in e.g. Oakeshott's own interpretation and the examples of Chinese history and philosophy. See, e.g. Oakeshott 1947, *Rationalism in Politics*, RP, p. 14n. Compare with I. Berlin 1988, pp. 8-10.

[140] R. Rorty 1989, p. 59.

[141] M. Oakeshott 1950, *Rational Conduct*, RP, p. 122.

Thus, for Oakeshott, rationality is culturally bound as opposed to a universal 'product' of reason, for instance. Reason, however, does have a place in Oakeshott's conception of politics: It is not "*to take the place of* habits of behaviour, but to act as *the critic* of habits of behaviour, keeping them from superstition etc."[142] In addition, the 'irrationality' of human beings can be evaluated against the idiom of activity, which means that not *everything* is equally rational (or irrational) for Oakeshott. In this sense he is, at the very least, protected against accusations that he supports the more extreme forms of 'relativist' thought. For Oakeshott, an irrational scientist is neither a man whose activity is ungoverned by pre-established rules and principles, nor a man who fails to achieve results, but is instead "the scientific crank and the eccentric."[143] He is labelled irrational both because of his unfaithfulness to the tradition of scientific inquiry and his ignorance with regard to how to carry out a scientific investigation. Thus, in this sense, we may consider Oakeshott to be a somewhat more conservative than Rorty, for whom the inventors of "new vocabularies" are the heroes of his ironic liberal culture (Oakeshott can be legitimately regarded as one such hero). Rorty says that he wishes to drop the words "rational," "argument", "foundation" and "absolute" from the ironic, liberal vocabulary.[144] Oakeshott, for his part, wishes to retain the notion of rational, but also naturally takes into consideration those inescapable changes in practices and customs that modify cultures further. Oakeshott sees the concept of 'rational', which he puts in quotation marks, as worth defending if used in the 'right' way, unlike the term reasoning.[145] Oakeshott describes 'rationality' as "the certificate we give to any conduct which can maintain a place in the flow of sympathy, the coherence of activity, which composes a way of living."[146] In this sense, I think Rorty might accept the inclusion of the concept "rational" in the ironic, liberal vocabulary, but in 1989 he appears to have interpreted the 'semantic battle' over the meaning of the concept "rational" as having been lost. As such, the word has to be discarded.

---

[142] M. Oakeshott 1948, *A Letter to Karl Popper*.
[143] M. Oakeshott 1950, *Rational Conduct*, RP, p. 124.
[144] R. Rorty 1989, pp. 48-9.
[145] See Oakeshott 1950, *Rational Conduct*, RP, p. 105.
[146] Ibid., p.130.

In Rorty's view, the crucial move in the reinterpretation of the morality/prudence distinction towards a view in which liberals might be convinced that in our society loyalty to one's own society is a sufficient expression of morality, requiring no ahistorical backup, is:

> ...to think of the moral self, the embodiment of rationality, not as one of Rawls's original choosers, somebody who can distinguish her *self* from her talents and interests and views about the good, but as a network of beliefs, desires, and emotions behind it – no substrate behind the attributes.[147]

Thus, Rorty includes the Oakeshottian use of the term rationality in his earlier work, only to later abandon it from the vocabulary of his liberal utopia. Writing about the postmodern bourgeois society as the Hegelian attempt to defend the institutions of the rich North Atlantic democracies, he also moves closer to Oakeshott's understanding of human agency:

> For purposes of moral and political deliberation and conversation, a person *is* just that network, as for purposes of ballistics she is a point-mass, or for purposes of chemistry a linkage of molecules. She is a network that is constantly reweaving itself in the usual Quinean manner – that is to say, not by reference to general criteria (e.g., "rules of meaning" or "moral principles") but in the hit-or-miss way in which cells readjust themselves to meet the pressures of the environment. On a Quinean view, rational behavior is just adaptive behavior of a sort which roughly parallels the behavior, in similar circumstances, of the other members of some relevant community. Irrationality, in both physics and ethics, is a matter of behavior that leads one to abandon, or be stripped of, members in some such community.[148]

Agency is not a closed substance, but readjusts in different practices and situations. Herewith, we move on to a different view of human agency than that of the more conventional form of liberalism, as entertained by Berlin and Raz. Oakeshott's and Rorty's agent is neither an agent who only becomes realized within a 'state' called autonomy nor an agent for whom the 'outer world' and relationships primarily represent coercion, but, rather, he/she is an agent who is to some extent *composed* of the activities that take place in those relationships and practices. This notion is undeniably representative of a view of liberalism that has been nudged in the

[147] R. Rorty 1983, pp. 585-6.
[148] Ibid., p. 586.

Hegelian direction instead of towards Kantianism, though one should not forget that Oakeshott's conception also includes certain Hobbesian connotations.

This kind of examination of agency also implies the utilization of a different conception of *freedom* within the realm of liberal thought. It is neither exhausted in terms of the freedom *from* or freedom *to* – though it can entail both. Rather, it is *choosing* within a network that consists of outcomes of earlier choices and that is further changed by a new choice. Practices etc. do not create any *outside* coercion or even opportunities, but they are included in the situation of choice itself. Freedom in civil association, which I see Oakeshott as fostering, naturally includes rules that only have to be acknowledged while choosing; they are not commands but adverbial considerations to be contemplated by the agent. The issues of authority and civil association are, however, tackled later in this book without the burden of "ism" thinking, so I will not proceed any further down this path here. Yet in my interpretation, Oakeshott's distinct conception of freedom is quite relevant to liberalist discussions, because it implies that a liberal society consists of practices and rules that make *living* as an individual – in the 'fullest sense' of an agent making choices for him-/herself – possible.[149] There is a difference in meaning here to the conception – like that of Raz's – that a government must offer as many *options* as possible for its citizens to choose from, as here these options are the premeditated ends in the act of

---

[149] If we can refer to Oakeshott's conception as a 'fourth' concept of liberty, there must of course be "a third concept of liberty," which is relevant to the contemporary discussions on liberalism, i.e. freedom from dependence. Q. Skinner 2002a, p. 18. This conception was devised during the Roman Republic and then revived by a "number of spokesmen in the English Parliament," who began to apply the conception in their criticism of the Crown in the early decades of the 17th century. Ibid., p. 17. According to Skinner, the essence of the argument is that freedom is restricted by dependence. Rights are illusory and therefore not real if their existence depends on the benevolence of the monarch or some other authority: "To live as subjects of a monarch is to live as slaves." Ibid., p. 18. In this view, it is only possible to enjoy one's liberty if one lives as a citizen of a self-governing republic. Skinner also recommends this view "given our current predicament," in which civil liberties are often suppressed in times of emergency, often in the name of freedom and democracy. The use of this kind of language is, for Skinner, to speak the language of tyranny. We may also find some parallels to this conception of freedom in Oakeshott's conception of the 'benevolent ruler' of *universitas*, who – by applying e.g. 'distributive justice' – renders people his dependent *subjects*. There is no freedom for Oakeshott in such a state, as it has been replaced by the enjoyment of assured benefits. OHC, p. 317. See also, P. Pettit 1997, pp. 80-109.

choosing. In contrast, in my reading, in the Oakeshott-Rortyan liberal society[150] – or utopia, if you wish – the authority would only be responsible for maintaining and adjusting conditions and practices to the extent that they remain adverbial considerations, open to *many* options and chances that are often *unknown* in advance. Thus, in this sense, Oakeshott's conception of agency and freedom can be contrasted with the views of both Hobbes and Hegel as anti-teleological. It is also in Hobbes's thinking that human beings are actually provided with the option of whether or not to enter into a contract or to remain in a state of nature. However, the consequences of doing so are seen as so unpleasant that his political philosophy actually presents a kind of teleology as regards entering into a social contract.

In Rorty's view, whatever is referred to as 'true' in a liberal democracy becomes esteemed as true in a free conversation. The political discourse of Western democracies is the exchange of Wittgensteinian "reminders for a particular purpose" – "anecdotes about the past effects of various practices and predictions of what will happen if, or unless, some of these are altered."[151] In Oakeshott's words, political discourse consists of:

> ...the effort to address ourselves to real and imaginary situations; and the effort to support our proposals with relevant arguments in which conjectures are not confused with certainties nor opinion with demonstrable truth.[152]

It is here, too, that Oakeshott's and Rorty's conceptions of politics differ from those entertained either by Berlin or Raz. For Oakeshott, what makes politics – as well as other practical activities – rational is its place in a "flow of sympathy, a current of moral activity."[153] In a more recent definition, politics in *respublica* is to "consider the desirability or otherwise of the conditions prescribed in a practice."[154] Politics is precisely this 'keeping in trim' of the rules and their continuous modifica-

---

[150] I use the term "society" here for the purpose of convenience, yet it must be noted again that Oakeshott, in his late production, did not approve of the use of the term, or put it in quotation marks in order to avoid false connotations to totalities. Here, one can also substitute the term for "association" if one wishes to remain faithful to Oakeshott's thought.

[151] R. Rorty 1983, p. 587.

[152] M. Oakeshott 1991, *Political Discourse*, RP, p. 95.

[153] M. Oakeshott 1950, *Rational Conduct*, RP, p. 129.

[154] OHC, p. 161.

tion. Thus, I argue that this conception bears none of the connotations of stagnation that are present in Raz's, and to some extent Berlin's scheme with its 'permanent' moral horizon. Here, we may refer to this 'Rortyan-Oakeshottian' version of liberalism as a 'politics of change and conversation', which certainly adds to and contests features of the 'politics of consensus' and the 'politics of conflicts' of Raz and Berlin.

Of course, there is some expression of conservatism in the work of both Oakeshott and Rorty. For example, according to Rorty, the contemporary liberal society already contains the institutions necessary to facilitate its own improvement.[155] However, the important point to remember here is that these institutions are not rooted in any external standard that would be necessary in order to ensure their protection and without which they would collapse. Rorty's thought of course includes the notion of the avoidance of cruelty as one of the virtues of a liberal citizen, but this quality is as much a form of historical contingency as anything else in the language of morals. The same applies to the Oakeshottian individual, who values making choices for him/herself. Nor do they point in the direction of any government *policy*, as is the case with both Raz and, to a lesser extent, Berlin.

However, contrary to a commonly held prejudice, 'Oakeshottian liberalism' is not right-wing libertarianism, but he does, for example, acknowledge that a modern state accommodates certain features that do not belong to the theoretical abstraction of civil association. In Hegel, "who was an unequivocal modernist," Oakeshott finds someone with a sophisticated view of the matter. For Hegel, "modern poverty was a relative not an absolute condition and it was the counterpart of modern wealth rather than a sign of personal inadequacy."[156] Oakeshott's account is that:

> ... great disparities of wealth were an impediment (though not a bar) to the enjoyment of civil association; and this hindrance could and should be reduced by imposing civil conditions upon industrial enterprise (similar perhaps to those designed to prevent fraud or the pollution of the atmosphere), and where necessary by the exercise of a judicious 'lordship' for the relief of the destitute.[157]

---

[155] R. Rorty 1989, p. 63.
[156] OHC, p. 305.
[157] Ibid., 304-5n.

Both Rorty and Oakeshott have a certain level of trust in the prevailing liberal culture and its possibilities, although its only 'guarantee' is the existence of people who are willing to unflinchingly stick to their own convictions. For both Oakeshott and Rorty, foundationalist conceptions such as human nature are not prerequisites for the understanding of and desire for the continuity of liberal cultures and states. In addition, both of their contributions to liberal theory include some new vocabulary and new ways of conceptualizing a liberal society whose citizens are conscious of their own contingency and that of their society.

3: Conservatism

The connection of the ideology or doctrine of conservatism to Oakeshott's thought is more complex than that of liberalism. Namely, one can interpret Oakeshott as having contributed *some* interesting and beneficial aspects to the theory of liberalism, whereas he has been largely interpreted as *the* representative of twentieth century British conservative thought. Thus, his entire political philosophy is seen either as having laid down the ideological foundations for conservatism or as simply continuing the tradition of conservative thought. One example of the combination of both outlooks is Robert Nisbet's grouping of Oakeshott with "the Jouvenels and Kirks" of the "'pre-political strata'," who are linked with the "Thatchers and Reagans of the 'political strata'."[158] He also considers the tradition of conservative thought – extending from Edmund Burke down to Russel Kirk, Bertrand de Jouvenel and Oakeshott – as unproblematic, thus viewing Burke (somewhat justifiably) as the Marx or Mill of conservatism; *Reflections on the Revolution in France* is said to have marked the beginning of anti-Enlightenment production, which went on to include such names as de Maistre, Chateaubriand, Coleridge and Hamilton.[159] In these types of interpretations, Oakeshott appears as a kind of "Rawls" or "Nozick" of conservatism.

Oakeshott has also been given a considerable role in various textbooks as having modified some of the central aspects of conservatism, such as skepticism, the rejection of political ideals, a limited and rule-based government, the reliance on tra-

---

[158] R. Nisbet 1986, p .x.
[159] Ibid., pp. 1-2.

dition, as well as even organicism and communitarianism.[160] This commonly held view of Oakeshott as a figurehead of contemporary conservatism has also spawned a great deal of criticism. For example, Jeremy Rayner has summed up Oakeshott's reputation as "the legend of Oakeshott's conservatism," and he denies – along with Oakeshott himself – that "a preference for civil association has anything to do with a preference for a limited or noninterventionist style of government."[161]

However, Rayner does acknowledge the existence of certain links with conservative thought by attributing to Oakeshott a preference for a more limited role for politics: "Civil association could happily exist without politics."[162] In his view, this is the "grain of truth" in the criticisms of contemporaries ranging from Bernard Crick to Bikhu Parekh. Placing authority at the centre of political life, Oakeshott undermines the importance of politics as activity. This is precisely what I wish to challenge in this book; my claim will eventually be that Oakeshott's view becomes a qualified praise of political activity.

Maurice Cranston has written an additional insightful interpretation of Oakeshott as a conservative. For him, Oakeshott's voice is unique: It is a combination of traditionalism without traditional beliefs, individualism with a preference for Hegel over Locke, and a marvellous sense of style.[163] According to Cranston, viewing Oakeshott as one of Burke's successors would be a mistake as he does not share Burke's championing of the Christian order, Natural Law or the Right to Property. Instead, Oakeshott should be acknowledged as a kindred spirit of David Hume, with whom he shares a reliance on tradition, habit and custom because there is nothing else to rely on: "No God, no Natural Law, no Rights."[164] Furthermore, he attributes a manifest devotion to freedom against régimes and concentrations of power to the heart of Oakeshott's thinking – an interpretation with which I generally agree.

However, it is less frequently noted that the *early* Oakeshottian discourse also converged with some of the central aspects of *old* conservatism, which are often listed as trust in

---

[160] G. Thomas 2000, p. 206. See, e.g., R. Dahrendorf 1995, p. 515.
[161] J. Rayner 1985, p. 335.
[162] Ibid., 334.
[163] M. Cranston 1967, p. 82.
[164] Ibid., p. 84.

experience and tradition over abstract thought and revolutionary politics, a belief in authority – not only of the state but also of the family, local community and church – the organic growth of a society, hierarchy, and religion. A human being is seen as an inseparable totality made up of physical matter, moral, religious and other mental features, and here conservatism diverges from liberalism, which – from a conservative point of view – oversimplifies human beings and contributes to the birth of mass society and the idealization of economic growth.[165] For example, in the essay *The Authority of the State*, Oakeshott wrote about the Church, the trade union and the family as organs of a state.[166] Some of the points he expressed during the 1940s are also reminiscent of Edmund Burke's views. Firstly, Oakeshott speaks of political tradition as if there was only *one* in any given society and as if it offered politicians the possibility to consult the voice of the past. Additionally, Oakeshott seems to entertain a view of *parliament* that is similar to that of Burke. For Burke, the parliament was "a *deliberative* assembly of *one* nation, with *one* interest, that of the whole."[167] A member of parliament does not present local prejudices or purposes but acts first and foremost as a member of parliament. In 1948, Oakeshott acknowledged the politician's need for policy and programme, but denied that the conservative view had anything to do with "catchwords, slogans and visions," i.e. with a rhetoric that he seems to see as appealing to inexperienced voters.[168] Oakeshott also speaks of parliament as emphatically 'one' body in a society; a politician, whether in government or the opposition, must understand that his primary *function* is to disperse dangerous concentrations of power in a society. These statements, along with the essay *Rationalism in Politics* (1947) and his letter to Karl Popper (1948), suggest that Oakeshott's ideal model of politics originated from the period before the introduction of the 1867 Reform Act. It is my view that it took decades for Oakeshott to completely diverge from this 'original' conception.

The 'mediating phase' of Oakeshott's work, which spanned the late 1940s and 1950s, tends more often to be interpreted in terms of *modern* conservatism, which has retained many of the

---

[165] See, e.g., R. Harisalo & E. Miettinen 1997, N. O'Sullivan 1976, pp. 119-53.
[166] Oakeshott 1929, *The Authority of the State*, RPML, p. 85.
[167] E. Burke 1774, p. 64.
[168] M. Oakeshott 1948, *Contemporary British Politics*, p. 486.

features of the older type of conservatism, with the exception of, for example, religion and hierarchy. Oakeshott is often linked to conservatism in terms of his critique of rationalist politics and his emphasis on traditions and practical knowledge.

Oakeshott's later work, on the other hand, has been interpreted as representative of *new* conservatism, which is seen to emphasize the authoritarian framework of the state while fostering the working of free-market mechanisms and undermining the authority of intermediary organizations.

Below, I will concentrate on the latter two phases of Oakeshott's claimed conservatism and the interpretation of them. Because the aforementioned claim of the development of Oakeshott's political thought constitutes an important part of the argument in this book, in this chapter I will briefly examine the question of Oakeshott's conservatism through other influential interpretations of him as a conservative, leaving chronology in the background. My approach here is also more critical than in my examination of liberalism, as, in my opinion, it is precisely the persistent 'myth of conservatism' that has partially prevented Oakeshott's work from being read by a broader audience. His label as a leading figure of British conservative thought has certainly kept those who entertain other political commitments from taking an interest in his thought. Thus, in this chapter I would like to contribute to the undermining of Oakeshott's reputation as a *partisan* conservative while not, of course, denying his unique understanding of the entertainment of a conservative *disposition*.

Here, then, I distinguish between two alternative yet partially complementary interpretations of Oakeshott as a representative of conservatism, namely the *philosophical* and *political* interpretations of conservatism. The latter usually represents Oakeshott as a theoretician of conservatism from whose thought one can rather directly draw conclusions with regard to practical politics as understood as a policy. One example of this kind of interpretation can be found in Robert Devigne's book, *Recasting Conservatism*. With regard to the former interpretation, I focus particular attention on Bernard Crick's interpretations. This examination is intentionally a bit fragmentary, as a more profound inquiry into one of the central concepts of these interpretations, namely that of tradition, is carried out later, also including some views put forth by Crick. By philosophical conservatism I am referring both to Wittgenstein's phrase that philosophy "leaves everything as it is" – attributed also to Oakeshott – and to the idea that Oakeshott has (re)formulated a coherent philosophy of conservatism. Although this distinction between the two types of conservative interpretations may seem trivial, I find it to be a rather solid one, as the representatives of a philosophical interpretation usually deny the existence of a direct party-bias in Oakeshott's thinking, whereas political interpreters draw parallels between Oakeshott and Conservative Party policies.[169]

On Bernard Crick's Critique

The tone of Bernard Crick's view of Oakeshott leaves little room for misinterpretation:

> A spectre is haunting the LSE and (please don't forget) Political Science. For ten years the skeptical, polemical, dandiacal, paradoxical, gay and bitter spirit has been haunting, rather than filling, the Chair of Political Science formerly held by Harold Laski.[170]

His interpretations of Oakeshott stand out in the crowd of so-called "ism" interpretations in their explicit and persistent critical approach towards Oakeshott's *oeuvre* since the 1960s, and it is precisely in terms of conservatism that Crick interprets his thought. The most evident watershed between the authors is Crick's commitment to the Socialist doctrines – a feature which he, of course, does not wish to hide. He also points out his discontent with Oakeshott's election to the Chair of Political Science at the London School of Economics and Political Science in 1951, as it altered the school's previously 'activist' style of political science towards that of historical study. However, this does not represent the entire picture of the relationship between Crick's and Oakeshott's thought. Namely, I also see Crick as responding to Oakeshott in his own theorizing, although he seldom mentions Oakeshott's name in this connection. For example, along with Oakeshott, Crick wishes to reserve a special role for politics:

---

[169] See, e.g., C. Covell 1986, p. 93.
[170] B. Crick 1963b, p. 65.

> The attempt to politicize everything is the destruction of politics. When everything is seen as relevant to politics, then politics has in fact become totalitarian.[171]

Along similar lines, Crick also defends politics against ideology and technology. For him, as for Oakeshott, political activity cannot be reduced to a system of beliefs or a set of goals, nor must politics be understood as a 'science'.[172] The following quote could easily be mistaken as having been written by Oakeshott:

> Politics is not, then, a grasping for the ideal; but neither is it a freezing of tradition. It is an activity lively, adaptive, flexible, and conciliatory.[173]

Yet Crick does not attribute this kind of conception of politics to Oakeshott. Instead, Oakeshott's "understanding of politics is entirely that of a preservative activity rather than one having possibility of being innovative."[174] In short, the cornerstones of Crick's critique are: Oakeshott's opposition to a reformist conception of politics, his conception of tradition and – perhaps most importantly – his skepticism.

In Crick's view, it is precisely Oakeshott's skepticism that located him "beyond the fringe of normal conservative experience," rendering him a kind of *ultimate* conservative. Oakeshott not only attacked metaphysics in the spirit of Wittgenstein but was also critical of the possibility of any theoretical knowledge about politics and society, thus remaining completely skeptical of the view that any political doctrines can have any philosophical foundations.[175] It appears as though the difference lies primarily in the understanding of the theory/practice relationship:

> Now it is not, I agree with Oakeshott, the special business of a political philosopher to offer advice to politicians or to presume to make people's minds up for them. For one thing, their minds are almost always made up already. But it is part of our business to follow truths and their implications, whether we see them as theories or doctrines, and to debate...on a level above both political opinion and political theory (as contingency and relativity).[176]

---

[171] B. Crick 1962, p. 151.
[172] Ibid., p. 54.
[173] Ibid., p. 55.
[174] B. Crick 1991, p. 123.
[175] B. Crick1963a, p. 65.
[176] Ibid., p. 13.

He is, of course, correct in maintaining that Oakeshott denies the existence of a direct relationship between philosophy and politics in the sense that one could conclude that philosophical principles are 'put into practice' in politics. Yet Crick misunderstands Oakeshott's conception of the modes of practice and philosophy by maintaining that he denies the possibility of possessing any theoretical knowledge of politics and society, as Oakeshott's point is actually quite the opposite. For Oakeshott, political philosophy is theorizing *on* and *about* politics, but it is done in another language, by applying an explanatory idiom that lacks injunctive force.[177] The role of political doctrines is not denied either, although Crick is correct in maintaining that Oakeshott completely rejects the notion of doctrines as being based on philosophical foundations. In fact, according to Oakeshott, there cannot be philosophical foundations for *anything*; philosophy is a parasitic activity:

> …it springs from the conversation, because this is what the philosopher reflects upon, but it makes no specific contribution to it.[178]

Yet doctrines are abridgements of traditions and appear in the form of principles, theories and ideologies. They can be used as aids in the reflection of political conduct. Oakeshott has "no horror of principles," as he noted in the reply to a critique by D.D. Raphael. [179]He emphasizes having "only a suspicion of those who use principles as if they were axioms and those who seem to think that practical argument is concerned with proof. A principle is not something which may be given as a reason or a justification for making a decision or performing an action; it is a short-hand identification of a disposition to choose."[180] Thus, principles are possible aids in political reflection, although they do not present a solid foundation for politics itself.

Thus, Oakeshott is not completely skeptical of the possibility of acquiring a theoretical knowledge of politics, nor does he succumb to other accusations hurled at the conservatives of that time, i.e. that they approximated politics with empiricism. As Stuart Hampshire put it:

---

[177] Oakeshott 1962, *The Study of 'Politics' in a University*, RP, pp. 212-8.
[178] M. Oakeshott 1959, *The Voice of Poetry in the Conversation of Mankind*, RP, p. 491.
[179] M. Oakeshott 1965, *Rationalism in Politics: A Reply to Professor Raphael*, p. 292.
[180] Ibid., p. 92.

> There is a tired lull in English politics, and argument on general
> principles has largely died. This may be taken as a sign of political
> health; for there is the view that abstract arguments and general
> ideas must mislead in politics: better stick to practical solu-
> tions...[181]

For Hampshire, this means that both political parties are now
tied to the conservative attitude by having anchored themselves to day-to-day experience. This view of politics is, however, condemned in a rather sarcastic tone by Oakeshott as
reminiscent of "waking up each morning and considering
'What would I like to do?'"[182] He refers to this conception as
"politics without a policy." From a theoretical point of view, it
represents a misunderstanding of politics as impossible to
achieve. From a practical perspective, an approximation of it is
to be found in the politics of "the wall-scribbler" and "the
vote-catcher."[183]

Along with the accusation of extreme skepticism, Crick's
categorization of Oakeshott as an opponent of innovation in
politics also implies that Crick's own view of politics is inherently rationalist. This is not, however, the case. Instead, he,
rather surprisingly, praises Burke's aphorism about the need
to reform in order to preserve as the most profound characterization of the method of political rule to date.[184] For Crick, as
for Oakeshott, *politics is primarily an activity*. The former
emphasizes it as a means of ruling divided societies without
undue violence, oscillating between the grasping of ideals and
the pursuit of self-interest. For the latter:

> Politics is the activity of attending to the general arrangements of
> a collection of people who, in respect of their common recognition
> of attending to its arrangements, compose a single community.[185]

And it is apparently to this definition of politics that Crick so
intensively attaches the label of conservatism, since Oakeshott
describes this activity as springing from the existing traditions
of behaviour and as being a pursuit of their intimations. In
Crick's view, tradition alone is too weak to perform an

[181] S. Hampshire 1953, p. 947.
[182] Oakeshott 1951, *Political Education*, RP, p. 46.
[183] Ibid., pp. 46-7.
[184] B. Crick 1962, pp. 24-5.
[185] M. Oakeshott 1951, *Political Education*, RP, p. 56.

"anthropological function of politics as preserving a community within a complex society."[186]

There are a couple of keen observations in Crick's critique of Oakeshott's conception of tradition, which were presented immediately after the publication of the first edition of *Rationalism in Politics* in 1962. His first thesis is that it is a mistake to align politics so closely with tradition. Tradition may be a necessary condition of politics, but it alone is certainly not sufficient.[187] His objection stems from Oakeshott's neglect of the role of conscious goals in politics; it is not enough to keep the ship afloat on an even keel but, rather, the "ship's masters... usually have some idea of where they are going."[188] As mentioned above, Oakeshott has responded to criticism regarding the role of principles in politics, but it is not at all surprising that contemporary critiques such as Crick's have taken on such tones.

In 1940s and 1950s, Oakeshott sometimes uses the concept of tradition as if encompassing in connection with politics and society. Thus, in terms of presenting a critique of Oakeshott's work, the choice of which texts to read and with what emphasis is important – and in Crick's case, the emphasis has naturally been on an interpretation through conservatism. It is not difficult to find evidence in support of this idea in the following quotation, for example:

> In short, political crisis (even when it seems to be imposed upon a society by changes beyond its control) always appears *within* a tradition of political activity: and "salvation" comes from the unimpaired resources of the tradition itself.[189]

In my view, Crick is not entirely mistaken in claiming that in the essay *Political Education* the concept of tradition becomes very closely related to that of ideology – one offering a way of understanding everything, the other providing a means of explaining everything.[190] For Crick, it becomes gravely difficult for a conservative to describe any criteria for choosing between differing traditions and their intimations, and therefore he or she will tend to turn to a conception of *one* tradition in a society:

---

[186] B. Crick 1962, p. 24.
[187] Ibid., p. 117.
[188] Ibid., p. 118.
[189] M. Oakeshott 1951, *Political Education*, RP, p. 59.
[190] B. Crick 1962, p. 119.

> But in the unfamiliar mode of Oakeshottian irony we hear, in fact,
> a familiar hortatory voice telling us that for any politics there
> *should* be one dominant tradition... *The* tradition then becomes
> seen as simply the tradition of the governing class.[191]

Oakeshott has actually responded to this kind of critique by
saying that "the absence of homogeneity does not necessarily
destroy singleness," adding that he has explored how the legal
structure of a society is reformed and amended.[192] As to the latter point, it seems not to have convinced Crick, who stresses
the importance of the continuous adaptation of a state to
changing circumstances in order to survive, but denies – I
think incorrectly – that this characterization exists in Oakeshott's thought.

Yet, I think Crick is correct in highlighting the most obvious
point of what we might go so far as to refer to as Oakeshott's
party conservatism, namely his choosing *between* ideologies
and traditions. That is, Oakeshott much more critically labels
the policies (or claimed policies) of the Labour Government as
belonging under the title of rationalism: He draws parallels
between Cromwell and Attlee, tyranny and the Labour Party,
while in the same breath he says that "Conservatism has no
incentive to promote despotism."[193] Thus, conservative politics would be more open to the intimations of traditions than
the politics of other parties, and in this sense, e.g. the essays
Contemporary British Politics and *The Political Economy of Freedom* contain an open party bias. It is Crick's view that Oakeshott's conservatism becomes more conventional, favouring
certain specific social and economic doctrines in a particular
time and place and resisting inventiveness, innovation and
conscious dexterity in a society.[194]

Crick has not been alone in his critique of Oakeshott's conservative conception of tradition. For example, Hanna Pitkin
wrote that the "appeal to tradition, then, is useful only to the
privileged, both in the sense that one must already be blessed
with a healthy tradition in order to make such an appeal, and
in the sense that only those already granted privileges by that

[191] Ibid., p. 120.
[192] M. Oakeshott 1962, *The Pursuit of Intimations. Appendix to Political Education*,
RP, p. 69. The critique was presented by R.H. Crossman (1958) in his *The Charm
of Politics*, although Oakeshott does not mention him by name.
[193] M. Oakeshott 1948, *Contemporary British Politics*, p. 485. See also, M. Oakeshott
1947, *Rationalism in Politics*, RP, p. 11.
[194] B. Crick 1962, p. 120.

tradition can expect further privileges from it."[195] It is not that I wish to say that there is nothing to these kinds of criticisms; as in Rorty's thought, there are also indications of this type of thinking in Oakeshott's work, as he clearly does not favour any 'utopian' conception of politics. Yet, it must be stressed that Oakeshott has never explicitly attached his thinking to any particular 'social class', and his notion of the pursuit of intimations can be interpreted in a wide range of ways. For example, Chantal Mouffe refers to the "radical potential of his arguments."[196] Oakeshott's discussion of the "legal status of women" through the vehicle of understanding political activity as "the exploration of sympathy present but not yet followed up, and the convincing demonstration that now is the appropriate moment for recognizing it" is viewed as useful in the extension of 'democratic principles'. For Mouffe, Oakeshott's notion of the heterogeneous, open and ultimately indeterminable character of traditions can be used in the context of democratic tradition as playing certain aspects of tradition against others.[197] As to resisting innovation, Oakeshott famously pointed out that the "plan to resist all planning" found in Friedrich Hayek's *Road to Serfdom* is as rationalistic as other rationalist plans.[198]

Thus, as I noted above, one might to a certain extent agree with Crick's criticism if one were to concentrate on Oakeshott's *Rationalism in Politics* essays, which were written in the 1940s and early 1950s. Crick's reading implies that Oakeshott has reformulated a philosophical doctrine of conservatism that has evolved around the concept of tradition. In addition, it is also evident that Oakeshott did actually listen to his critics, as he substituted tradition with "practices" in his later work. However, a broader picture of the development of Oakeshott's work in a new direction begins to emerge when we pay careful attention to the content of the entire book, particularly to the essay *On Being Conservative* (1956). In this essay, a conservative disposition centres foremost:

> ...upon a propensity to use and to enjoy what is available rather than to wish for or to look for something else; to delight in what is

[195] H. Pitkin 1973, p. 264.
[196] C. Mouffe 1993, p. 16.
[197] Ibid., p. 18.
[198] M. Oakeshott 1947, *Rationalism in Politics*, RP, p. 26.

present rather than wish or to look for something else; to delight in what is present rather than what was or what may be.[199]

For Oakeshott, this propensity to enjoy the present represents the opposite of ignorance and apathy, instead breeding attachment and affection. The 'postmodern' understanding of 'life politics' bears echoes of this kind of conception of politics, in which a subject is understood as necessarily situated within a given time and place and as making the best of it. More explicitly with regard to politics, Oakeshott favours governing as "a specific and limited activity: not the managing of an enterprise, but the rule of those engaged in a great diversity of self-chosen enterprises."[200] Thus, he also prefers a plural society and agrees with Crick that the task of a government is "to keep its subjects at peace,"[201] which is more a 'liberal conservative' view than that of "a High Tory."[202] As to innovation, Oakeshott's stance is, like Crick, rather Burkean:

> Innovation, then, is called for if the rules are to remain appropriate to the activities they govern. But, as the conservative understands it, modification of the rules should always reflect, and never impose, a change in the activities and beliefs of those who are subject to them, and should never in any occasion be so great as to destroy the *ensemble*.[203]

Innovation, as a moderate change in present conditions, is thus part of Oakeshott's conception of political activity in this essay. This view also takes the unintended consequences of innovations into account since every improvement generates a new and complex situation of which the actual innovation is merely one component: "The total change is always more extensive than the change designed; and the whole of what is entailed can neither be foreseen nor circumscribed."[204] As such, it becomes understandable that Oakeshott prefers piecemeal innovations to great, rapid changes. Additionally, it should always be kept in mind that the opposite of Oakeshott's conservative politician is an imaginary picture of a rationalist politician who approximates politics to engineering or science. Thus, it is also always Oakeshott's intention to

[199] M. Oakeshott 1956, *On Being Conservative*, RP, p. 408.
[200] Ibid., p. 429.
[201] Ibid.
[202] B. Crick 1962, p. 33.
[203] M. Oakeshott 1956, *On Being Conservative*, RP, p. 431.
[204] Ibid., p. 411.

protect the understanding of politics as a situated, reflective activity as opposed to that of a 'planning mentality'.

If Crick's earlier reading of Oakeshott is blind to some of the nuances in both Oakeshott's 'conservatism' and the conservative disposition, his late criticism seems to be even more misguided. After the publication of *On Human Conduct* (1975), I find it difficult to sustain the claim that "Oakeshott seems to set himself against any possibility of conscious change."[205] First of all, all agency *is* reflective consciousness and all action is thus a reflected, i.e. a chosen action. Secondly, politics in a civil association is:

> … concerned with an imagined and wished-for condition of *respublica*, a condition in some respect different from its current condition and alleged to be more desirable. It is deliberation designed to specify and find reasons for, utterance designed to recommend and give reasons for, and action designed to promote the change from the one to the other.[206]

Oakeshott's understanding of politics in *On Human Conduct* is thus very much that of being conscious change. Furthermore, Crick claims that Oakeshott's citizens are not really citizens at all, but are rather the good subjects of a *Rechtstaat*. They must behave themselves and "only take part in politics to protect the laws."[207] Regarding Hanna Pitkin's similar critique of *cives* as "all good boys," Oakeshott said that he never used the word 'obey' in this connection.[208] Oakeshott's *cives* are not defined as litigants but as suitors to a court; "he is one who has a court to go to if he needs it."[209] Similarly, Oakeshott's citizens 'go into politics' when they feel there is a need for change in – or preservation of – the rules ascribed in *respublica*.

Robert Devigne and Oakeshott's New Conservatism

If Crick's interpretation of Oakeshott as a representative of modern conservatism does not apply to his major work, *On Human Conduct*, is there still a possibility for another kind of conservative interpretation? Robert Devigne has attempted this in his book, *Recasting Conservatism. Oakeshott, Strauss, and*

---

[205] B. Crick 1991, p. 123.
[206] OHC, p. 168.
[207] B. Crick 1991, p.123.
[208] M. Oakeshott 1976, *On Misunderstanding Human Conduct. A Reply To My Critics*, p. 356.
[209] Ibid.

the Response to Postmodernism (1994). Whereas Crick interpreted Oakeshott from a more 'philosophical' perspective,
saying that Oakeshott prefers to be thought of as being "above
politics,"[210] Devigne wishes to highlight his relevance to an
actual political situation in Great Britain, i.e. Thatcher's
regime. His theoretical constellation is also different; Oakeshott is seen as responding to a postmodern situation. According to Devigne, Oakeshott, in contrast to Hayek, did not fear a
peaceful, legal road to totalitarianism but, rather, a postmodern world of barbarism or nihilism. This world appears as
a political order without authority; a fragmented, incoherent
society based on competing interpretations of the truth.[211]
Thus, the 'new' conservatism, which Oakeshott represents
here, is not a version of libertarianism, concerned exclusively
with enlarging the individual's private domain; it is a response
to the loss of civil tradition, morality and authority.[212]

Devigne traces the origins of Oakeshott's new conservatism
back to his (and Hayek's) criticisms of "the middle way" or
"Butskellism" in British postwar politics.[213] Oakeshott criticized the state's attempts to direct patterns of activity within
the society towards rational political goals, as doing so causes
them to lose their coherence and their ability to dictate the procedures of the pursuit of private goals.[214] Devigne's doctrinaire interpretation of this phase of Oakeshott's thinking
claims that Oakeshott advocated a return to the "consti-
tutionalism" of conservative thinking. The state's focus
should be on the high politics of foreign policy, as well as on
sterling and the preservation of a diffusion of power within
the society. Low politics, such as the distribution of social services, should only be attempted if "political subunits or civil
institutions were faltering and threatening the independence
of the central state."[215] Thus, Devigne acknowledges the difficulties Oakeshott had in following his own 'program' of
non-partisan political philosophy and uses the opportunity to
translate his language into that of practical politics.

Concerning Oakeshott's later period, Devigne attaches his
discussion of Oakeshott's new conservatism to the debate

[210] B. Crick 1962, p. 111.
[211] R. Devigne 1994, p. 10.
[212] Ibid., p. xii.
[213] Ibid., p. 5.
[214] Ibid., p. 10.
[215] Ibid., p. 11.

between the *garantiste* constitutionalists and the supporters of parliamentary sovereignty in the Conservative Party in the 1970s and 1980s, which began with Edward Heath's "U-turn" and ended with Margaret Thatcher's second parliamentary victory in 1983.[216] He views the central issue as the controversy between the rule of law and the authority of the rule-making centre. *Garantiste* constitutionalists, i.e the 'Hayekians', placed the central state under the rule of higher laws in order to restrict arbitrary power. Supporters of parliamentary sovereignty – 'Oakeshottians' in this reading – emphasized that the legislative centre of the national government was to regain its authority and become the sole lawmaking centre of the polity. As Oakeshott was opposed to alleged unconditional principles of *jus*, such as the Bill of Rights, he is seen as having established the power of the ultimate authority and having undermined the importance of intermediary organizations. The state would be the legitimate centre of political action and the market would be introduced as the central organizing mechanism of the economy.[217] Both liberty and order would be enhanced by the re-establishment of spontaneous discipline through the price system. "These theorists and writers," notes Devigne, "produced a new mixture of Tory ideas of authority and individual liberty in order to establish the legislative office of the central state's undivided authority."[218] In Devigne's interpretation, the Thatcher governments introduced precisely those reformations recommended by the Oakeshottians.

Devigne is naturally correct in maintaining that the concept of authority is central to Oakeshott's theorization of civil association, but the practical – and in fact economical – conclusions he draws from it seem to me to be rather seriously flawed. In Jeremy Rayner's view, though favouring civil association, Oakeshott' animus was, however, "directed against those confused parodies of civil association he discerned in modern conservatism."[219] Oakeshott denied that civil association has anything to do with the preference for a limited or non-interventionist style of government that would endorse the market mechanism. He also denied that civil association has

---

[216] Ibid., p. 25.
[217] Ibid., pp. 27-30.
[218] Ibid., p. 28.
[219] J. Rayner 1985, p. 335.

any necessary connection with capitalism, which denotes an arrangement regarding the satisfaction of needs. A civil association is in no way a "free enterprise association," and although it would increase the aggregate prosperity of its members faster than other forms of association, this is no reason to recommend it. In short, "Oakeshott is not willing to recommend civil association in terms of its likely consequences at all."[220] Of course, it is to some extent possible to see Oakeshott's view of the rule of law as something which "bakes no bread" in relation to 'non-interventionist' views, but, according to Rayner, his unwillingness to recommend civil association because of its consequences should be given more weight. Oakeshott clearly distinguishes himself from those who recommend certain forms of association according to their promised material prosperity or freedom, as freedom, too, is not a consequence of civil association but intrinsic to it in terms of its requirement that the associates merely acknowledge their obligation to take the relevant laws into account in their conduct.

Devigne finds a further link to the new British conservatism in Oakeshott's rejection of the ideal of social justice. By this he refers to the idealist legacy of the notion that all morality is an artifice to be learned, which implies that there are no external principles of, for example, social justice – a notion that particularly Shirley Letwin has emphasized in her writings. In addition, Devigne highlights Oakeshott's denial of the existence of so-called 'distributive justice' in his ideal character of civil association.[221] In Devigne's interpretation, as opposed to serving as an instrument of the achievement of particularistic goals, the authority of the state encourages respect for uniform laws and rules. Oakeshott in particular and British conservative theory in general maintain that the authority of the state can be ensured only if the central state remains above the pressures exerted from all other sources. By avoiding setting programmatic goals and by operating according to its own rules, the state "creates public belief that it is 'In Authority' – thereby building a uniform procedural framework that sustains social and political interaction."[222] Hence, Oakeshott can be seen as responding to a postmodern situation with the revival of

---

[220] Ibid.
[221] R. Devigne 1994, p. 84.
[222] Ibid., p. 85.

morality and authority. The new British conservatism largely neglects the Church. Instead, the state is endowed with the authority to maintain public interaction and coordinated activity, thus preventing the society from dissolving. "Public compliance with uniform laws will create morality whereby respect for rules becomes the reference point for good and bad behavior."[223]

Devigne's argumentation may initially seem convincing to those who are only fragmentarily acquainted with Oakeshott. And it is precisely through the fragmentary nature of his selection of specific features of Oakeshott's thought that Oakeshott may be viewed as defending Authority and Morality against the postmodern situation. The connecting of his theory with conservative economic theory once again results in the translation of Oakeshott's 'own' language into a foreign language. As such, his important, original emphases and nuances are lost. Namely, it is precisely *freedom* that is essential to Oakeshott's theorizing in *On Human Conduct*. All human conduct is inherently free, as it is an act of reflective intelligence. Authority and laws in civil association emphasize this freedom further: Oakeshott's careful dissociation of laws from commands stresses their nature as merely adverbial considerations upon which an agent may freely base his/her actions. Devigne's political interpretation of Oakeshott's conservatism also entirely neglects the role of *politics* in civil association. It is not so much that the state creates 'uniform morality' through laws, but politics in a way mediates the current morality into laws. Another central aspect of Oakeshott's thought is that this morality need by no means be inherently uniform, but, rather, he stresses that the practices and traditions within a given state are plural in nature. Therefore, it is impossible to view Oakeshott's thought as belonging to the category of the new conservatism, with its championing of markets and heralding of a new form of moralism.

4: Idealism

Next, I will discuss and consequently reject the philosophical "ism" of idealism as a comprehensive interpretative framework of Oakeshott's political philosophy.[224] In doing so, I rely

---

[223] Ibid., p. 118.
[224] Compare, e.g., with R. Tseng 2003.

on Steven S. Gerencser's provocative and profound reflection on the topic in his *The Skeptic's Oakeshott* (2000), which I think deserves to be examined carefully in this context.

For Gerencser, the essential change in Oakeshott's conception of philosophy is its simultaneously increasing degree of skepticism and diminishing level of idealism, which Gerencser considers significant also in terms of the effects it has on Oakeshott's political thought.[225] The dominant element in Oakeshott's early work is that of his being an "absolute idealist" for whom theory and practice are strictly separated and "philosophy alone can integrate a unified world of coherent ideas."[226] However, there are already indications of skepticism in *Experience and Its Modes* in the form of "skeptical idealism." Apart from philosophy, the other modes of experience are described as resting on presuppositions and thus as being incapable of achieving the unmodified and absolutely coherent totality of experience. This skeptical idealism examines "the implicit and often unrecognized presuppositions that limit each of the modes, undermining their claim to absolute certainty."[227] The idea here is not to deny that they express truth, but to understand its partial and relative quality. Thus, the pursuit of philosophy as the "totality of experience" separates it from the modes which were otherwise to lose their modal quality and become a complete experience. Philosophy is thus irrelevant to the sphere of practical life, to which politics belongs.[228]

In the next outline of philosophy, *The Voice of Poetry in the Conversation of Mankind* (1959), Gerencser sees Oakeshott as having abandoned absolute idealism. Philosophy is seen as facing the same limitations and cautions as the other modes, and is conceived as one "voice" amongst many. For many interpreters, such as Franco and W.H. Greenleaf, this is a "mere modification of detail or nuance," but for Gerencser it represents a "vital alteration."[229] Skepticism becomes a disposition against the final certainty of any one voice and thus also

---

[225] S. Gerencser 2000, p. 7.
[226] Ibid., p. 6.
[227] Ibid., p. 29.
[228] Ibid., pp. 24-9.
[229] Ibid., p. 37.

guarantees their independence against any irrelevant claims of authority.[230]

I do not have any difficulties in generally agreeing with this view, especially as Gerencser convincingly traces the roots of this change back to the late 1940s. In the posthumously published *Political Philosophy*,[231] Oakeshott maintains that a person is a philosopher in respect of his skeptical predisposition and not in respect to something he ultimately achieves at the end.[232] Here, Oakeshott has abandoned many of his idealist presumptions, although he continues to hold on to the notion of the separation of philosophy and politics. Mixing the two would inevitably lead to the hindrance of the reflecting impulse of political philosophy by rendering it servile to politics, or to a confused political activity. However, Oakeshott no longer claims that "all nonphilosophical experience is 'confused and distracted', nor does he insist that all forms of experience must be kept completely separate."[233] The *superbia* view of philosophy is beginning to vanish in order to culminate in *The Voice of Poetry*.[234]

Gerencser also re-dates the posthumously published essay *The Concept of a Philosophy of Politics* to the late 1930s, whereas Timothy Fuller, the editor of the *Religion, Politics and Moral Life* collection, estimates it to have been written in the mid-1940s.[235] The reasons he gives for this re-dating are its resemblance to *The Concept of Philosophical Jurisprudence*, which was published in 1938. The likeness of the two, complete with a number of identical paragraphs, stresses its distinction from *Political Philosophy*, which is estimated to have been written between 1946 and 1950. In *The Concept of a Philosophy of Politics*, the earlier idealist language of philosophy now also applies to the philosophy of politics, although without the pejorative conception of 'pseudo-philosophy' expressed in *Experience and Its Modes*. It performs the function of transforming the understanding of practical politics into the notion of the coher-

---

[230] Ibid., p. 41.
[231] The essay is estimated to have been written between 1946 and 1950 by Timothy Fuller, the editor of the RPML collection.
[232] S. Gerencser 2000, p. 38.
[233] Ibid.
[234] I think it is worth emphasizing here that "coherence" as a 'result' of philosophical thinking is ultimately unattainable and is also more indicative of a criterion of the impulse of philosophy in *Experience and its Modes*.
[235] Ibid., pp. 68-9.

ent world of ideas or the totality of experience. This operation would, in the 'earliest' conception of philosophy, be condemned as contradictory, as the destruction of the original concept.[236] Gerencser sees Oakeshott as defending idealism against the position that "Hobhouse had abused Bosanquet,"[237] i.e. against the notion of the general will as something which never consciously occurs in political activity, but may still be the ultimate definition of what is present in consciousness. Gerencser asserts that Oakeshott quietly abandoned this type of absolute idealism after the 1930s, never to return to it again. *Political Philosophy* provides a contrast for the understanding of philosophy in the 1930s. In this essay, it is the never-resting, skeptical, radically subversive attitude that prevents philosophy from contributing to politics, *not* the complete *definition* of political concepts.[238]

After concluding this analysis, Gerencser explores the shift in Oakeshott's notion of political philosophy in greater detail. The keys to Gerencser's reading are Oakeshott's changing notion of authority, his increasing skepticism and nominalism, as well as his inherent 'Hobbism'. Gerencser begins by examining Oakeshott's first essay on political philosophy, *The Authority of the State,* which was published in 1929. Here, Oakeshott begins exploring the understandings of authority and state, a continuity that extends to his later work, thus indicating that his reflection on political philosophy is not a derivative branch of his 'Philosophy'. Though Oakeshott did not situate himself within any specific debate in this essay, Gerencser has no difficulty in identifying his thought with the concerns of the earlier idealists. The essay can also be read as a revival of the idealist conception of the state, which, along with British idealism in general, had suffered the "same mortal fate."[239] I will not go into detail with regard to Gerencser's reading, but this view of Oakeshott as defending the British idealist tradition and Bosanquet against H.J. Laski's, A.D. Lindsay's and most notably L.T. Hobhouse's criticism is convincing.[240] In keeping with Franco, Gerencser sees Oakeshott as presenting a full-blown Hegelian definition of the state in

[236] Ibid., p. 72.
[237] Ibid.
[238] Ibid., pp. 74-5.
[239] Ibid., p. 54.
[240] Ibid., pp. 54-5.

which its separation from society is rejected and it is seen as an all-inclusive set of relations, the social equivalent of monism.[241] The authority of the state consists of the whole ground of beliefs or action and relies solely in the completeness of the satisfaction that the state affords to the needs of concrete persons.[242] Gerencser sees the seeds of the skeptical element in Oakeshott's political philosophy in this location of authority in the beliefs of those who are obligated to the state rather than in some external criterion. Yet, although Hobbes makes an appearance in the last lines of *The Authority of the State* as providing an example of the "absolute and inescapable authority" of the state, Oakeshott still "spends another decade working through philosophical idealism."[243]

In this early idealist conception of the state, one distinguishing aspect in contrast to Oakeshott's later production is his connection of the state to the satisfaction of needs. Gerencser notes this connection and he adds that Oakeshott bypassed the question of 'needs' very quickly here, providing no explanation as to what these needs might be.[244] Still, it must be emphasized that in the later division between civil and enterprise association, the satisfaction of needs is very explicitly confined to the latter.[245] Along with the observation of this significant change in Oakeshott's use of vocabulary, I think one could reflect more on one other important difference between the mainstream British idealists and Oakeshott. Namely, that it can hardly be argued that Oakeshott shared the political sympathies usually associated with idealism – not necessarily in terms of idealist argumentation, but in its 'utilizations' in practical politics. One vital difference that is already clear in Oakeshott's early work is that he does not support more direct state activity in the form of the activity of government. The expression of these 'needs' – which are 'satisfied' partly by the Government, regulated in a limited sense by the law, and which have the Church, the trade union and the family as its organs – might just as easily be indicative of Oakeshott's phase as a traditional conservative than of any kind of thorough ide-

---

[241] Ibid., pp. 60-1.
[242] Ibid., p. 63.
[243] Ibid., p. 65.
[244] Ibid., p. 62.
[245] Ibid.

alist re-thinking.[246] There is already more or less of a balance between these elements in *The Authority of the State*, and the consideration of authority as belonging to the sphere of everybody's own judgement and its completeness in the state may well be read as justifying the status quo. Thus, the seeds of social radicalism, often connected to philosophical idealism in Great Britain, are in no way present in Oakeshott's conceptions.

According to Gerencser, the interest in Hobbes is an essential element of Oakeshott's metamorphosis into a skeptic and a nominalist. It is not Gerencser's aim to argue the supremacy of Oakeshott's reading of Hobbes. Rather, he hopes to trace the effect that Oakeshott's focus on Hobbes had on his political thought by examining it in greater detail. Gerencser aptly refers to this effect as 'sympathy'.[247] More specifically, Oakeshott appreciated Hobbes's ability to retain the notions of authority and law even while rejecting their natural or absolute foundations.[248]

The essay *Thomas Hobbes* was written by Oakeshott in 1935. Hobbes was presented in it as a philosopher who presents much more than mere political opinions in his analysis of political life. He offers a political philosophy that is not as time-bound as common sense. The traditional reading of Hobbes as primarily a materialist did not satisfy the 'idealist' Oakeshott, and he criticized it thoroughly in the famous piece *Introduction to Leviathan*, published in 1946.[249] Oakeshott rejected the view that in Hobbes's philosophy a "mechanistic-materialist politics is made to spring from a mechanistic-materialist universe."[250] Another view of Hobbes was equally rejected, i.e. that while Hobbes intended to present a materialist understanding of nature, he was unable to extend it to include politics. For Oakeshott, Hobbes was, however, successful in creating a philosophical system, as it would be wrong to expect a philosopher to be coherent in the sense of conforming to an architectural analogue of a system. Instead, the coherence of Hobbes's philosophy lies in one single "pas-

[246] M. Oakeshott 1929, *The Authority of the State*, RPML, p. 85.
[247] S. Gerencser 2000, p. 78.
[248] Ibid.
[249] Ibid., pp. 79-80.
[250] M. Oakeshott 1946, cited in S. Gerencser 2000, p. 80.

sionate thought."[251] Oakeshott then emphasizes that for Hobbes, philosophy is *reasoning*. The misunderstanding of Hobbes as a materialist and a mechanist stems from the language of causes and effect that he uses to express philosophy as reasoning. The point of Oakeshott's interpretation is that although Hobbes normally uses the "word science as a synonym for philosophy," the distinction between them still exists, although it is only "imperfectly achieved."[252] In short, a scientist interprets the causes and effects of sensations by relying on the assumption that they are reliable and transparent. A philosopher, too, views sensations as a point of departure, but finds them alone to be insufficient. Philosophy relies solely upon reasoning and thus also questions sensations. Gerencser stresses that this perhaps "subtle distinction" is fundamental to Oakeshott's work.[253] The world was literally a machine for the scientist, whereas Hobbes understood it in terms of its being the analogy of a machine. It is not science but philosophy that is fundamental to Hobbes's thought, and its authority lies not in observation but in reasoning.

Thus, Oakeshott rejects the primacy of the alliance of Hobbes's philosophy with the beginnings of modern science, and, as Gerencser importantly emphasizes, he substitutes it for another association. Oakeshott finds a connection between Hobbes and the philosophy of the Middle Ages. Oakeshott places Hobbes "within a tradition of scholasticism, nominalism, and a brand of skepticism."[254]

Contrary to many other interpreters, then, Hobbes can be seen here as having inherited tradition as opposed to revolting against it. Hobbes's novelties may well be startling, but they are still the moves of a master player adhering to medieval rules.[255] Hobbes was more like his contemporaries in his thorough skepticism, in this case in his extreme methodological doubt. Scholasticism and skepticism are brought together by the inheritance of medieval nominalism in Hobbes's thought. For Hobbes, language is "something both grand and humane," and it allows for the existence of universal truths, although his skepticism is based on doubts regarding the cer-

[251] Ibid., p. 81.
[252] M. Oakeshott 1946, cited in S. Gerencser 2000, p. 82.
[253] Ibid., p. 83.
[254] Ibid.
[255] Ibid., p. 84.

tainty of the world. It is this kind of "skepticism" that is essential to Gerencser's interpretation of the 'sympathy' and affinities between Hobbes and Oakeshott:

> It is the creation of meaning by humans, yet its reference is only internally to that construction, not a world external to it. The result is that the only guide for its use is its own consistency and coherence. A universal truth has that character within the universe of the users of language whose conventions recognize such as a truth, not in some 'Universe' at large. This skepticism, which Oakeshott finds exhibited in Hobbes's thoughts on language, reflects the character of his own skepticism concerning the modes in *Experience and Its Modes,* and the voices in "The Voice of Poetry".[256]

"Extreme nominalism" is the philosophical basis for skepticism; for Oakeshott, Hobbes's notion of language is arbitrary and conventional.[257] Gerencser distinguishes two aspects in this view. Firstly, "language is the giving of names to thoughts or images in the mind, not the things in the world."[258] Secondly, this naming is not a reasoned procedure, but the arbitrary precondition of all reasoning. Philosophy thus concerns universal propositions that can be true, but only hypothetically. There is no ultimate information available about the world, but the "after-images" initiated through the senses can be ordered through language and reason.

As noted earlier, Gerencser does not actually argue that this interpretation of Hobbes's 'language' and 'philosophy' is superior or even interesting as such. Instead, "Oakeshott's Hobbes" reveals the sympathy between their philosophy and civil philosophy. The notion of human beings as being the *makers* of themselves and their worlds is both an interpretation of Hobbes and also reflects Oakeshott's own ideas.[259] Taking into account earlier reflections on Oakeshott's idealism, Gerencser makes yet another observation. In *Introduction to Leviathan,* Oakeshott writes that, according to Hobbes, philosophical knowledge is conditional as opposed to absolute knowledge. Again, this may appear to be a rather minor detail, but given

[256] Ibid., p. 86.
[257] Ibid., p. 87.
[258] Ibid.
[259] Ibid., p. 92.

Oakeshott's own shift, Gerencser writes, his presentation of Hobbes's philosophy is significant.[260]

Later in his book, Gerencser makes the case for "Mister Hobbes's Oakeshott," i.e. Oakeshott became to increasingly describe Hobbes's political philosophy in terms that were reminiscent of his own political philosophy. Oakeshott's interpretation includes both "projecting oneself onto text" and "exposing oneself to it," as Gerencser quotes Paul Ricoeur as noting.[261] When comparing the versions of the *Introduction* from 1946 and 1975 via the 1961 publication of *The Moral Life in the Writings of Thomas Hobbes*, Gerencser specifically directs his attention to terms like "acknowledgement" and "recognition," asking if these are "fair terms to use in place of 'covenant' and 'consent' for Hobbes"?[262]

Thus, the 'impact' is mutual, although it is more indicative of the changes in Oakeshott's own thinking on politics than vice versa. In Hobbes, Oakeshott is attracted to a "skeptic who instead of landing in nihilism and resignation, developed a political theory of authority that can serve to abate the dangerously random existence his skepticism tells him is his plight."[263] In Gerencser's reading, Oakeshott's conceptions of both authority and civil association are in this respect deeply Hobbesian. Yet, in the final chapter of his book, Gerencser criticizes precisely Oakeshott's concept of authority for not being skeptical enough to maintain the division between enterprise and civil association. Civil association retains the element of consensus, which had been intended to be eliminated, while not allowing "incoherence in beliefs about authority."[264]

It is here that I will conclude my examination of Gerencser's views for now, although I will return to them later in this book, as I have a number of things to add and contest with regard to the changes of vocabulary in Oakeshott's postwar production. However, I see Gerencser's interpretation of Oakeshott's idealism and skepticism as having been sufficiently argued to the

---

[260] Ibid., p. 94. Again, I wish to note here that the language of idealism may well be quite 'deceptive' in this respect, and that perhaps this is one reason why Oakeshott used it more cautiously in his later work. The concepts of 'permanent' and 'absolute' as applied in Oakeshott's early vocabulary do not, in my interpretation, refer to a correspondence theory of truth in the Platonic sense any more than in a 'positivist' sense.

[261] Ibid., p. 100.

[262] Ibid., p. 114.

[263] Ibid., p. 121.

[264] Ibid., p. 165.

extent that I can in good conscience refrain from carrying out a thorough discussion of Oakeshott's pre-war work in this study.

5: Conclusion

In this chapter, I have examined Oakeshott's relationship to the three "isms" to which his name is most often connected: liberalism, conservatism and idealism. I began by examining the differences and similarities between Oakeshott – when read as a liberal thinker – and Joseph Raz, Isaiah Berlin and Richard Rorty.

The difference between foundational and anti-foundational thinking has been most visible when comparing Oakeshott with Raz. For example, the endeavour to diminish the significance of rights in political discussions is argued in almost entirely differing terms. Whereas Raz sees rights as existing only in the service of a greater good which serves as a foundation of his theory, Oakeshott regards them as clumsy political arguments in a political discussion. Despite the different intentions of the two authors – one normative and one explanatory – I hope to have successfully illustrated some critical points at which Raz's theory might even benefit from taking Oakeshott's points into account.

Berlin was introduced as a proponent of liberalism in which negative liberty plays a central role. This, of course, differs quite dramatically from Raz's liberalism, in which positive liberty plays the primary role. Although we can take value-pluralism as a true cornerstone of Berlin's liberalism, the notion of human nature still renders him a foundationalist in comparison with both Oakeshott's and Rorty's thought. Both Oakeshott and Rorty are anti-foundationalist thinkers in the sense that they see liberal cultures and states as contingent facts requiring no other basis than the contingent conviction of excellence or the desirability by their citizens. I think Oakeshott's contribution is best exemplified by his conception of human agency and choice as full of possibilities in contingent situations. It is precisely *because* we do not have any common human nature that an agent, valuing individuality yet also conscious of his own contingency, appreciates the conditions of civil association which allow individuality to blossom, perhaps even in as yet unknown directions. In my view, this understanding is one significant aspect of the crucial role played by Oakeshott in current political thought. His thought is relevant not only to our philosophical, but also our ideological and perhaps even practical political reflections, although it must not be taken as a system of ideas to be put into practice. This applies both to his more 'ideological' texts as well as to his 'explanatory philosophy', which was also discussed here in terms of liberalism. We will return to this point in the concluding chapter by reflecting on the theory/practice relationship in Oakeshott's thought.

Secondly, I examined Oakeshott's relationship to conservatism, which is *the* "ism" that cannot be overlooked when viewing Oakeshott's understanding of politics and its influence in contemporary and present-day discussions. I examined two styles of interpreting Oakeshott as a representative of conservatism.

In Bernard Crick's critique, Oakeshott appeared as a conservative philosopher whose philosophy is nihilist in its refusal to offer any foundations for political activity. I disagreed with Crick that this refusal infers nihilism, because Oakeshott certainly does not deny the possibility of possessing theoretical knowledge of politics. For Oakeshott, political philosophy is not the act of searching for truths for practical politics to follow, but reflection on political experience in another idiom.

It would appear as though in Crick's eyes Oakeshott has reformulated a rather coherent philosophical doctrine of conservatism around the concept of tradition. In this connection, Crick has, for example, criticized tradition as a general means of explaining everything as regards political activity. I agreed with some of his criticism and thus accept conservatism as an appropriate context for interpreting Oakeshott in some cases. This examination will continue in the next chapter, although the idea of conservatism as a general framework for studying Oakeshott's thinking is rejected. Instead, I attempt to uncover the sometimes surprising similarities and differences in the uses of concepts linked to political activity by different authors who write under different 'commitments' and positions.

In this chapter, we have seen how persistently viewing Oakeshott through just one doctrine may hinder and even distort our understanding of the changes in his conceptions of political activity. I pointed out the similarity between Crick's and Oakeshott's understandings of politics. Both have regarded politics as a reformative activity, although Crick claimed that Oakeshott's conception of politics was entirely centred on its being a preservative activity. In the following chapter, I argue that this critique is more applicable to Oakeshott's earlier conception of politics than to the criticized *Rationalism in Politics* essays. In addition, we will see how Oakeshott's late conception of political activity very much entails the notion of conscious change, which does not fit into Crick's interpretation of him as a conservative.

Robert Devigne's interpretation introduces us to Oakeshott as a conservative philosopher whose thought has practical implications. Since I do not see this view as entirely 'illegitimate' as such – our thinking and acting in politics may well also be affected by political philosophy – this rather common connection of Oakeshott to Thatcherism deserves attention. Devigne, however, makes the mistake of going too far in likening the thought of 'Oakeshottians' to Oakeshott's own thought. In addition, he misinterprets the nature of civil association. Authority in *On Human Conduct* is not seen as a means of repairing a fragmented, postmodern morality; it is intrinsically linked to civil freedom and the plurality of moralities. In fact, Devigne's interpretation serves here as an example of a fragmentary reading of Oakeshott's production. It reveals how events in (subsequent) practical politics and the tenets of new conservative ideology have led to picking bits and pieces from Oakeshott's thought.

Finally, I briefly examined Oakeshott's philosophical commitments and argued that idealism, too, is not a general framework in which to interpret Oakeshott's (political) philosophy. I agreed with Steven Gerencser's thesis of Oakeshott's increasing skepticism and diminishing level of idealism over the decades. The presentation of this shift lays the groundwork for understanding changes in his conceptions of politics. There are elements of coherence and 'truth' in, for example, the concept of tradition, which are difficult to understand if one is unfamiliar with Oakeshott's idealism. On the other hand, recognition of his increasing skepticism and nominalism allows us to understand how his conception of political activity moves towards an emphasis on individual action, choice and reflection. Acknowledging that the human world is 'essentially' an artifice also allows us to better understand why and how Oakeshott pays so much attention to different vocabularies of politics and their use in his political philosophy.

CHAPTER III

The Changing
Conception of Politics

1: Introduction: Politics: Corrupted and Proper

Kenneth Minogue has characterized Oakeshott's production as "the work of a radical individualist and one with no taste for surrounding himself with disciples."[1] According to Minogue, Oakeshott "often seemed to inhabit a different universe from that of his professional colleagues." Without going into biographical detail, there is no reason to question any of this view. W.H. Greenleaf, on the other hand, noted that despite the differences, there are also similarities between Oakeshott and the prevailing school; between T.D. Weldon's rejection of political foundations and Oakeshott's repudiation of ideology, for instance.[2] In this chapter, both the specificity of Oakeshott's thought and its relationship to other authors' views are taken into account when examining his postwar conception of political activity.

Shortly after the war, Oakeshott wrote about the effect of the "perverting tendency of current politics" on political philosophy.[3] The last fifty years had been quite scant in terms of the development of political philosophy as:

> The febrile political activity of the period was not the most inspiring background for philosophical reflection; intense concern with the practical and the transitory, where it does not produce pseudo-philosophy, is apt to inhibit philosophy altogether.[4]

In Oakeshott's view, the politically hectic periods before and after World War II were unfavourable contexts in which to practice philosophy. Yet according to his own understanding,

[1] K. R. Minogue 1976, p. 144.
[2] W. H. Greenleaf 1966, p. 96.
[3] M. Oakeshott 1949, A Review of J.D. Mabbot: *The State and the Citizen*, p. 379.
[4] Ibid.

political philosophy stems from the analysis of the current human predicament. In the essay *Rationalism in politics* (1947), this identification of contemporary politics as entirely rationalist or near-rationalist serves as a platform for the historico-philosophical examination of political activity. The "intellectually corrupt age" of the postwar years thus certainly inspires and informs Oakeshott's own thinking on politics. [5]

As to the theme of the theory/practice relationship in relation to political activity: for Oakeshott, political philosophy represents the idiom of explanatory language, whereas practical politics accommodates, for example, the language of persuasion and recommendation. Thus, Oakeshott's conviction that "what is farthest from our needs is that kings should be philosophers" remained largely unchanged throughout his career. [6]The aforementioned passage from *Experience and Its Modes* suggests that philosophers are the "victims of thought" and "self-confessed betrayers of life, and must pursue their way without the encouragement of the practical consciousness, which is secure in the knowledge that philosophical thought can make no relevant contribution to the coherence of its world of experience. The world of concrete reality must, indeed, supersede the world of practical experience, but can never take its place." Yet the ironic tone which is present throughout the entire book is directed more toward the world of practical experience and the pressure it puts on philosophy.

In *On Human Conduct*, on the other hand, Oakeshott deplored the character of a *theoretician* who acts as if his philosophical wisdom would endow him with the superiority to give instructions on practical conduct. Here, Oakeshott does not seem to be as concerned with safeguarding philosophy from the pressures of practical life as he had been in the earlier account. As regards political philosophy, we may conclude that this safeguarding becomes increasingly irrelevant alongside his growing appreciation of political activity as such. This shift also becomes visible in this chapter in conjunction with the presentation of Oakeshott's changing attitude and description of politics.

My intention below is thus to enquire into the relationship between the 'detached' and the more 'worldly' Oakeshotts. I wish to produce an interpretation of Oakeshott's central con-

---

[5]   M. Oakeshott 1948, A Review of K.B. Smellie: *Why We Read History*, p. 766.
[6]   EM, p. 321.

cepts -- such as authority, ideology and tradition -- by viewing their relationships to his conceptions of political activity. I also relate his thought to other contemporary British thinking and to some more current lines of political philosophy.

As I have already mentioned, Oakeshott's conceptions of politics appear here as *plural* and as occupying different levels of reflection, and they also include internal changes in his usage of related concepts. Accordingly, the concept of ideology, for example, does not remain the same during the period under examination. My enquiry follows more of a thematic than a chronological order, one reason being that the changes in Oakeshott's conceptions do not necessarily occur all at once. A given text may, for example, simultaneously conform to both the institutional and activity concepts of politics.[7]

I would like to emphasize that I am not aiming at any kind of 'neutral', 'true' or 'final' reading of Oakeshott here, but my specific point is to read him from a *political* perspective and to combine historical and philosophical readings. Thus, Oakeshott's distinction between history, as 'conditional' knowledge dealing with (constructed) 'facts' or traces from the past, and philosophical knowledge, as directed by an unconditional impulse to understand, is to a certain extent fused in this chapter. All in all, my examination is qualified by the word politics and thus 'philosophy' here becomes political theorizing, following Oakeshott's late classification.[8]

My approach can be seen as the translation of Oakeshott's texts and concepts within and between different contexts, a procedure which, according to the 'Weberian perspectivist' Kari Palonen, is an omnipresent procedure that takes place even between two speakers of the "same" language due to differing contexts and interpretations.[9] Contexts are both read *out* of Oakeshott's texts by following their intimations and read *back* by viewing the influence of his texts, for example based on the reception they received from his contemporaries.

Utilization of the political perspective explains the selection of the concepts examined here. That is, although, for example, the concept of a politician is not central to Oakeshott's texts, its significance in terms of clarifying the shift in Oakeshott's attitude towards politics becomes more visible from this point of

---

[7] See K. Palonen 2003a.

[8] See M. Oakeshott 1973, *What is Political Theory?*, WH, p. 401, OHC, p. 11.

[9] K. Palonen 2003c, pp. 16-7.

view. On the other hand, some notions which are generally accepted as central to Oakeshott's thought, such as practical knowledge, modes of understanding or freedom and rule of law, take on rather supporting roles. Furthermore, since Oakeshott considers *morality* as the appropriate context for understanding politics,[10] for example the notion of tradition naturally represents an important consideration here.

The thread I wish to follow leads from Oakeshott's near contempt for politics to a qualified laudation of political activity through the changes and continuities in his use of the concept of politics and related terms. The voyage of his dual understanding of politics begins from the juxtaposition of 'traditional' and rationalist politics, continues via the confrontation between parliamentary, conversational politics and popular government and mass politics, and ends with an antithesis of deliberative and teleocratic politics.

The duality refers to the fact that, according to Oakeshott's understanding, there is a divide between two understandings of politics in the European history of political thought. Acknowledging the fact that these ideal types or characters rarely occur as 'pure' types even in political philosophy, Oakeshott wishes to arrange his own examinations around these culminations. In practical politics, these types of political activity appear together, although their proportions may vary. The extremities express "the range of meaning" around which the ambiguous European political vocabulary moves.[11]

The fact that Oakeshott is perhaps most famous for his notion of *rationalism* in politics at least partially explains his reputation as someone who dislikes politics in general. However, in a nutshell, by rationalist politics Oakeshott is referring to the incorrect assimilation of politics into some other activity. His notion of rationalist politics can be seen as an umbrella concept for criticizing various attempts to reduce 'politics' to administration, economic fabrication, engineering, or a scientific understanding. It must also be taken into account that Oakeshott's view of contemporary politics was particularly pessimistic in the essay *Rationalism in Politics*, in which he most forcefully outlined this notion. Hence, if taken as a prime

---

[10]   M. Oakeshott 1958, *Morality and Government in Modern Europe*, MPME, pp. 26-7.

[11]   M. Oakeshott 195?, *The Idea of 'Character' in the Interpretation of Modern Politics*, WH, p. 276.

example of his understanding of politics, this essay can easily lead to the false assumption that Oakeshott possesses a general disregard for politics. The duality according to which Oakeshott operates should always be kept in mind, however. The negative conception as a description of a 'corrupted' or 'perverted' understanding of political activity is usually accompanied by a description of 'normal' or 'proper' political activity. Roughly put, 'rationalist politics' is politics understood as the aspiration of attaining some premeditated ideal. And 'politics', without pejorative prefixes, is an activity of attending to the general arrangements of a community according to some established ways of political behaviour.

With regard to terminology, it should be noted that I use mainly the notions of 'rationalist' and 'rational' politics as descriptive terms of the duality in Oakeshott's conception of political activity. Yet I acknowledge that 'rationalist' politics as such belongs to his late 1940s concepts. And 'rational' is a prefix that I have attached in order to emphasize that this type of politics represents a 'good', 'proper' or 'uncorrupted' type of politics for Oakeshott. His comprehension of this latter type of politics is also the one that changes most visibly during the period examined in this book. All in all, my aim here is to (re)construct as complete a picture as possible of Oakeshott's vision of political activity in his postwar period.

2: Power/Authority

Is all politics merely a question of the aspiration for *power*? Or can power be defined more comprehensively, such as Steven Lukes's famous formula: "...A has power over B ... when A affects B in a manner contrary to B's interests..."?[12] These are familiar questions about power in Anglophone political thought. In light of Oakeshott's views, however, they are more representative of a banal view of politics. Namely, Oakeshott views power mainly as an *instrument of critique,* which is importantly linked to his general critique of rationalist politics. Certain specific features of Oakeshott's view of the human being and the political agent become visible in relation to the concept of power – a human being does not merely aspire to the fulfilment of his or her own needs or wants.

---

[12] S. Lukes 1974, cited in T. Ball 1988, p. 89.

In general, it may be argued that one of the 'greatest fears' of the postwar years expressed in political discussions was the fear of great concentration(s) of power. This was due in part to the recent memory of the immense power exercised by totalitarian governments throughout Europe, although the direction of domestic policy also raised concerns in Great Britain. These fears were most intensely expressed by George Orwell in his classic works *Animal Farm* (1945) and *Nineteen Eighty-Four* (1949). Oakeshott, too, saw the potential danger of 'Continental influences' on British politics. Parliamentary institutions were not as deeply rooted on the Continent as they were in Britain, and what "fascism rejected was something which Germany and the continent generally enjoyed only fitfully and never understood, the institutions and values of parliamentary government; what it represented was something that Germany and the Continent understood very well – rationalistic politics."[13] Parliamentary institutions were not the offspring of rationalism, as was often believed, but, rather, an antidote to it. However, in the essay *Rationalism in Politics* (1947), the informality of English politics had already been surrendered to rationalism, and a year later the "general name for all forms of political disease is the concentration of power."[14]

Thus, during the postwar years Oakeshott associated power with the negative side of political life, and this conception bears a certain resemblance to liberal thought as manifested, for example, by Berlin. In liberal thought, power is presented predominantly as an antithesis of freedom that must be limited. Notions of power are also closely connected to various conceptions of what it is to be human; gloomy pictures of power as a disease of modern political life often mingle with the notion of humans as creatures who primarily aspire towards power, as presented, for example, by Hans Morgenthau.[15] Oakeshott's view, however, differs from this interpretation, although without fully cohering to the liberal notion of 'essentially' free human beings. Instead, Oakeshott's later views bear some resemblance even to Michel Foucault's notion of individuals as being *created* by power, although Oakeshott's conception is more limited in this sense. A similar type of analysis, or critique, of methods of discipline can be

[13] M. Oakeshott 1947, *Scientific Politics*, RPML, p.102.
[14] M. Oakeshott 1948, *Contemporary British Politics*, p. 486.
[15] See H. Morgenthau 1946, p. 9.

found in both *On Human Conduct* and Foucault's *Discipline and Punish* (*Surveiller et punir. Naissance de la prison*, 1975). In a Foucaultian manner, the increased apparatus of power, the "overseers and instructors," foster the disposition of an "'anti-individual'" in modern men.[16] The 'anti-individual' finds comfort in similarity with his alikes, and thus 'normality' is a counterpart of governing which includes "the continuous exercise of supervision, courts of morals, sumptuary regulations, inquisitions, informers, secret agents at home... overseers of schools and universities, tests, accusations, warnings..." etc.[17] In addition, government as understood and practised in the form of education or therapy creates subjects who are "understood in relation to 'sanity', that is, a uniform normality."[18]

In Oakeshott's late examinations of political vocabulary, however, power 'as such' was purged from negative connotations, and Oakeshott connected it to the conception of the "office of power" of the state.[19] By this he was referring to the equipment of the enforcement of authoritative law, which, as such, is a prerequisite in a state, but which in its present form has become rather overbearing in terms of its meaning.

As I mentioned earlier, authority already made its debut in Oakeshott's political philosophy in the 1920s. Only the final authority, such as our world of ideas as a whole, has the power to coerce belief or action. Oakeshott denies the contrast between authority and reason and places authority in judgement, thus deviating from the construal of authority as "emotivist,"[20] as based on 'feelings'. Nor does he adhere to the "epistemocratic" model, as his authority does not rely on claims of expertise and specialized knowledge. In fact, it is this conception to which Oakeshott is most explicitly opposed; his pejorative ideal type of a rationalist relies solely on the authority of his own 'reason' and is the enemy of authority, prejudice and anything traditional, customary or habitual.[21]

In the postwar years, an understanding of *tradition* as a prerequisite of politics is more central to Oakeshott's thought than the concept of authority, which usually only occurs in the

[16]   OHC, p. 268.
[17]   Ibid., p. 284.
[18]   Ibid., p. 310. See also D. R. Mapel 1990, p. 404.
[19]   Oakeshott 1975, *Talking Politics*, RP, p. 445.
[20]   T. Ball 1988, p. 110.
[21]   M. Oakeshott 1947, *Rationalism in Politics*, RP, p. 6.

presence of the concept of tradition. Oakeshott's longing for things like "parental authority" also adds conservative nuances to his use of the concept.[22] In the 1950s, his changing notions of authority are connected to his changing character-ization of politics as an activity, and both imply the more accentuated role of individuality and contingency in Oakeshott's political thinking. Changes in vocabulary reflect this shift: "government rests upon the acceptance of the *current* activities and beliefs of its subjects."[23] Furthermore, *governing* is characterized as the maintenance of the authority of an arbi-ter, which both enables a great diversity of self-chosen enter-prises and diminishes frustrating collisions of interests. Governing and authority are not applied as entirely synony-mous, but they instead postulate each other within durable associations between human beings. And politics postulates governing; it is a question of the determination of the manner and matter of governing, discussing and criticizing author-ity.[24] Oakeshott's work in the 1970s also essentially connects *authority* to the concept of freedom. Thus, it is precisely author-ity that enables political action. Accordingly, Oakeshott avoids the rocky areas of the more conventional theories when dealing with the concept of authority, as it is presented in the debate between deontological and communitarian liberalism.

It is not unusual, however, to encounter different kinds of interpretations, especially in the case of the concept of author-ity in *On Human Conduct*. Hanna Pitkin, for example, wrote: "Oakeshott is interested not in self-government but in obedi-ence – obedience that is obligatory though not unchosen, anal-ogous to our obedience to God as law-giver."[25] Here, Pitkin sees Oakeshott as a Hobbes-authoritarian, an old-fashioned conservative. I wish to contest this interpretation, although I naturally admit that the meaning of the concepts of authority and power are by no means standard throughout Oakeshott's entire production. Oakeshott's famous original style of writ-ing requires special attention during the analysis of his thought. For example, his use of such terms as rule or *jus* and *lex*, adopted from Roman law, does not naturally mean that he defines them in a manner identical to earlier authors. Instead,

---

[22] Ibid., p. 41.
[23] Oakeshott 1956, *On Being Conservative*, RP, p. 429, emphasis SS.
[24] Oakeshott 1958, *The History of Political Thought*, MPME, p. 8
[25] H. Pitkin 1976, p. 310.

the terms must be viewed in the context of the entirety of whichever of Oakeshott's own texts happens to be in question. By making these distinctions I hope to accentuate in this chapter that one can only speak of Oakeshott's "authoritarianism" in a very specific sense, i.e., as Roger Scruton put it, as advocating a government based on an established system of authority as opposed to one based on explicit or implicit consent.[26]

Below, then, I examine the positions and meanings of the concepts of power and authority in Michael Oakeshott's thinking. These concepts are sometimes used synonymously in the Anglophone political discourse, but it can generally be argued that authority is the 'milder' of the two terms. Authority usually refers to right, whereas power is linked to force, might and also coercion.[27] For the most part, this type of division also applies to Oakeshott's use of these concepts. Here, however, I concentrate on those aspects that are specific to and characteristic of Oakeshott's use of these concepts.

Power and the Critique of Rationalist Politics

In 1939, Oakeshott contrasted the doctrine of representative democracy with that of national socialism. The concept of the individual was presented as fundamental to the former, but the latter doctrine was "merely a programme of power masquerading as a social ideal."[28] Fascism, communism and national socialism represented authoritarian doctrines that were to be resented; the notion of power as a primary goal of politics was criticized. One of the central principles of the tradition of representative democracy, on the other hand, was that "a society must not be so unified as to abolish vital and valuable differences, nor so extravagantly diversified as to make an intelligently co-ordinated and civilised life impossible, and the imposition of a universal plan of life on a society is at once stupid and immoral."[29] Power politics is presented here as a foe of diversity and individuality, and thus the rather concrete contemporary 'model' of the famous dualism of Oakeshott's political thought would appear to lie in this rather neglected text.

---

[26]   R. Scruton 1983, cited in A.W. Sparkes 1994, p. 41.
[27]   Ibid., p. 36.
[28]   SP, p. xxii.
[29]   Ibid., p. xix.

Oakeshott outlined the main lines of the critique of rationalist politics in the 1940s and 1950s, i.e. at quite a tumultuous time in political philosophy and theory; the 'illusions' were dissolving and statistical methods were gaining popularity. In British day-to-day politics, the functions of the state were extended during the reign of the Labour Government, and the Conservative Party also moved closer to Labour in this respect. "Full employment" was a popular slogan which was regarded as being one of the aims of the state. Typical of the time, for example William Beveridge stated in his report in 1944 that full employment cannot be achieved without a significant extension of the state's responsibilities and powers.[30] For him, to aspire to full employment, while simultaneously opposing the expansion of the state's sphere of responsibilities, was comparable to aiming towards an end while denying the means necessary in order to achieve it.[31]

Viewed in this context, Oakeshott's *The Political Economy of Freedom* (1949) and its critique of the growing power of the state or government appears to be an attempt to defend traditions against new trends. It is in this text that Oakeshott presents the concepts of authority and power as opposing yet simultaneously overlapping. Defining "the most general condition of our freedom" as the lack of overwhelming concentrations of power in "our society," Oakeshott seems here to incorporate the concept of power – as might and property – into the very heart of his political thought in a fairly conventional manner.[32] Power is "with us" dispersed between different interests, organizations, organs of government as well as "the Administration and the Opposition," and all of these diffusions represent the general conditions of our freedom.[33] Since Oakeshott sees property – either as mental or physical capacity or the means of production etc. – as an inherent form of power, he considers it particularly important to oppose monopolies as power concentrations. It is precisely this point that makes Oakeshott's reputation as even a party conservative or a committed right-winger understandable. The most

---

[30] R. Barker 1997, p. 36.
[31] Ibid.
[32] Oakeshott 1949, *The Political Economy of* Freedom, RP, pp. 388. Compare with, e.g. F.A. Hayek 1944.
[33] Ibid. The extent to which this argumentation can be attributed to H.C. Simons 1948, *Economic Policy for a Free Society*, which Oakeshott here reviews quite favourably, is not always clear.

dangerous property monopolies were those of labor, having "shown themselves more capable than enterprise monopolies of attaining really great power, economic, political and even military."[34] In the same token, the dangerous centralization of governmental power as collectivism and a society of complete control are connected particularly to terms that are customarily associated with the Left, i.e. with communism, socialism, economic democracy and centralized planning. In retrospect, we may argue that Oakeshott overesti- mated the potential impacts of the Labour Government on British society. Additionally, as I noted earlier, he comes close in this article to being what he later referred to as a theoretician, engaging in a prescriptive theory of politics.

Yet in *The Political Economy of Freedom*, the concept of power also includes aspects of the use of power as a tool of the critique of rationalist politics. In a sense, Oakeshott's power is an economic concept which can simultaneously be used to criticize economic thinking in relation to politics. For Oakeshott, the greatest fear that may arise as a result of the power of one's own government is the fear of *control*, which at worst means "day-to-day intervention – controls of prices, licenses to pursue activities, permissions to make and to cultivate, to buy and to sell, the perpetual adjustment of rations, and the distribution of privileges and exemptions – by the exercise... of the kind of power most subject to misuse and corruption."[35] This view of power or "discretionary authority" does not represent politics itself but rather a threat to it.[36] Oakeshott positions the rule of law, i.e. the existence of general laws that bind the governors and the governed alike, as the most significant measure against the "fear of the power of our own government," the fear of huge concentrations of power.[37]

In other words, here, power is connected to economico-rationalistic 'politics' in which the freedom of individuals is, to say the least, compromised. A human life that centres exclusively on the satisfaction of wants is, for Oakeshott, rather barbaric. The enterprise of increasing prosperity comprises our common dream: "It informs all our politics; it binds us to the necessity of a 4 percent per annum increase in productivity;

[34] Ibid., p. 401.
[35] Ibid., p. 399.
[36] Ibid.
[37] Ibid.

and it is a dream we have spread about the world so that it has become the dream common to all mankind."[38] By focusing on the satisfaction of wants, "*Homo Sapiens*" and "*Homo Laborans*" suppress "*Homo Ludens*" and corrupt the most civilized human activity, i.e. "'play'," the realm to which the activities of explanation and understanding belong.[39] I think that this is one of the possible reasons for Oakeshott's insistence on keeping philosophy and politics separate: philosophy, history and science belong to a world of play, whereas a corrupted, contemporary politics is subordinated to economics and the satisfaction of wants. Thus, it is to be noted here that this conception later undergoes changes, and in *On Human Conduct* the 'disciplined imagination' required for political reflection also moves towards the concept of play.

Yet, it must be noted that Oakeshott's view differs from many contemporary socio-economical views on economics as such. Importantly, he treats economic institutions as ways of being active, not as pieces of machinery.[40] Thus, economy may be interpreted not only as a 'sphere' that suppresses the sphere of 'proper' politics, but also as a type of activity that seeks to replace it with another kind of activity. Properly, politics should be understood as a limited activity of the "readjustment of human relationships (and not the administration of things)."[41] Human individuality is comprised of the capability to engage in various kinds of activities. It is not a natural occurrence, but a "great human achievement,"[42] and it thus becomes understandable that "'maximum productivity' is one of the most damaging of the moral superstitions of our time."[43]

However, not only economic but all kinds of concentrations of power are dangerous in Oakeshott's eyes. In this sense, Oakeshott deviates slightly from, for example, Friedrich Hayek, whose power is more easily equated with property or wealth, although there are similarities in their opposition to a 'society of one plan'.[44] For Oakeshott, coercive power means

[38] M. Oakeshott c. 1960, *Work and Play*, WH, p. 307-8.
[39] Ibid., 306-10.
[40] M. Oakeshott 1951, A Review of Thomas Wilson: *Modern Capitalism and Economic Progress*, p. 506.
[41] M. Oakeshott 1948, *Contemporary British Politics*, p. 489.
[42] Ibid., p. 488.
[43] M. Oakeshott 1951, A Review of Thomas Wilson: *Modern Capitalism and Economic Progress*, p. 506.
[44] See F.A. Hayek 1944, p.19.

an attempt to establish external 'norms' of conduct (or behaviour). Therefore:

> The general name for all forms of political disease is the concentration of power in the hands of a part, whether that part is a private individual, a corporation, a union, a party, a majority, a minority or a government.[45]

The business of a *politician* is to prevent the concentration of power in a society and to break up all existing concentrations of power. By opposing concentrations of power to individual freedom he appears to cherish political pluralism. In a rare comment on political parties, Oakeshott writes that in politics, which makes use of past achievements and endeavours to add to those achievements:

> ... there is still room for differences of programme, for difference of opinion about what to do next and for differences of judgement about where the current damages lie. And these will be the *differentiae* of political parties. What there is no room for is a party whose leaders seek to establish a despotism and to fix upon society an external order.[46]

A concentrated power, whether in the form of a single party or some other form, thus always means despotism. In this sense, Oakeshott's conception of power and its proper limits is not far from Berlin's liberal thought, in which the negative concept of liberty counters incommensurable human goals and values:

> Pluralism, with the measure of 'negative' liberty that it entails, seems to me a truer and more humane ideal than the goals of those who seek in the great disciplined, authoritarian structures the ideal of 'positive' self-mastery by classes, or peoples, or the whole of mankind. It is truer, because it does, at least recognise the fact that human goals are many, not all of them commensurable, and in perpetual rivalry with one another.[47]

As I have already mentioned, it is important to recognize that the plurality of rights and duties are not derived from human nature in Oakeshott's view. Instead, particularly in the British context, they were the gift of parliamentary institutions. They "were the fruit of experience of the British people."[48]

---

[45] M. Oakeshott 1948, *Contemporary British Politics*, p. 486. At this point in this book review, Oakeshott favourably reviews Quintin Hogg 1947, *The Case for Conservatism*.

[46] Ibid., p. 489.

[47] I. Berlin 1958, p. 241.

[48] M Oakeshott 1948, *Contemporary British Politics*, p. 490.

The defence of authority is incorporated into the picture by connecting the concept with tradition and politics. It is a contributory factor in the general condition of freedom; authority is diffused between past, present and future, and we are free because politics in such a society can be seen as a conversation in which "each has a voice" but none dominates permanently.[49] Oakeshott points out that the "political economy of freedom" is not concerned with 'economics' but with *politics*; a politics which is not the "science of setting up a permanently impregnable society" but the "art of knowing where to go next in the exploration of an already existing traditional kind of society."[50] As this knowledge also entails a prevailing understanding of government as the prevention of coercion and, for example, the protector of minorities against the power of majorities, here too it is ultimately authority and not only the mechanical distribution of power that is linked to (political) freedom.

Oakeshott's postwar ideas bear some similarity to the British politician Enoch Powell's combination of conservatism and libertarianism in the 1960s.[51] However, although it is true that Oakeshott was opposed to collectivism, resisted inflation and entertained a somewhat libertarian view of the diffusion of power in *The Political Economy of Freedom*, in general, he did not wish to associate the opportunities provided by the "nation" mainly with "free enterprise,"[52] as Powell did. Regarding Oakeshott's later production, the differences between the two figures grow deeper still. Since the activities and vocabularies of economics and politics are distinct in Oakeshott's view, he could not have agreed with Powell that the "free enterprise economy is the true counterpart of democracy."[53]

Oakeshott's emphatic understanding of the historicity of all human life adds a certain 'Foucaultian flavour' to his conception of power; the more a given activity (economics) occupies human life, the more people 'internalize' its rules, which then become a part of conduct as such.[54] For Oakeshott, it is also possible to seek power simply for power's sake, as the Party

[49]   M. Oakeshott 1949, *The Political Economy of Freedom*, RP, p. 388.
[50]   Ibid., p. 406.
[51]   R. Barker 1997, p. 199.
[52]   E. Powell 1969, p. 33.
[53]   Ibid.
[54]   See also, D. R. Mapel 1990.

does in *Nineteen Eighty-Four*. He quotes R.G. Collingwood favourably:

> Power means the exercise of force: it corrupts by undermining a man's will and reducing him to the level of his own slaves. A slave-driver, getting out of the habit of explaining to his slaves what he means them to do, gets out of the habit of formulating his intentions even to himself... The lack of free will, the inability to resist the pressure of emotional forces, which makes the slave a slave, is also what makes a tyrant a tyrant.[55]

Although Oakeshott is reviewing Quintin Hogg here, this quotation also reveals his own views. According to Oakeshott, it is because there is no human nature that both leaders and people can easily begin to appear as banalized seekers of needs and wants, allowing themselves to become corrupted by power. In this sense, Oakeshott deviates, for example, from his contemporary Hans Morgenthau, for whom the lust for power lies precisely in the realm of human nature and the chief mischief of rationalism is its refusal to recognize *this* fact.[56]

To recapitulate, for Oakeshott, the understanding of mere economic success as the rational goal of mankind involves a "revolting nothingness, which has only to be successful in order to reduce human life to absolute insignificance."[57] Although he is writing here in reference to a Marxist book, his critique of the understanding of "the good life" as "nothing more than the enjoyment by more and more people of more and more everything" also applies to capitalism.[58] Similarly, he rejects the majority and scientists as attempting to set goals for everyone. He refers to Howard Selsam, whom he characterizes as a "true believer," although also as a "quiet, reasonable writer," as supporting the notion of the "'socialist' society."[59] The critique, however, can also applied more generally:

> The desires of the masses (in so far as desire is allowed to appear at all) are to be the standard for everyone, and the result is a tyranny of the majority. Or, when 'need' is substituted for 'desire', the result is the tyranny of those who determine need, the 'scien-

[55] R.G. Collingwood 1942, cited in M. Oakeshott 1948, *Contemporary British Politics*, p. 487.
[56] H. Morgenthau 1946, p. 9.
[57] Oakeshott 1949, A Review of Howard Selsam: *Socialism and Ethics*, p. 694.
[58] Ibid.
[59] Ibid., p. 692.

tists'. Of the two, any sane man would no doubt choose the former; but it is a desperate alternative.[60]

Oakeshott repeatedly criticizes the tendency towards the overwhelming power of the masses by sheer virtue of their number, as I will elaborate in more detail below.

In Oakeshott's more philosophical writings, the concept of power is predominantly linked to elements which come from 'outside' the sphere of politics and aspire to domination in the conversation. For him, when applied directly as a style of 'politics', both economic and scientific thinking represented the form of rationalism into which nearly all politics had been altered. Since proper politics is connected to authority and tradition in Oakeshott's view, his definition of the "'disposition of the rationalist'" speaks for itself: "At bottom he stands (he always stands) for independence of mind in all occasions, for thought free from obligation to any authority save the authority of 'reason'."[61] As I have already noted, the rationalist is the "enemy of authority, of prejudice, of the merely traditional, customary or habitual," but he never doubts the "power of his 'reason'." In Oakeshott's eyes, all this is due to a large extent to the Baconian notion that "knowledge is power," which Oakeshott himself famously described as "technical knowledge," whereas in "practical knowledge" authority occupies a significant space as acquiring knowledge from and respecting practices.[62] However, I would like to stress that Oakeshott is not, of course, opposed to 'reason' or its use as such. He objects to a doctrinaire belief in the inherent and unconditional abilities of the 'abstract mind'. He does not claim that a human being acts more on grounds of mere feelings or traditions and thus irrationally, but denies the significance of such dichotomies. It is precisely the vulgarized version of the Baconian or Cartesian belief in the sovereignty of 'reason' as certain techniques or methods that has rendered Rationalism "the *stylistic criterion* of all respectable politics" as opposed to its being one of many political styles.[63]

In short, in Oakeshott's vocabulary immediately after the war, the concept of power is above all attached to the critique of rationalist politics and its manifestation as increasing the

---

[60] Ibid.
[61] M. Oakeshott 1947, *Rationalism in Politics*, RP, pp. 5-6.
[62] Ibid., pp. 14-15.
[63] Ibid., p. 26.

power of the state. The primary 'model' of rationalist politics is war: a situation in which a society is overridden by one common goal – its survival and maintenance. During times of war or national emergency, it is a good thing that the state has power, precisely in the sense of controlling the world of humans and things. This power enables it to act quickly and efficiently. In a normal situation, however, it would be destructive to both human freedom and politics.[64]

Many contemporary thinkers saw this concern of imposing war-like practices upon peacetime politics as the main predicament of that time, and their general analysis is reminiscent of Oakeshott's. For example, the idealist 'Oxonian Hegelian' G.R.G. Mure stated that:

> In times of stress when mankind is afflicted by war and by acute material shortage and dislocation, the economic aspect of life is bound to overshadow the more strictly political... And the aftermath of war very evidently breeds politicians and civil servants for whom planning has become an end in itself.[65]

According to Mure, the economic aspect of life overshadows the more exclusively political aspect, and since the last war, the hopes of the people have centred on economic rather than political salvation. In his view, government guides the direction of the community as a whole and "standard government action" should be moral as opposed to economic.[66] In Oakeshott's words:

> Now, we cannot too often remind ourselves that, in politics and in every other activity: war is a blind guide to civilized life. In war all that is most superficial in our tradition is encouraged merely because it is useful, even necessary, for victory. *Inter arma silent leges* is an old adage which can support a wide interpretation; not only the laws suspended, but the whole balance of the society is disturbed.[67]

Although this passage includes some traits of Oakeshott's idealism in terms of understanding a society as comprised of its customs and laws in their entirety, the aim of this essay is more to emphasize pluralism as an essential feature of the experience of the British society. Warlike politics, which in peacetime

---

[64]   See M. Oakeshott 1948, *Contemporary British Politics*, pp. 475-9; 1949, *The Political Economy of Freedom*, RP, pp. 399-400.
[65]   G.R.G. Mure 1949/50, pp. 542-3.
[66]   Ibid.
[67]   M. Oakeshott 1949, *The Universities*, VLL, p. 133. Here, Oakeshott examines W. Moberly 1949, *The Crisis in the Universities*.

may appear as the pursuit of absolute principles or the ends of ideologies by means of the power exerted by the 'whole state', does not accommodate Oakeshott's view of a free society.

Power and the Critique of Popular Government

Oakeshott continued his critique of rationalism in politics by analyzing the 'political' disposition of the 'individual *manqué*' or the 'anti-individual' in the late 1950s. This disposition, longing for communal warmth and shunning the freedom of choice, emerged in 16th century Europe as what might be referred to as a mirror image of the "individual."[68] The 'anti-individual' is a person whose "sole distinction" is "his resemblance to his fellows and whose salvation lay in the recognition of others as merely replicas of himself."[69] In other words, all "must be equal and anonymous units in a 'community'."[70]

In Oakeshott's reading, both the "godly prince" of the Reformation and the "enlightened despot" of the 18th century are "political inventions for making choices for those indisposed to make choices for themselves."[71] Subsequently, anti-individuals came to require "'leaders'", whereas associations of individuals called for "rulers."[72] Leaders were to tell the 'anti-individuals' what to think, to help them to realize their desires and to make them aware of their power, which in relation to the modern masses refers, of course, to numbers. At this

---

[68] Oakeshott 1961, *The Masses in Representative Democracy*, RP, p. 371.

[69] Ibid., p. 375.

[70] Ibid. As Oakeshott is predominantly examined from a contemporary perspective in this study, his impressive analysis of the formation of the state and the dispositions of the individual are, for example, mostly neglected. However, the essays *On the Character of a Modern European State* in OHC and *The Vocabulary of a Modern European State* (1975) are conceivably the most representative works in this respect.

[71] Ibid., p. 373.

[72] Ibid. This distinction bears a striking resemblance to a conception put forth by Bertrand de Jouvenel, who also gave lectures at the LSE in the 1950s: for de Jouvenel, in 1953, *dux* was the leading force and *rex* the harmonizing force of an aggregate. De Jouvenel 1953, p. 457, originally delivered as a lecture at LSE, 1953. De Jouvenel's conception of the duality of leadership in terms of *dux* as referring to a conductor or a leader and *rex* as "the man who regularises or rules" seems to have effected Oakeshott's later distinction between the vocabularies of power and authority and enterprise and civil association. Ibid. In a review of de Jouvenel's *Sovereignty* (1957), Oakeshott says that de Jouvenel's distinction between *rex* and *dux* as "the two poles of every durable association" help "in construing the ambiguity which this disposition has imposed upon our political vocabulary." M. Oakeshott 1957, A Review of Bertrand de Jouvenel: *Sovereignty*, p. 43.

point, it is important to note that Oakeshott's notion of the 'mass man' does not refer to any specific *group* of people, but instead refers quite emphatically to the disposition that is shared by all modern, western people to varying degrees.[73] In light of the formation of political life and theory, it is important to notice that the new 'rights' of freedom of choice and the pursuit of happiness were seen as burdens by the 'mass men'. They were substituted with the right to "'enjoy happiness'", that is "Security," as a common good.[74]

Here we can detect similarities to the Foucaultian notion of "pastoral power", which is also presented in *On Human Conduct*. Foucault's metaphor of the shepherd–flock game in relation to pastoral power implies the view in which the welfare of the people is seen as a more important consideration than their liberty.[75] In Foucault's reading, this metaphor is alien to the contractarian and republican traditions of Western political thought,[76] which in the Oakeshottian context foster individuality as opposed to the disposition of a 'mass man'.

In the Anglophone jargon, Anthony de Crespigny, an historian and political theorist, speaks about "inducive power," which means "the capacity of *A* to get *B* to act in conformity with his intentions, and as *B* would not otherwise act, by providing or securing something attractive to *B* in order to gain his compliance or by undertaking to do this if *B* complies."[77] De Crespigny thus distinguishes between coercive power, which is based on making things unpleasant or threatening to make things unpleasant for *B* if he fails to comply,[78] and inducive power, which is based on the promise of rewards or benefits. Although inducive power extends the concept of power from that of mere coercion, and although de Crespigny also notes that the offered inducements often entail constraints, it still refers to the relationship between two 'complete' subjects who are not constituted by power, as both

[73]   Ibid., p. 381.
[74]   Ibid., p. 378.
[75]   B. Hindess 1996, p. 118.
[76]   Ibid.
[77]   A. de Crespigny 1968, p. 198.
[78]   Ibid., p. 197.

Foucault's concept of "discipline"[79] and Oakeshott's notion of the disposition of the 'mass man' indicate.[80]

In Oakeshott's reading of the two modern dispositions, the 'mass man' aspires to give governments enough power in order to satisfy the desire for security by the means of 'the vote' and the sheer power of numbers.[81] This requires that 'parliamentary government' be modified into a 'popular government', in which the parliamentary representative acts not as an individual but as a *"mandataire"* charged with the task of imposing the substantive condition of human circumstances required by the 'mass man'.[82] Accordingly, the parliament becomes converted into a "work-shop" instead of a "debating assembly."[83] Although the parliamentary practises have, according to Oakeshott, thus far been able to accommodate these modifications while still remaining parliamentary, authority and power have been affected in two distinct ways. Firstly, the authority of sheer numbers has been confirmed, although it is an authority that is alien to the practice of parliamentary government. Secondly, it has given "governments immensely increased power."[84] In Oakeshott's view, however, the mandate was an illusion from the very start. Being incapable and unwilling to make choices, the 'mass man' cannot instruct a delegate who, as a 'leader', relieves "his followers of the need to make choices for themselves" by "the familiar trick of ventriloquism."[85] The 'mass man' thus gives a leader the "unlimited authority" to make choices on his behalf and is thereby "saved" from the burden of choice.[86]

Oakeshott shared his apparent concern about the power of the 'masses' – or more preferably their leaders – with his contemporaries. The precedents for these attitudes can be found earlier in the century, for example in José Ortega y Gasset's *The Revolt of the Masses* (*La rebelión de las masas*, 1929), as well as in

---

[79]   M. Foucault 1979.
[80]   The "politics of faith" welcomes power and aims to associate it with the project of perfection so as not to exploit or waste any available resources: "Not as a defect but as a virtue, in proportion to the power at its disposal, the activity of governing in this style of politics will be minute, inquisitive, and unindulgent: society will become a *panopticon* and its rulers *panoverseers*." PFPS, pp. 28-9.
[81]   M. Oakeshott 1961, *The Masses in Representative Democracy*, RP, p. 379.
[82]   Ibid.
[83]   Ibid.
[84]   Ibid.
[85]   Ibid., p. 380.
[86]   Ibid.

various explanations such as 'mass psychology'. In Great Britain, the future of democratic institutions was often considered to be under threat by political thinkers. The act of voting as a means of ensuring democracy was questioned; the connection between democracy and representation was refuted:

> If an assembly is an exact microcosm of a nation, then it need admit of no limits to its authority, since its every action will presumably accord with the popular will.[87]

The means of keeping excessive authority and power at bay were often seen as more important than mere 'comprehensive' representation. The diversity of a society was seen as profoundly valuable.

For those who see all politics as power politics, democracy as a concept is vain, as it is only a mask for oligarchy. Eugen Weber's arguments on this view are reminiscent of Oakeshott's thought, though in a sharpened form. For this historian, electorates are mostly naive and:

> Political sophistication, like the little girl's enlightenment, is simply the technical understanding of a craft which, like every craft, is a 'mystery' to the uninitiated.[88]

A certain amount of elitism as regards politics was not unusual at the time, and Oakeshott's views are reflective of this general mood. The doctrine of the mandate in connection with party discipline was connected both with an unseen amount of authority as well as the power of the democratic leaders.[89]

This argument was not alien to the committed writers and politicians of the Left either. Many of them thought that as a result of the Attlee government the growth of state power had come to the end of its (desirable) path and argued for a diffusion of power.[90] The Labour MP John Strachey drew on the ideas of "Talmon, Oakeshott, Berlin, Beloff and Utley" with regard to criticizing the tendency of concentrated, economic power to submerge political power.[91] Yet the general argumentation of the Left, crystallized in the views of thinkers such as C.A.R. Crosland, supported the strengthening of the provision of public services and the reduction of income differ-

---

[87] R.E. Dowse 1961/62, p. 343.
[88] E. Weber 1953/4, p. 415.
[89] See e.g., J. MacCallum 1955/56, p. 199.
[90] J. Strachey 1956, p. 276, R. Barker 1997, p. 185.
[91] R. Barker 1997, p. 187.

ences, which was in opposition to Oakeshott's views.[92] Oakeshott's conception of freedom in this sense is more decisive; he wished to avoid the 'unseen string' of what could be called the inducive or pastoral power.

All in all, Oakeshott was by no means alone in his defence of parliamentary government and thus a *conversational* political culture.[93] For Oakeshott, most party politics represented rationalist politics in terms of suppressing individual choice and opinions under a common scheme or plan. A parliament, which is organized around the actions of its individual members as opposed to tightly binding group commitments, is more conducive to Oakeshott's view of politics as "identified, in the first place, as practical activity concerned with making a response to situations of a certain sort: political situations."[94]

Furthermore:

> A political situation may be identified, first, as a condition of things recognized to have sprung, not from natural necessity, but from human choices or actions, and to which more than one response is possible. Thus, politics may be said to be the activity of responding to conditions of things already recognized to be the product of choices.[95]

Oakeshott's understanding of political activity as responding to contingent situations which are products of choices represents a direct opposition to deterministic or mechanistic models of politics. For him, a political situation is "'public'" and the ingredients of political activity are "a situation of a certain sort and a response to it by somebody recognized to have the authority to respond to it."[96] If we see a political situation as usually arising through someone with the 'political imagination' to interpret a certain circumstance as being in need of change and through her/his assignment of the matter to the parliament, where it will be discussed and then presented to

[92] Ibid., p. 188.
[93] Oakeshott's metaphor of conversation is naturally much more versatile than this; it also refers, for example, to tradition – as a conversation between the past, present and future – and to the relationship between the different modes or voices and thus to civilization; these nuances appear later in this book.
[94] Oakeshott 1991, *Political Discourse*, RP, p. 70. The essay was first published in the 1991 edition of RP, but in my estimation, it was written some time around the mid-1960s.
[95] Ibid.
[96] Ibid., p. 71.

the government for further discussion, I think we come rather close to Oakeshott's notion of good political conduct on a practical level. At no point is there any *necessary* response to a given political situation. The openness to conversation refers to the contingency of politics; the idiom of political discourse is persuasive, not demonstrative. It is:

> ... the effort to understand our 'principles' and our 'admitted goods' in such a way as to recognize each as a choice we have made for ourselves on our own moral responsibility, and in such a way that each is given its due and none becomes a tyrant; the effort to address ourselves to real and not imaginary situations; and the effort to support our proposals with relevant arguments in which conjectures are not confused with certainties nor opinion with demonstrable truth.[97]

Oakeshott emphasizes the importance of responsibility in politics; political aspirations and decisions are bound to be made without reference to any demonstrable truths, but a politician must rely on her/his own judgement. Thus, Oakeshott again disconnects politics from the idea of the 'power of knowledge'. For him, "'the end of ideologies',"[98] in the sense of the search for information that would provide "'correct' diagnoses of political situations," represents a current form of the search for "demonstrative political deliberation."[99]

In the critiques of both rationalist politics and the politics of the 'mass man', one can then clearly recognize that Oakeshott attaches the concept of power to what he regards as the negative phenomena of political life, to the avoidance and restriction of the freedom of individual choice. It is evident, however, that the critique of rationalist politics, which he presented at the end of the 1940s, is too extensive to be taken literally. During that time, for example, he often considered all modern party politics as inherently rationalistic. Furthermore, with regard to the notion of 'mass man', it is difficult to avoid ending up with a bit of an elitist picture of Oakeshott's political philosophy if the only proper form of politics is seen as parliamentary debating.

Here, however, I hope to point out the importance of Oakeshott's use of quotation marks when referring to the terms 'mass men', 'leader' and 'rights'. I think that in the case

---

[97] Ibid., p. 95.
[98] Ibid., p. 93.
[99] Ibid., p. 92.

of the first two, the quotation marks indicate that he is simply using these words for lack of anything better, as these two terms had already been established, as well as to mark their theoretical character. They are also quite likely used in order to emphasize that there are often no sharp lines to be drawn between them. Oakeshott's metaphor of the "familiar trick of ventriloquism" and the notion that 'masses' are, in a way, the inventions of their 'leaders' are open to even further possible interpretations. A modern human being, having the propensity of both an individual and an 'anti-individual', exists in a situation in which voting is the first thing that comes to mind when considering political activity. For Oakeshott, as we have seen, this is in many senses merely an apparent freedom of choice in relation to politics. What is more important is that we 'as anti-individuals' have the disposition to endow government with enormous power and authority and are unable to distinguish a ruler from a 'leader'. It seems to me that Oakeshott wishes to draw our attention to how authority here merges itself with power and its implications. When authority is understood as the right to make choices for others, it becomes *fetters* instead of a condition of political freedom. As to 'rights', in addition to highlighting the sarcasm related to the 'perverted' understanding of, for example, economical security as a right, the quotation marks are used here once again to emphasize that there are no cores or foundations in Oakeshott's nominalist view of history or political philosophy. I think he is making a strong point that the defence of individuality on the grounds of certain inviolate, fundamental and natural rights is rather flimsy. The dichotomies that Oakeshott applies are thus used in order to stress a point, and, as such, are to be understood as instruments of thinking, not as images of reality.

The Problem of Oakeshott's Concept of Authority

Steven Gerencser raises a question regarding the concept of authority, found in Oakeshott's later work, as not being skeptical enough to maintain the division between enterprise and civil association. Although civil association does not require approval of its rules or a consensus regarding a common purpose but merely the recognition of its authority, it still retains the element of consensus by not permitting "incoherence in beliefs about authority."[100] Gerencser is not content with Oakeshott's conception of politics as "the critical discourse regarding the desirability of the particular rules of association,"[101] but wishes to include "critical deliberation concerning the authenticity of the various procedures and offices from which *lex* or rule, generates."[102] In the Harvard Lectures (1958), however, Gerencser interprets Oakeshott as allowing for the critical discussion of the composition and conduct of authority:

> Politics is an activity, not of governing, but of determining the manner and matter of government, and where those are predetermined and are regarded as immune from choice or change, there is no place for 'politics'. Thus political activity, the activity in which the composition and conduct of authority is considered, discussed, determined, criticized, and modified, may be said to be an invention of Western Europe which has spread about the world from this center.[103]

Still, Gerencser also discerns some hints of critical reflection on authority in *On Human Conduct*, for example in the expression "that the *respublica* shall, so far as possible, adequately reflect what is currently held to be civilly desirable."[104]

In the late essay *The Rule of Law* (1983),[105] Oakeshott applies the concept of *jus* to his discussion on politics. *Jus* is what he uses to identify "a rule understood in terms of the 'rightness' or 'justice' of what it prescribes."[106] Thus, the idea of "justice" is included in politics as a consideration of the desirability of conditions, but the authenticity of *lex* is separated from *jus*; an *injus* law can still be authentic and thus authoritative, and in this sense, Oakeshott's view resembles accounts of legal positivism. In addition, the criticism presented against legal positivism can also often be applied to Oakeshott: in the school of legal positivism, the law has "indeed no scientific basis other than the fact that this is the currently accepted doctrine and that it is practically acted upon in the individual states and in the community of nations."[107] It is to be noted, however, that in

---

[100] S. Gerencser 2000, p. 165.
[101] Ibid., p. 151.
[102] Ibid., p. 148.
[103] M. Oakeshott 1958, cited in S. Gerencser 2000, p. 144.
[104] Ibid., p. 146.
[105] OH, pp. 119-64.
[106] M. Oakeshott 1983, cited in Gerencser 2000, p. 146.
[107] A. Brecht 1959, p. 183.

Oakeshott's view, despite his attempts to separate legality from all other considerations, John Austin, in a quite Benthamite manner, "understood a state to be an enterprise association the purpose of which was to maximize the general happiness."[108] Instead of thinking in terms of civil association, Oakeshott maintains that, for Austin, "acknowledgement of the authority of law was, ideally, deference to a legislator's superior knowledge of the conclusions of an inductive science of happiness, but that (owing to the somewhat primitive condition of this science) it was in fact deferring to the opinion of those whose knowledge was only marginally more reliable than his own."[109] Thus, since Oakeshott's concept of authority has no reference at all to 'scientific knowledge', one must not associate Oakeshott too closely with legal positivism.

Gerencser identifies one of the problems of Oakeshott's political thought as lying in his "warding off from politics any critical examination of the basis of authority, any consideration of disagreements about beliefs about the authoritative, any deliberation concerning whether current legal or constitutional arrangements reflect changing beliefs about authority."[110] Gerencser's account of Oakeshott's view of authority is appealing and in many respects convincing, and as it is also quite comprehensive, I will limit my own examination accordingly. Instead of introducing Oakeshott's conception of authority in full, I will concentrate here on attempting to find an 'explanation' of the *problem* of authority in Oakeshott's thought. In addition, on this basis, I think we can also broaden our view on Oakeshott's politics with regard to questions of authority, and thus take the contingent nature of authority more seriously. Accordingly, we can formulate the question regarding the importance of interpreting Oakeshott's conception of politics in relation to authority as follows: Should we take his 'hints' towards allowing a critical examination of authority in *On Human Conduct* more seriously?

As I mentioned earlier, in the late 1940s and 1950s, Oakeshott connected the concept of authority with that of tradition. A principle of tradition is:

---

[108] OHC, p. 171n.
[109] Ibid.
[110] S. Gerencser 2000, p. 151.

...a principle of *continuity*: authority is diffused between past, present and future; between the old, the new, and what is to come.[111]

Traditions have authority in regard to human conduct, and therefore we can interpret authority as also being connected with Oakeshott's notion of rationality. As we saw in the discussion of Oakeshott and Rorty earlier, for Oakeshott, "rational conduct" meant acting in a way that preserves and possibly even enhances the coherence of the idiom of the activity of human conduct.[112] Rationality is not something fixed or finished; the knowledge of how to pursue an activity is ever-changing in faithfulness to the coherence of the activity. Oakeshott's assignment of authority to the sphere of judgement in his early work is echoed here. Practical human conduct is considered 'rational' with respect to its faithfulness to a tradition of moral activity – it is rational in its place within a "flow of sympathy, a current of moral activity."[113] In other words, traditions and idioms of behaviour have authority, and "'rationality' is the certificate we give to any conduct which can maintain a place within the flow of sympathy, the coherence of activity, which composes a way of living."[114] No authority is 'absolute' here, as only complete adherence to the coherence of the idiom of activity would be embraced, but Oakeshott always allows for the freedom of the individual in both the performance and modifications of traditions, as well as of idioms and later practices.[115]

Oakeshott distinguishes between the more fluid and firmer characteristics of traditions; the rule of law as "the greatest single condition of our freedom" and as a "known and settled protective structure" belongs to the latter category.[116] In the conversation of politics in a society, however, there is a diffusion of authority between past, present and future so that *"none permanently dominates."*[117] Here, Oakeshott's conception of authority thus also includes the notion of the possibility of

[111] M. Oakeshott 1951, *Political Education*, RP, p. 61.
[112] M. Oakeshott 1950, *Rational Conduct*, RP, p. 122.
[113] Ibid., p. 129.
[114] Ibid., p. 130.
[115] Terry Nardin pointed out that the first use of the word "practice," in the sense of a manner of activity, was in the essay *On the Activity of Being an Historian* (1958). T. Nardin 2001, p. 76.
[116] M. Oakeshott 1949, *The Political Economy of Freedom*, RP, p. 391.
[117] Ibid., p. 388, emphasis SS.

change: Oakeshott's conception of authority is neither connected to any idea of 'Natural Law' nor to a fixed constitution. Rather, in my interpretation, *politics* as an activity of the modification of rules is directly linked to the composition of authority. Procedures can be changed despite the fact that there is no room within Oakeshott's conception of politics for what we might refer to as a 'total' change, such as the sudden overthrow of a constitution.

However, Oakeshott's treatment of authority in the late 1940s and 1950s as a kind of 'hidden' concept, mainly in relation to the traditions of behaviour and less so to government and politics, indicates *the problem of equating the concept with general conditions of activity*. The intimate connection of authority with tradition also implies that the governing authority always has a safe 'backup' tradition. T.D. Weldon's notion thus also applies to Oakeshott's conception:

> But however 'authority' is being used, it is true that when a number of people begin to ask in a mutinous and not a theoretical tone of voice 'Why should I obey X?' X has already lost, or is in process of losing, his authority, for his orders are not being treated as the orders of those who are correctly said to have authority are treated.[118]

It seems that both 'antifoundationalists', Oakeshott and Weldon, to a certain extent exclude the questioning of authority from their understanding of the concept. They limit their examination to the existing "laws" and "political organizations" not,[119] for example, to the origins of their authority. Thus, Oakeshott is not immune to the critique that Karl Popper presented against "ethical positivism."[120] In his view, ethical positivism reduces norms to facts, which are to be understood sociologically as "the actual existing norms." Since, the "existing laws are the only possible standards of goodness," he criticizes this kind of "might is right" thinking for often being an expression of ethical nihilism accommodated by authoritarian and conservative quarters. In his eyes, a belief in the arbitrariness of norms implies a distrust of man and his possibilities; it is precisely this kind of critique that has always fallen upon Oakeshott. Yet I do not think that one can say that this kind of critique drains Oakeshott's conception.

---

[118] T.D. Weldon 1953, p. 56.
[119] Ibid.
[120] K. Popper 1945, p. 71.

Oakeshott's similarity to, for example, Peter Winch's Wittgensteinian account of authority of rules, which he presents in his *The Idea of a Social Science and its Relation to Philosophy* (1958), is clear. Both Winch and Oakeshott emphasize that no traditional behaviour ever remains fixed.[121] Although Oakeshott has emphasized the authority of traditions, he has also always 'allowed' for and cherished individuality. He shares Winch's view that the judgement of right and wrong *also* depends on one's own, individual thinking, although all behaviour or conduct belongs to the sphere of the participation in rule-governed activities. Thus, Oakeshott cannot entirely be criticized for expressing the view that it is "society which provides the code by which the individual must be judged."[122] Although according to Winch's interpretation, Oakeshott denies "the *possibility* of reflection" as essential to the adaptability of traditional ways of behaviour,[123] we must keep in mind that Oakeshott's division of traditional behaviour and "*the reflective application of a moral criterion*"[124] as a part of "*the selfconscious pursuit of moral ideas*" is to be treated as an "ideal extreme"[125] and not as an image of moral conduct in real life.

Nonetheless, as regards political activity, during the 1940s and 1950s, Oakeshott may occasionally have had some difficulty distinguishing between "sociological" and "legal" authority.[126] This is due in part to his concentration on the history of British politics and parliamentarism, which he clearly assumes to be authoritative in both senses, although he does view them as having been 'infected' by rationalism. Thus, other forms of governing and their authorization remain clearly unproblematized.

In John Day's view, if sociological authority means the "voluntary acceptance" of the rule of the governing authority, "very often in practice… the actual, 'sociological' authority is sooner or later given a constitutional backing."[127] Furthermore:

---

[121] M. Oakeshott 1948, *The Tower of Babel*, RP, p. 471, see also, P. Winch 1958, p. 63.
[122] K. Popper 1945, p. 71.
[123] P. Winch 1958, p. 63.
[124] M. Oakeshott 1948, *The Tower of Babel*, RP, p. 472
[125] Ibid., p. 477.
[126] J. Day 1963, p. 257.
[127] Ibid., p. 263.

Political success breeds legality. The old constitution is changed for a new one, which gives 'legal' authority to the 'sociological' authority. This happens after successful revolutions and after civil wars in which the established government is overthrown.[128]

Oakeshott's later conception of "constitutional histories" as being related to the beliefs of rulers and subjects about authority coheres with Day's understanding.[129] Where they differ is in their understanding of civil war. According to Oakeshott:

Dissent from the authority of *respublica* is giving notice of a resolve to terminate civil association, and genuine dissentients are either secessionists who design to place their investment in civil intercourse elsewhere, or they are disposed to destroy the civil condition in civil war. And whoever embarks upon either of these courses has renounced politics in favour of exile or subversion.[130]

The total resolution of authority is not a condition of politics for Oakeshott and this is one of the inherent tensions also in his (late) theorizing: By what means is a new authority built if not by politics?

In general, Oakeshott has kept the questions "Who shall rule and by what authority"? and "What shall government (composed and authorized in whatever manner we think proper) do"? separate.[131] Although Oakeshott mainly avoids setting any 'permanent' criteria for his understanding of different concepts, it is to be noted that there is one common criteria of success that applies to both politics and authority in the 1950s – that of "modifying the reign of arbitrary violence in human affairs."[132] A government that "rests upon the acceptance of the current activities and beliefs of its subjects" and whose "only appropriate manner of ruling is by making and enforcing rules of conducts" also provides "a sufficient force to maintain the authority of an arbiter" in any collision of interests.[133] To cite Oakeshott:

At least, a 'government' whose authorization can be withdrawn as soon as it has been given, on the least pretext or none at all, and one which is obliged to share its responsibility with persons or bodies which have not received the same or any authorization,

---

[128] Ibid.
[129] OHC, p.189.
[130] OHC, p. 164.
[131] PFPS, p. 3.
[132] Ibid., p. 19.
[133] M. Oakeshott 1956, *On Being Conservative*, RP, p. 429.

seems to me to be qualified in a manner in which most governments in modern times are not in fact qualified.[134]

Here, Oakeshott emphasizes the importance of the continuity of authority in order for a government to remain an arbiter in the clashes of interests. Importantly, in the skeptical understanding of governing, the maintenance of order is the primary object of government, although it is of equal importance to seek out improvements "and where appropriate to improve the system of rights and duties and the concomitant system of means of redress, which together compose the superficial order."[135] *Politics* is thus essentially linked with authority:

> … this activity of 'improvement' is not an independent activity additional to the activity of maintaining order; it is itself the maintenance of an appropriate order… And on this account the activity of improvement is not, strictly speaking, a second object of government; it is merely an aspect of the first and only object.[136]

Authority lies in an established system of rights, duties and means of redress and has never been designed as a whole. It can and must be changed through a political process, but preferably slowly and in close connection with tradition and thus subjects' beliefs about authority.

In contrast, the Baconian understanding of the governing authority as authorized rather by its power and intention of conferring 'well-being' on its subjects treats authority as almost external to the society, as something that regulates it from outside. In this kind of understanding, for example democracy is superior to monarchy in that it generates more power. Conversely, in the politics of skepticism, democracy "is superior to 'monarchy' because it more effectively protects the community against the pursuit of favourite projects by government; a plebiscite cannot compete with a House of Commons as a means of exercising continuous control over government; and every extension of the franchise is recognized as giving a broader base and more authority to this control."[137] Thus, the authority of numbers is also recognized here by Oakeshott as a means of controlling the power of governments, which he saw as a typical modern malady. Although authority is generally understood as a given 'fact', he also

---

[134] PFPS, p. 27.
[135] Ibid., p. 34.
[136] Ibid.
[137] Ibid., p. 131.

assigns authority instrumental value in a democracy as a counterforce of governmental power.

In sum, in the 1940s and 1950s, Oakeshott connects authority with the rules of behaviour, although he is not always clear on the difference between the traditions of behaviour, laws and the more 'fixed order' of constitution, and this adds a certain conservative nuance to the concept. It must be emphasized, however, that no government or constitution is naturally 'perfect' for Oakeshott, although he does have some faith in parliamentary democracy. In *The Politics of Faith and the Politics of Skepticism* and the texts from the mid-1950s on, politics as disagreement, conversation and the suggestion of improvements are always permitted and emphasized in relation to authority. Thus, for example, the fact that the authenticity of procedures is not questioned tends to be a nuance of normal peacetime; procedures, too, can always be changed politically when necessary. The authority of *respublica* depends on its continuous acknowledgement by *cives*, and over the course of time this recognition supposes that the procedures and offices of authority can be modified.[138] The problem that remains is the construction of a new authority. When politics is closely connected to authority, a situation without a clear framework of authority becomes easily equated with chaos.

Oakeshott and Hobbes – On Authority by Reason and Political Authority

I will continue my examination of Oakeshott's thought, particularly his later conception of authority and its relation to political activity, by reflecting on his texts on Hobbes as well as on *On Human Conduct*, both of which are highly relevant in the facilitation of our understanding of Oakeshott's conceptions of power and authority.[139]

"[I]t is Reason, not Authority, that is destructive of individuality," remarks Oakeshott in his well-known *Introduction to Leviathan*.[140] Conversely to the common tradition of interpretation, Oakeshott views individualism as a central and *enduring*

[138] OHC, p. 154.
[139] As Gerencser (2000) has made a substantial contribution to our understanding of 'Oakeshott's Hobbes', this part can again also be read as both partially complementary to and partially a response to his text.
[140] M. Oakeshott 1975, *Introduction to Leviathan*, RP, p. 282.

part of *Leviathan*. The authorization of the sovereign does not mean the relinquishment of one's individuality, because the unity of an association, born out of the agreement on authorization, "lies solely in the singleness of the Representative, in the *substitution* of his one will for the many conflicting wills."[141] Instead of supposing some kind of common will or concord of wills, one must understand that the representative's choice is not his/hers *per se*, but is made on his/her behalf. The law is not equated with reason or even custom, so the authority of the sovereign is not derived from the truthfulness or correctness of his choices. According to Oakeshott, the Hobbesian sovereign is primarily a lawmaker whose rule is not arbitrary but 'the rule of law'; "Hobbes is not an absolutist precisely because he is an authoritarian."[142] As Oakeshott sees it, the freedom of the individual does not disappear in the commonwealth. The Authority of the sovereign is derived from a free "act of will of him who is obliged," and the sovereignty of an individual over himself is preserved in the silences of the law.[143]

It is important to take Oakeshott's readings of Hobbes into account in order to understand the central emphases of Oakeshott's own authority/power concepts. That is, his vocabulary is full of Hobbesian expressions, which are of course very difficult to avoid in Anglophone political philosophy. In Oakeshott's case, however, there is more to it. Namely, he names Hobbes along with Hegel as his most important predecessors as theorists of civil association.[144] As such, particularly when reading *On Human Conduct,* it is important to note that the vocabulary Oakeshott 'adopts' from his predecessors must be seen in relation to *theorizing of civil association*, its most important aspects being the stress it places on individualism, its skepticism towards the omnipotence of reason – whether it be of a human being or an artificial sovereign – and reliance on the rule of law.

Along with civil association, another 'ideal type' of a human relationship, which has no direct empirical referent and which is also strongly connected to the concepts of authority and

[141] Ibid., p. 281.
[142] Ibid., p. 282.
[143] Ibid., p. 283.
[144] M. Oakeshott 1976, *On Misunderstanding Human Conduct. A Reply To My Critics,* p. 310.

power, is enterprise association. To put it very briefly, Oakeshott uses this concept in order to describe an association structured by a common goal, in which freedom is based on voluntary membership to (and withdrawal from) the association and in which the authority derives its legitimacy from a common purpose. Enterprise association is also, by definition, terminable; it can be abolished by mutual agreement or when the agreed goal is reached. When this happens, the rules of enterprise association also naturally lose their validity because they are first and foremost means of achieving a desired end. Civil association, rather, is based on known rules. Members of a civil association do not necessarily have anything in common other than their acknowledgement of the authority of these rules. They approve these rules as adverbial considerations for their activities. Unlike instrumental rules, these rules cannot prescribe any *particular* act, and people are thus free to choose their own actions in different situations. The fact that acknowledgement of authority is the single common 'factor' relating the *cives* to each other also means that being associated does not "threaten the link between belief and conduct which constitutes 'free agency'."[145] In Wittgensteinian manner, Oakeshott thus compares the rules of civil association to a vernacular language that makes a certain utterance possible without determining its 'content', although certain rules must be complied with in order to make oneself understood. This recognition thus has nothing to do with the desirability of the rules in question, nor is it bound to the decision to remain associated in order to achieve whatever common goal has been set.[146]

When theorizing on states, Oakeshott uses the corresponding Latin terms *societas* and *universitas*. For Oakeshott, these concepts are essentially *instruments* which can help us to understand the complicated, historical nature of modern European states. *Societas* and *universitas* are complementary and competing understandings of the state, neither of which is usually found in its purest form, even in philosophy. Furthermore, when we are aware that in Oakeshott's view states are not based on any other 'foundations' than historical and contingent "human dispositions," we may better understand why it is that he specifically reads Hobbes as a '*societas*-theorist',

---

[145] OHC, p. 158.
[146] Ibid., p. 157-8.

although many central passages of *Leviathan* clearly belong to the sphere of the *universitas* vocabulary.[147] Namely, in Oakeshott's interpretation, Hobbes's disposition, his emphasis on human will and the artificiality of the *Leviathan*, clearly promoted the development of "the morality of individuality" as opposed to the "morality of communal ties or the common good."[148] In Hobbes's *civitas*, the "independent rights of spurious 'authorities' and of collections of individuals such as churches" are excluded, while the freedom of the individual is not.[149]

In relation to the concepts of authority and power, it is to be noted that peace or security as *purposes* or necessary consequences do not conform to Oakeshott's conception of civil association. More appropriately, they may be seen more as potential, yet by no means inevitable, 'by-products'.[150] In comparison with, for example, the essay *On Being Conservative* (1956), this *emphasis* on the exclusion of these purposes from civil association signifies the development of his own, stricter vocabulary in relation to his theorization of civil association. The authority of the rules in civil association is thus not linked to any kind of guaranteed success with regard to, for example, maintaining peace. The obligation does not disappear in the face of the potential failure of the task at hand, as is the case in *Leviathan* and implied in Oakeshott's earlier theorizing. Correspondingly, the authority does not have uncomplicated power in relation to the citizens; obedience is not part of the vocabulary of *societas*.[151]

Since abstract individualism and the notions of contract and consent are also not part of Oakeshott's theorizing, we can understand civil association as radically contingent and historical. There is no foundationalism in Oakeshott's conception of civil association. It does not provide any answers to 'fundamental questions' such as: "Why should I obey"?[152] Neither obedience nor power (in the sense of a command) can structure civil association. Moreover, Oakeshott does not explain why citizens should go on recognizing certain forms of contin-

---

[147] See B. Parekh 1982.
[148] M. Oakeshott 1962, *The Moral Life in the Writings of Thomas Hobbes*, RP, p. 296. Originally delivered as a lecture at the University of Nottingham 1960.
[149] M. Oakeshott 1975, *Introduction to Leviathan*, RP, p. 282.
[150] OH, p.161.
[151] M. Oakeshott 1975, *Talking Politics*, RP, pp. 441-5.
[152] I. Berlin 1962, p. 64.

gent authority. This latter point is thus often viewed as a weakness in Oakeshott's thinking in comparison to, for example, Hobbes's theorizing.[153] He merely states that since belonging to a state has *so far* been understood as compulsory, then *societas* is the only morally tolerable type of state. There is no compromise between freedom and authority in *societas*, whereas an obligatory enterprise association is a contradiction in terms. For Oakeshott, there is no such thing as collective choice.[154]

Oakeshott seems to embark on his dissociation from the vocabulary of British idealism and old conservatism through his reading of Hobbes. The denial of the existence of totalities in the concept of civil association represents a particularly clear distinction from his earlier thought. Oakeshott had previously emphasized that the authority of the state not only refers to government and law, but is also based on the completeness of the satisfaction of needs that is produced by the state itself. Only that which in itself is complete may be authoritative in the full sense of the term.[155] This kind of rhetoric could no longer be accommodated by Oakeshott in 1975, and especially in connection with the concept of *cives*, he stressed the acknowledgement of authority as lying only with citizens as artificial persons. It is not suitable to speak of trade unions, the church or the family as the organs of civil association because these concepts presume a kind of collective morality. In addition, I think that this clearer differentiation between the vocabularies of authority and power is based in part on Oakeshott's reading of Hobbes. In particular, the connection of power to the satisfaction of wants (as the ability to do so) links power to the kind of activity that cannot constitute a civil association in the Oakeshottian sense.

It is easy for me to agree with Parekh that Oakeshott's formalistic "thin theory" on civil authority has clear advantages in comparison with, for example, John Rawls's "thick theory" on authority.[156] Since Rawls's conception of authority relies on certain "principles of justice," it is difficult for him to justify why those rejecting these principles should, by and large, recognize the legitimacy of authority. On the other

---

[153] B. Parekh 1995, p. 178.
[154] OHC, p. 119.
[155] M. Oakeshott 1929, *The Authority of the State*, RPML, p. 87.
[156] B. Parekh 1995, pp. 177-8.

hand, Oakeshott stresses the contingent nature of all authority, although he does not explain why *cives* should go on acknowledging it.[157]

Noting this criticism, however, I think it is important to stress that according to Oakeshott himself, the greatest difficulty in theorizing civil association was the fact that his predecessors had written on it as if it were a desirable and objective model for a modern state; the level of abstraction may not ultimately be sufficient in *On Human Conduct*.[158] Yet I tend to see *Oakeshott's* silences concerning authority as significant too. By leaving the exact content of, for example, laws (*lex*) and especially justice (or rightness) unspecified, he also leaves room for various interpretations of the 'prevailing morality' and its relation to civil intercourse in civil association at any given time and thus also for various choices with regard to the actions that are best suited to his 'Hobbesian' individualism.

As I have already mentioned, Oakeshott's authority does not cohere to the "epistemocratic models" of authority:

> *Respublica* is not a system of theorems alleged to be true or offering themselves to be accepted on trust, and what is loosely called 'believing on authority' (that is, deferring to the opinion or judgement of another believed to be better informed than oneself) has no place whatever in that relationship between a subject and *lex* which constitutes civil association.[159]

Although Oakeshott uses the term "acquiescence" in relation to authority in *On Human Conduct*, he also stresses that a critical attitude, too, has its own important place in *respublica*. Here, politics:

> ...is thinking and speaking about a rule of civil intercourse which has been notionally resolved from being an authoritative prescription into a conclusion in order that what it prescribes may be distinguished from its authority and thus be made available to be considered in terms of its desirability; or it is thinking and speaking in order to reach a conclusion which may then be transformed into a rule by an authoritative act.[160]

The interpretation of what has been notionally resolved from being an authoritative prescription must be made by individuals and politicians with no permanent guidelines upon which

[157] Ibid.
[158] M. Oakeshott 1976, *On Misunderstanding Human Conduct. A Reply To My Critics*, p. 364.
[159] OHC, p. 171.
[160] Ibid., p. 165.

to lean. Politics is not a technical but rather a practical activity, which may have an unforeseeable impact on authority.[161] By emphasizing politics as a *conscious* activity that amends laws or rules, Oakeshott separates his conception of authority from the earlier implication of its being equated with customs or general conditions of behaviour. That is, this shift separates authority from any implications of its having a 'direct' or 'automatic' connection to customs and traditions. Oakeshott's late theorizing stresses the point that politics as an appeal to an authoritative quarter to preserve or change a law is always qualified by individual judgement.

Talking Politics

I will close my examination of the relationships between the concepts of authority, power and politics by concentrating on the essay *Talking Politics* (1975),[162] and, to some extent, *On Human Conduct*. Here, Oakeshott's theorizing is presented perhaps in its most distinguished mode, the language requiring the careful attention of its readers. I hope, however, that my examination has both provided a sufficient basis for the contextualization of these texts in relation to Oakeshott's wider production and emphasized the importance of paying specific attention to the changes in it.

In Oakeshott's view, the (European) vocabulary of political discourse aims to express "the conflicts, the tensions, and the alignments of political belief and design which are characteristic of modern states."[163] It is composed of expressions used to diagnose situations and intended to call for redress in the form of an official response. It can be used in order to express and recommend beliefs, doctrines or dispositions. Although political discussions are inevitably temporal and local, it will not be long "before one of those haunting words is uttered (democracy, freedom, rights, justice) and we become aware that we are talking about a state."[164] Political discourse has been formed in conjunction with the development of the modern state, thus reflecting those special characteristics of the state that are the focus of political attention at any given time. The vocabulary of political discourse is complex, historical and

---

[161] See T. Ball 1988, p.119.
[162] Published first by *National Review* on December 5, 1975.
[163] M. Oakeshott 1975, *Talking Politics*, RP, p. 438.
[164] Ibid., p. 457.

contingent, and it is always mutable, like the type of association referred to as the state. For Oakeshott, however, this discourse is now full of vague, "all-purpose" expressions that are incapable of resolution. This is particularly true in the case of expressions such as 'free speech' and 'laissez faire', both of which Oakeshott interprets as relatives that have been transformed into absolutes; into sloganish, empty unconditional claims.[165] In *Talking Politics*, Oakeshott thus implores us to recall what political discourse has been all about in terms of its connection to the modern state "as it emerged from a medieval realm, a patrimonial estate, a military protectorate, or a collection of colonial settlements."[166]

There are three distinct features of a modern state that have never been abandoned: it is "an office of authority, an apparatus of power, and a mode of association."[167] The vocabularies of both authority and power thus belong to the vocabulary of politics, although as concepts they are categorically distinct. The fact that a person has power does not necessarily mean that he or she is in a position of authority. On the other hand, "to be acknowledged to have authority does not, itself, endow a man or an office with power."[168] The distinction that Oakeshott makes between the *vocabularies* of authority and power is of crucial importance when compared with their synonymous use by many other thinkers.

By the office of authority Oakeshott is referring to the way states are constituted as associations, i.e. in terms of the acknowledgement of the authority of the rules and arrangements of the state. Oakeshott does not thus imply that the acknowledgement of authority requires the approval of what is prescribed, but it does require the recognition of the antecedent right to prescribe rules or laws (*lex*). We thus recognize the shape or constitution of the office, but we do not recognize the quality of its enactments or their outcomes.[169] In the civil condition, the twin pillar of civil authority is civil obligation; authority is always endowed by those whom it obligates.[170] And over the course of the histories of modern states, powerful dissent from the authority of *respublica* (manifold of rules)

[165] Ibid., p. 440.
[166] Ibid., p. 441.
[167] Ibid.
[168] Ibid., p. 445.
[169] Ibid., p. 442.
[170] Ibid.

has usually led to civil war.[171] According to Oakeshott, a state's constitutional history is ultimately the history of beliefs related to authority. In all their detail, Oakeshott sees the actual constitutional forms as "the most substantial expressions of the fluctuating beliefs that endow an office of rule with authority."[172] The use of rather vague general expressions, such as 'democratic', 'liberal', 'parliamentary' or a 'revolutionary-democratic dictatorship', is common.[173] These words belong to the vocabulary of authority. Thus, in Oakeshott's view, when referring to democracy as a 'method of governing' that fabricates rules in order to promote our specific interests, we are 'guilty' of contributing to the ambiguity of political talk. On a more serious note, if we look for the authority of the association in the unanimous approval of its performances, we are no longer referring to the modern state, as a modern state never includes this kind of authority.[174]

Oakeshott defines the word power within political vocabulary as follows: "It is a human relationship, which means the ability to procure with certainty a wished-for response in the substantive conduct of another. And, since it is a relationship of human beings, and thus depends upon both the ability and the disposition of the respondent to make the wished-for response, this certainty can never be absolute and power can never be irresistible."[175] The existence of a relationship in terms of power presupposes a fear of injury or the elevation of a want into a need, as a human being without any fears or needs cannot be drawn into a power relationship.[176]

In relation to the modern state, an apparatus of power is annexed to the office of authority. Interestingly, in Oakeshott's view, although the *ingredients* of this apparatus are "durable," consisting of greatly increased "information about what is going on and the certainty with which it may be controlled" with the aid of different procedures, devices, machines etc.,

[171] Ibid., pp. 442-3, OHC, p. 149; p. 164.
[172] M. Oakeshott 1975, *Talking Politics*, RP, p. 443.
[173] Ibid.
[174] Ibid, pp. 443-5.
[175] Ibid., p. 445.
[176] Ibid. Oakeshott's 'Hobbesian' use of vocabulary is very clear here: he also uses terms like 'aversion' when speaking of power.

this is not power as such.[177] In Oakeshott's thought, the nature of power as a relationship is one example of his deviations from more traditional views of someone possessing power. For him, these 'ingredients' compose an apparatus of power only when "they are mobilized and deployed to exact, under threat of injury or disadvantage, specific performances from assignable agents."[178] In the modern state, "the only legitimate use of this apparatus is to enforce subscription to the rules and arrangements to which the associates are already obliged to subscribe."[179] Thus, it is the failure to fulfill an obligation – not mere fears or wants – that turns a person into a *subject* of the apparatus of power. It is only then that the demand can be made for an assignable agent to perform a specific act, such as paying a fine. According to Oakeshott, ruling may only be equated with the exercise of power when the conduct enforced is in compliance with the demands of powerful persons. Thus, a 'ruler' is identified as a 'tyrant'. The case is similar to the belief that obligations derive from God or Nature as opposed to the authority of the office of rule. Oakeshott takes the "fanciful doctrine of the Declaration of Independence" as a prime example of this kind of thinking.[180] In it, governments are said to exist only to secure rights, which they do not have the authority to prescribe. Furthermore, the alleged consensus can only legitimize the apparatus of power which is necessary in order to provide that security.

I wish to emphasize, however, that although Oakeshott sees power as the most abused word in our language of politics, it is it is by no means the notion of power (or the apparatus of power) that in itself 'corrupts' the vocabulary of politics. For him, it is perfectly proper to reflect on, for example, excesses in the use of power in political discourse. The fact, however, that the vocabulary of power incorporates the vocabulary of authority causes confusion.[181]

Politics as an activity is not directly related to the 'ruling authority' or the apparatus of power, but to the shape of the association, i.e. to how persons are related to each other and to the engagements of the office of rule. In an enterprise associa-

---

[177] Ibid., p. 446.
[178] Ibid.
[179] Ibid.
[180] Ibid., p. 448.
[181] Ibid., p. 447, OHC, p.195.

tion, the rulership (or the 'lordship' more aptly) means managerial engagements, and the *persona* it thus establishes is a servant to a specific purpose. 'Politics' in an association of this kind can be described in terms of the Lasswellian "contention about who gets what, when and how, urging upon managers some marginally different 'alternative' purpose, and voting them into office in a rare occasion when they are not *coup d'étatistes*."[182] In a civil association, on the other hand, the 'ruler' is the custodian of rules, and persons are associated only in terms of their obligation to these non-instrumental rules as 'citizens'. Obligations, rules, practices and laws are to be taken into account as conditions for choosing. They do not thus negate the possibility of choice, but instead they negate a "notional unconditional choice," made as if in a void.[183] In Oakeshott's reading, the language of rights, for example, is one of pretended unconditionals, which are nothing more than empty utterances unless they are specified within a collection of described obligations.

Politics in a civil association is thus deliberation over the desirability of the conditions prescribed in *respublica*: to imagine them differently, to promote and withstand change. In one respect, politics may be understood as a private engagement. According to Oakeshott, an agent or association of agents bargains with others in order to satisfy a want in politics too. The primary distinction between politics and a private engagement is related to the addressed respondent of political activity, i.e. the occupants of legislative office. They have the authority to make or refuse the proposed changes in rules or laws. The desired outcome of political action is, however, not that others perform a certain act but that all *cives* should have a new civil obligation or be relieved of a current obligation. In other words, the desired 'result' of political action or a political utterance is the establishment of a rule prescribing the conditions to be subscribed to by all in unspecifiable future performances.[184]

We have now examined Oakeshott's views on the political vocabulary of the modern state as regards authority, power and politics. It is worth recalling that Oakeshott also mentions such metaphorical notions as 'matrimonial politics' and 'fac-

---

[182] M. Oakeshott 1975, *Talking Politics*, RP, p. 453.
[183] Ibid., p. 456.
[184] OHC, pp. 162-3.

tory politics'.[185] Yet Oakeshott thinks that 'proper' politics is intrinsically linked to the idea of civil association: in a modern state, political activity both moves within the limits of the acknowledgement of the authority and is made possible by the prevailing authority. At the same time, political activity is also the constant modification of the *respublica*. For Oakeshott, a modern state is in a perpetual state of change – it is never complete in any teleological or other sense.

The concept of enterprise association is also valuable. In relation to politics it operates at the very least as a tool of critique, but it also marks an important distinction by which we may attempt to better understand the unique character that Oakeshott attaches to political activity in his late production. In Oakeshott's later work, after all, political engagement is the most difficult of all human engagements because it allows no room for the consideration of interests.[186] Oakeshott's connection of political activity to the concept of authority and the emphasis on the freedom of human choice, along with his distinction between the power to secure obligations and the power exerted to satisfy a want, are important to our conceptualization of politics. In Oakeshott's view, we cannot assign political meaning to, for example, a "'capitalist state'" if a state itself is not understood as an enterprise.[187] It does not refer to a civil association that favours "'free enterprise'," for example.[188] In his later work, Oakeshott is very critical of all notions of a 'minimal state' and a 'capitalist state'. These notions belong to the sphere of the understanding of politics and state in the language of teleocracy.[189] Increase in productivity, even as the prime object of a *policy*, is strongly criticized by him, whether as part of a 'conservative' or any other form of party politics. The managerial understanding of ruling and the character of enterprise association imposed upon a state began to take on most of Oakeshott's earlier negative connotations of rationalist politics in the late 1960s and 1970s.

---

[185] Ibid., p. 162.
[186] M. Oakeshott 1975, *Talking Politics*, RP, p. 455.
[187] Ibid., p. 457.
[188] Ibid., p. 456.
[189] M. Oakeshott 1965, A Review of The Conservative Opportunity: *15 Bow Group Essays on Tomorrow's Toryism*, p. 26.

In my view, Oakeshott's historical examination of and conceptual differentiation between the vocabularies of authority, power and the mode of association are precisely what they claim to be: conceptual tools which facilitate our understanding of political activity, perhaps more profoundly than we are accustomed to. Thus, I still hope to emphasize that we are not referring here to 'real entities' but to political theorizing. In Skinner's terms, we may say that Oakeshott put forth a "rhetorical redescription" of the concepts of authority and power, keeping the 'conversation going'.[190] Oakeshott's concepts of authority and power are not absolute definitions. They are, however, an important part of Oakeshott's powerful defence of the human freedom that is intrinsic in human agency and its prosperity in a civil association. And, as a 'relationalist' defence, it does not fall into the dreaded category of an 'everything goes' type of relativism. That is, in the *Introduction to Leviathan* (1946, 1975) and *Rational Conduct* (1950), he evokes the understanding that a concept requires the right convention or tradition as its context in order to be properly understood; a convention which in this respect is not arbitrary. By his own redescription of the concepts of authority and power, he exemplifies a conscious reformation of the concepts within recognized conventions. Although the conventions are always changeable, his work instructs us on how historical knowledge can provide us with anchorages upon which we can modify and apply our concepts and language of politics more 'civilly' and consciously.

3: Ideology/Tradition

Another central pair of concepts in Oakeshott's political thought is that of ideology and tradition. It is a well-known fact that the concept of ideology generally appears with negative connotations in Oakeshott's work and is closely connected to his ideal type of rationalist politics. Ideology is described as a comprehensive, self-legitimating, and often pseudo-scientific program of action; a plan which intrinsically belongs to the strain of politics referred to by Oakeshott as rationalism. It is purported to be a set of independently premeditated abstract principles which supply in advance a formulated end (or ends) for a society to pursue. Tradition, on the other hand, is central to the understanding of Oakeshott's conception of politics as sailing on a "boundless and bottomless sea." The metaphor does not refer to any kind of full relativity as a situation that is conducive to politics, but tradition establishes a criterion against which 'good' politics is measured. Tradition establishes a criterion against which 'good' politics is measured. It refers to the entirety of conventions, customs and beliefs of a society, which generates political activity by supplying both its resources and the 'intimations' to be pursued. Ideology and tradition are not, however, merely counter concepts, but, rather, ideology usually relates to tradition as if it were its 'stepchild'; ideology is never merely born in people's heads but is an abridgement of some tradition or set of traditions.

Similarly to the case of authority and power, meanings and utilizations of the concepts of ideology and tradition have changed over the decades and also include internal variations in terms of their application by Oakeshott in various texts. Importantly, the concept of tradition is often substituted with the more modest and explicitly plural concept of practices from 1958 onwards, signifying a certain level of estrangement from more conventional conservative thought as well as a shift towards an emphatically contingent understanding of politics. Compared with the virtually 'all-encompassing' concept of tradition with its strong notion of continuity, the concept of practices (or traditions, idioms, languages) also emphasizes the role of an agent: "Practices are themselves the outcomes of performances."[191] I see this change both partly as a response to the critique against his notion of tradition and as a sign of the relationship between Oakeshott's thought and the so-called linguistic turn. Ideology, for its part, changes from a false model of activity into a stock of vocabulary and a tool of politics, which also implies Oakeshott's higher esteem for political activity in his later work. Ultimately, Oakeshott's understanding of ideology is thoroughly linguistic and, as such, an important and 'positive' part of political activity. Here, ideology acquires the meaning of a special *vocabulary* in terms of which we may respond within (and to) a political situation. In one sense, ideology can be considered as a set of beliefs that imposes a certain logical design upon political discourse because of the logical status given to its maxims. The most

[191] OHC, p. 56.

common logical design of the argument is to persuade without being able to prove. On the other hand, if an ideology is composed of beliefs regarded as axioms instead of maxims, a political argument presents itself as demonstrative. In Oakeshott's interpretation, the former takes its most classic form in Aristotle's *Rhetoric*, whereas the 'father' of the latter is Plato.[192]

Thus, after examining Oakeshott's more familiar conceptions of ideology and tradition, which he used in the years immediately following the war, I continue by examining Oakeshott's relationship to the linguistic turn. My scrutiny begins as a footnote to W.H. Greenleaf's insightful examination of the relationship between Oakeshott, modern (linguistic) philosophy and politics, and concludes by highlighting the underestimation of Oakeshott's work in relation to the understanding of language as constitutive of politics. One part of my argumentation is that, in relation to the concept of ideology, Oakeshott's concept of tradition suffered a sort of 'weak' "Sorelian crisis."[193] He seems to have become even more skeptical of the 'reality' and 'truth' of tradition or, at the very least wanted to distance his own political philosophy from this possibility of ideological interpretation as taking the form of 'nostalgia' towards traditions or understanding traditions as 'moving' individuals. His replacement of the 'strong' concept of tradition with a weaker one, which he lists as belonging to the sphere of practices, idioms and languages, reflects this more accentuated consciousness of the lack of foundations in politics or life in general. The scope of this change is described here as ranging from the juxtaposition of 'ideological' and 'traditional politics' to the understanding of ideologies and traditions *in* politics.

The Practical Doctrines

Where does Oakeshott's conception of ideology stem from and why did it play such a central role in his view of (rational-

---

[192] M. Oakeshott 1991, *Political Discourse*, p. 78; p. 82.

[193] P. King 1968, p. 383. By the Sorelian crisis, Preston King is referring to the account that in the modern age, beliefs "may in no wise be viewed as embodying truth, but, instead, may be consciously manipulated in order to marshal the activities of people to achieve a frankly unquestioned goal. Ideologies often have a genuine strength when accepted as actually true. They lose their strength when consciously conceived as tools, or instruments of control (at least for those persons who consciously view them as such)." Ibid.

ist) politics until the late 1950s? It seems to me that precisely in this respect we can rather safely argue in Skinnerian terms that political life posed a major problem for the political theorist.[194] When reading texts on politics – at any 'level' – written in the years immediately prior to and after World War II, it becomes clear that an author who did not comment or take a stand on international politics in relation to ideologies was a rare exception, and Oakeshott was not one of them.

Again, Oakeshott's *Introduction* in *The Social and Political Doctrines of Contemporary Europe* (1939), which he edited in 1939 at Ernest Barker's request, offers an interesting point of comparison to his political essays of the late 1940s and early 1950s, especially to the classic essay *Rationalism in Politics* (1947), in which Oakeshott most forcefully stated his negative comprehension of the role of ideologies in politics, as well as to the controversial inaugural lecture *Political Education* (1951). Namely, Oakeshott's characterization of individual doctrines as claiming to be universally applicable – each being not merely a political doctrine "about the nature of the state and the ends of government, but also a social doctrine, a conception of society and of the place and function of the individual in society" – could be directly applied to his later conception of ideology.[195] He also considers doctrines in relation to the Mannheimian perspective on ideologies, which was difficult to avoid at the time, and states that even if one did understand all such doctrines as the products of social conditions, it does not necessarily follow that the examination of the doctrines themselves is worthless or that "such an examination is to assert (by implication) that these doctrines are independent of the social circumstances of their construction."[196] The crucial difference in his conception of ideology, however, is Oakeshott's treatment of Catholicism as a "doctrine in terms of Natural Law; it belongs, that is, to the most ancient of the Western European traditions of social and political thought. So far as Catholicism is concerned this tradition received a definitive statement in the philosophy of St Thomas Aquinas. But in modern times an admirable restatement of it was made in Leo XIII's remarkable series of Encyclical Letters."[197] Although

---

[194] See Q. Skinner 1978, p. xi, K. Palonen 2003b, p. 3.
[195] SP, p. xiv.
[196] Ibid., p. xiii.
[197] Ibid., p. 45.

Catholicism is to a certain extent an exception among the European political and social doctrines of the time, and although a certain break is indicated by the use of the word 'restatement', this sort of combination of the terminology of tradition, doctrine and social and political thought becomes impossible in Oakeshott's later use of the more distinctive concept of ideology. To heighten the point, no *ideology* provides any evidence that Natural Law or any other tradition of ideas "is not yet dead."[198]

The movement between 'practice' and 'theory' and the role of the critic is rather peculiar here. Oakeshott argues in idealist terms that a doctrine should not be condemned by "the intellectual critic" on the grounds of its being insufficiently coherent; "to dismiss Fascism because of the obvious confusion of Mussolini's mind."[199] Furthermore:

> The value of a regime, fortunately, does not depend upon the intellectual competence of its apologists; indeed, in most cases, practice is more coherent than doctrine and its superiority should be recognized. Nevertheless, when a regime chooses to rationalize its practice, chooses to issue an official statement of the social and political doctrine upon which it relies – and this is so with most of the regimes of contemporary Europe – the coherence of such a statement becomes a matter of importance; and if it can be convicted of intellectual confusion, that is not a fault to be brushed aside as insignificant. What the intellectual critic of a doctrine has to say is certainly relevant, though it is not all that can be said and is unlikely to affect the course of affairs.[200]

It is worth emphasizing that the most useful thing the philosophical critic can do in relation to political and social doctrines is to free them from parasitic philosophical ideas, such as the theory of knowledge in Marxism or Millian individualism, not to reveal them as 'false' as such. Instead, as doctrines, Oakeshott connects their relevance not to intellectual satisfaction or even coherence, but to practical success:

> Indeed, modern skepticism as to the efficacy of thought is unambiguously reflected in most of these doctrines. They do not trouble to hide their tendency to descend from reasoned statements to mere assertions and from thought to febrile activity as a substitute for thought.[201]

---

[198] Ibid., p. xix.
[199] Ibid.
[200] Ibid., p. xv.
[201] Ibid., p. xxiii.

They are not seen here as 'corrupting' politics, but as a part of political life not to be *judged* in terms of philosophical evaluation. In this sense, especially communism, fascism and national socialism, all of which were evaluated by Oakeshott at the time, were 'efficient' in "their remarkable success in subjugating whole communities" on the one hand, but more useless in "the comparatively small amount of damage which the doctrine of Representative Democracy has suffered from this bombardment" on the other.[202] Oakeshott also has an eye for political manoeuvres. He recognizes that by representing themselves as critiques of representative democracy, 'totalitarian' doctrines become compromised; they are either "merely verbal," as is the case with fascists attempting to pass themselves off as representing the truest form of democracy, "tactical," or assertive of the "complete liberty of creed and conscience."[203] Thus, here, Oakeshott applies doctrines in political activity in a similar fashion to the way in which he views ideologies as vocabularies to be utilized in his 1960s and 1970s theorizing; they are not only (falsely) understood as 'guides' of conduct by political actors.

What is surprising is that, despite many stylistic reservations, Oakeshott here endeavours to 'extract' a social and political doctrine from the tradition of ideas "under which the majority of civilized mankind still live," referring to it simply as "Representative Democracy."[204] The choice of name is made in order to distinguish it from the brand of "crude and negative individualism" apt to be associated with liberalism, which, for its own part, is usually contrasted with the creeds of the Labour and Conservative parties in Britain. For Oakeshott, this doctrine "is a tradition expressed, so far as this country is concerned, in the spirit of our laws rather than in the programme of any one party. Nevertheless, it is a Liberal doctrine."[205] Here then, the doctrine of representative democracy becomes merged into tradition as less systematic and rigid than the other doctrines, whose systems remain primarily on the surface. Importantly, Oakeshott writes:

> I do not wish to suggest (what I do not believe) that this doctrine
> of Representative Democracy is the final deliverance of the

[202] Ibid.
[203] Ibid.
[204] Ibid., p. xvii.
[205] Ibid., p. xviii.

human mind on questions of society and government (that is, what Mussolini and others accuse it of asserting itself to be, "outside history"), but it has the advantage of all the others in that it has shown itself capable of changing without perishing in the process, and it has the advantage (denied to all others save Catholicism) of not being the hasty product of a generation but of belonging to a long and impressive tradition of thought. It contains, I believe, a more comprehensive expression of our civilization than any of the others (though it is by no means either a complete or a satisfactory expression as it stands), and its adaptability is a sign of vitality rather than mere vagueness.[206]

In this text, written before the war, Oakeshott relies more heavily on the long, political tradition that the doctrine of representative democracy represents. Shortly after the war, his tone was much more pessimistic. In selecting the portions of text to represent this doctrine, Oakeshott hopes to convey its central principles:

That a society must not be so unified as to abolish vital and valuable differences, nor so extravagantly diversified as to make an intelligently co-ordinated and civilized social life impossible, and that the imposition of a universal plan of life on a society is at once stupid and immoral...[207]

*Oakeshott thus incorporates "Representative Democracy into our debate" by reading and selecting the most classic texts of the doctrine, which, characteristically speaking, are "a little behind the times," as well as by choosing some of its "fundamental" concepts.[208] The doctrine of representative democracy does not intend to impose a universal plan upon a society, and in this sense we can regard his conception of doctrine as more positive than his treatment of ideology in his postwar texts, in which not even 'liberal' ideology escapes the negative features of ideological thinking. He also makes an interesting distinction by placing the concept of the individual at the very heart of this doctrine:

A genetic treatment of this doctrine might show the conception of individuality springing from the conception and institution of property; but, as I have said elsewhere, I am not concerned with questions of genesis, and there can be no doubt that in the logical

---

[206] Ibid.
[207] Ibid., p. xix.
[208] Ibid., p. xvi.

structure of this doctrine the conception of property is subordinate.[209]

Here, in his overlapping treatment of tradition and doctrine, he emphasizes individuality as a more important element of representative democracy than property, and he sustains this emphasis throughout his career, especially when referring exclusively to the British political tradition.

In sum, as it is used here, the concept of doctrine includes certain active elements, such as the tactical use of the terminology of other doctrines or even the possibility of consciously constructing a doctrine for intellectual purposes, without the connotation of perverting the tradition of ideas. It is also important to note that the doctrine of Representative Democracy, as 'constructed' here by Oakeshott, clearly informs us of the 'positive side' of his dual conception of politics leading up to the final conception of politics in civil association or *societas*.

Ideology as a Distortion of Politics

In Preston King's view,[210] Christianity is the first and most pristine ideology to have emerged in the West, because it has always been very much aware of having marked a dramatically new beginning and thus as including a kind of geometry of myth.[211] He goes on to claim that ideological politics began with Christianity, which offered a mythological vision of the past, the future and a community of believers united in the acceptance of this vision.[212] Arendt, Friedrich and Brezezinski are listed as archetypical examples of those who have mistakenly conceived ideology as a recent historical phenomenom. For King, it is precisely this incorrectly foreshortened perspective that has also led writers to anticipate the end of ideology.

I think we can safely add Oakeshott's name to this list when emphasizing the use of the concept of ideology to describe and evaluate a distinctly *modern* political phenomena, although his specific emphasis on totalitarian ideologies is not accentuated to the same extent as in the texts of the aforementioned

[209] Ibid., pp. 3–4.
[210] In the volume *Politics and Experience* (1968), which was dedicated to Oakeshott on the occasion of his retirement from LSE. Thus, as the volume can clearly be read as a direct response to Oakeshott, it is of course interesting to note the similarity between King's newer view of ideology and Oakeshott's older view of doctrine in this particular instance.
[211] P. King 1968, p. 371.
[212] Ibid., p. 373.

authors. As already indicated, Oakeshott's replacement of the concept of doctrine with the concept of ideology can be interpreted as a self-correcting move by which he aims to more clearly distinguish tradition as 'a way of life', such as Christianity, and 'genuine philosophical traditions' from both the concept of *political* tradition and, most emphatically, from an ideology as a *distortion* of political tradition.[213] Ideology is a concept belonging to the sphere of political thought *per se*. This is not to say, however, that it would be impossible for Oakeshott to *ideologize* elements of, for example, Christianity, but again this is a 'new' construction, not the tradition itself. Thus, King's reasoning that "the fact that so many racialists, as in South Africa and the southern United States, are inveterate theologists as well, who demonstrate the correctness of *apartheid* and segregation by reference to biblical passages" proves that Christianity can be utilized ideologically is correct from an Oakeshottian perspective, but his conclusion that, for example, it is precisely for this reason that Christianity *itself* is an ideology is mistaken.[214]

Some general observations with respect to this shift, especially regarding the use of the concept of ideology, can be now stated. Firstly, 'since the time of Napoleon' to the present day, ideology has been a fairly obvious choice of terms in the evaluation of something as a negative aspect of political life. Secondly, there was a particularly intense discussion of the concept in the immediate aftershock of World War II and the climate of the Cold War. As I already mentioned, the sense of 'disillusionment' was perhaps the most general condition of political theorizing and can also be discerned in the British discussions. This disillusionment is crystallized in the essay *Rationalism in Politics* and its rather gloomy tone of discussion.

Although I do not entirely agree with the interpretations that insist on Oakeshott's claim of a single underlying tradition of political practice in Great Britain, John Gray's observation of Oakeshott as "treating the British – or to be more precise, the English – example as it were a paradigm of political experience" is quite accurate in terms of his conception of

---

[213] I am not arguing that Oakeshott entirely abandoned the term 'doctrine' in his political philosophy; as is the case with most terminological shifts in his *oeuvre*, the term continues to be employed, although with different emphases and in different positions to various degrees in relation to other terms.

[214] Ibid., p. 346.

'good' or 'traditional' politics – the opposite of which is naturally ideological politics.[215]

Before the war, 'a doctrine' was an apt term to apply to "the intellectual constructions on which the various regimes of contemporary Europe rely."[216] To some extent doctrines were complementary to each other, although they tended more to emphasize the idea that it is "foolish to attribute to our civilization a unity which it has lost."[217] In the late 1940s, however, the concept of ideology was assigned a double function in relation to the British/European political situation: it began to be used to criticize both certain 'false' types of political activity as ideological and false intellectual *interpretations* of such situations. The former approximates British politics more closely to Continental politics, whereas the latter indicates that it is precisely this interpretation that not only misunderstands the traditional nature of British politics, but also poses a danger to it. To accentuate this rather controversial point:

> The categories of British politics, according to both these writers [Quintin Hogg and John Parker, SS] are Left and Right. If this were really so it would imply a closer approximation of British to Continental politics than I had supposed to be the case, and it would deprive British politics of much of their individuality... There may be some faint approximation between the Labour Party and the continental parties of both the Left and the Right (in the politics of rationalism, that is continental politics, extremes are apt to meet); its roots are not as firmly fixed in the traditions of British politics as one would like... and when these categories of Left and Right are transplanted into the past, the writers who perform the operation merely make themselves ridiculous.[218]

In this passage, Oakeshott thus approximates Continental (and the Labour Party) politics to rationalist politics, although he ridicules those intellectuals who attempt to impose rationalist categories on British politics.

In a later and until recently unpublished account, Oakeshott deems as "'ideological' politics" such politics which draws us into the inquiry of the meaning of words like "communism" or "justice" as abstract nouns.[219] Subsequently, we are only ready to act once we have clearly defined the meaning of such words.

[215] J. Gray 1997, p.87. See also, e.g., B. Crick 1962.
[216] SP, p. xiv.
[217] Ibid.
[218] M. Oakeshott 1948, *Contemporary British Politics*, pp. 479-80.
[219] M. Oakeshott c. 1955, *Conduct and Ideology in Politics*, WH, pp. 245-54.

Secondly, in such politics we face the dilemma caused by the confrontation of ideological and practical judgement. How should we make political decisions in this type of situation? Oakeshott also suggests that these conflicts are more or less unavoidable. Thus, this account clearly continues Oakeshott's earlier reflections. This kind of ideological understanding of politics is mistaken and the ideological conduct of politics is impossible.

In addition, a reader interested in Oakeshott's character as an historian will likely notice the similarity between the afore-mentioned quotation and Oakeshott's later well-known notion of a "living past" as brought to existence by a mis-guided impulse of an historian.[220] Oakeshott also said that we "live in an intellectually corrupt age," which in the case of his-tory specifically implied its perversion for our own pur-poses.[221] Thus, one aspect of Oakeshott's concept of ideology began to take its form in the 1940s, i.e. the approximation of the concept to a certain type of 'theorizing', which is primarily an activity guided by an impulse (usually political) that is not appropriate to the mode, or activity, of philosophy or history. In addition, although Oakeshott's general emphasis is on the 'protection' of philosophy and history from the practical mode of politics, it is still important to note that there is an element of *the protection of the speciality of political activity* – as both transi-tional and local – from political philosophy, which at that par-ticular time was seen by Oakeshott as an "encounter with eternity."[222] The implicit assumption seems to be that different interpretations of history can be used appropriately in political argumentation, but mistaking it for proper history is one of the most serious and common fallacies of our time.

Oakeshott most clearly expressed the topicality of ideology in a letter to Karl Popper:

> ...under the inspiration of *true* rationalism you seem to me to break up political life into atoms of political action and to take the business of politics to be the right & reasonable solution of a series of problems. But political life only becomes this when it is gov-erned by ideologies: *normally*, in the 19th century, it was never this.[223]

---

[220] M. Oakeshott 1958, *The Activity of Being an Historian*, RP, p, 181; OH, p.19.

[221] M. Oakeshott 1948, A Review of K.B. Smellie: *Why We Read History*. p. 766.

[222] M. Oakeshott 1947, *Rationalism in Politics*, RP, p. 34.

[223] M. Oakeshott 1948, *A Letter to Karl Popper*, emphasis SS.

Oakeshott is here contrasting the time of 'normality' in politics in the 19th century to the age of rationalist, ideological politics. We will return to this point when discussing Oakeshott's conservatism in relation to his concept of tradition.

The argument can also be read as sharing the general concern regarding the equation of politics with engineering. In its brevity, the defence of the autonomy of political activity could be formulated as follows:

> The position of the statesman and that of the engineer are not analogous.[224]

Oakeshott uses the metaphor of conversation as an appropriate understanding of political activity and contrasts it with what Oakeshott views as Popper's "politics of argument."[225] Moreover, he emphasizes here that men are not only united by reason, but also by a common civilization or common habits of behaviour.[226] In the late 1940s, it was important to oppose the usage of the language of engineering, which represented ideological, rationalist politics.[227] The dual composition of Oakeshott's understanding of politics is again visible:

> How deeply the rationalist disposition of mind has invaded our political thought and practice is illustrated by the extent to which traditions of behaviour have given place to ideologies, the extent to which the politics of destruction and creation have been substituted for the politics of repair, the consciously planned and deliberately executed being considered (for that reason) better than

---

[224] T.D. Weldon 1953, p. 81.

[225] M. Oakeshott 1948, *A Letter to Karl Popper*.

[226] Ibid. 'The politics of innovation' is one apt term for describing Oakeshott's later view on politics (1956), which may – with some reservations regarding the fusing of different activities – even be compared with Popper's notion of social engineering. That is, if it is to be understood in a Weldonian limited way: "It is for these reasons that the confusion between puzzles, problems and difficulties which tends to infect political theory cannot be dismissed as a harmless eccentricity and phrases like 'social engineering' are to be regarded as something of a menace. Economic planning is rather like engineering in that both proceed from difficulties to problems and from problems to puzzle-solving. Provided that this is done consciously and the limitations of it are recognized (as they are, for instance by Professor Popper in his advocacy of 'piecemal' as distinct from 'utopian' engineering) there is much to be said for it." T. D. Weldon 1953, p. 82.

[227] It is to be noted that another activity to be kept separate from politics is economics. Oakeshott criticized the use of economical analogies in this respect already in 1930. See M. Oakeshott 1930, A Review of G.E.G. Catlin: *The Principles of Politics*, p. 400.

what has grown up and established itself unselfconsciously over a period of time.[228]

Ideological politics is thus analogous to a conscious, planned politics of destruction and creation and opposed to 'proper', unselfconscious politics. At this point, we can identify traces of the organistic conceptualization of society and thus politics in Oakeshott's thinking. The passage also reveals how Oakeshott does not yet emphasize the action of an individual, but, rather, that a change within the society as a whole is dependent upon the 'unconscious' changes inside tradition(s).

This aspect was also severely criticized by Oakeshott's contemporaries. For example, Thomas B. Peardon placed Oakeshott's thought along the same lines as the "new conservatism" and "traditionalism" with their "low estimation of speculation" and "deep skepticism about the possibilities inherent in political action."[229] It is to this type of critique that we can assume Oakeshott later responded by both developing the concept of ideologies as a tool of political activity and replacing the concept of tradition with practices.[230] It is also to be noted here that the *time-span* in Oakeshott's historico-philosophical conception of political activity is notably long, implying a (preferably) slow change which can then be viewed from the perspective of an 'entire' society. Although this perspective is not completely eliminated from Oakeshott's later thought, in the figure of civil association the time-span for political activity is clearly shortened along with the new emphasis on 'conscious' deliberation.

Still, for the postwar Oakeshott, *rationalism* is the most influential intellectual trend in post-Renaissance Europe, and the archetype rationalists were seen as the French *philosophes*,[231] which, of course, means that it was not a very novel

[228] M. Oakeshott 1947, *Rationalism in Politics*, RP, p. 26.

[229] T. B. Peardon 1955, pp. 491-2. See also, e.g., M. Postan 1947/8.

[230] Oakeshott was criticized as a successor of Laski for combining skepticism and the worship of tradition. Also, the 'other current' in English political thought was that of Weldonian liberal empiricism, which, despite certain differences, was united with Oakeshottian conservatism in its 'harmlessness to the status quo'. See, e.g., E. Gellner 1957.

[231] Compare with, Berlin's statement that *philosophes* of the eighteenth century failed over politics "because our political notions are part of our conception of what it is to be human." I. Berlin 1962, p. 79.

phenomenon. Yet the concept of ideology, which, of course, belongs to the 'scheme' of rationalist politics, is mainly used by Oakeshott to describe recent political experience in British politics, and, as such, he also admittedly uses it as a tool of argumentation when commenting on the political situation of the day. In terms of this specific type of use, most of the observations made earlier with regard to the concept of power also apply to ideology and thus need not be repeated here. Yet it is no surprise that his conception of ideology itself was often treated as 'ideological' by his contemporaries. The critique of a certain dismissal of deliberation in political activity referred to above is accentuated here. For example, J.W.N. Watkins said of Oakeshott that "having admitted that genuine speculation is possible, his own political philosophy would no longer be in danger of refuting itself."[232] The doubt surrounding Oakeshott's conception of ideology was condensed analogously to the well-known 'chicken-and-egg conundrum':

> But is it less extravagant to suggest that a tradition of political behaviour can come into being without some ideological preconceptions to preside at its birth and growth? Can politics be adequately explained as a self-generated activity or a game of follow-my-leader?[233]

And it is true that Oakeshott's conception of ideology in the late 1940s and early 1950s is also a sort of caricature that emphasizes the contrast between Oakeshott's notion of 'proper' politics and rationalist politics. Ideological politics represents the "imposition of a uniform condition of perfection upon human conduct," which means that it actually tries to extend itself beyond the limits of the sphere of politics.[234]

However, it is precisely this conception that has acquired a firm place in Anglophone (or British) political thought. For Minogue, ideologies "insist that no piecemeal solution is a proper solution, and that the ideological proposal is the solution to all problems."[235] In Oakeshott's view, ideological 'politics' is not actually politics at all, but "the abolition of politics."[236] This conception seems to appear as a 'given', even

---

[232] J.W.N. Watkins 1952, p. 337.
[233] Al Anon 1951, p. 341.
[234] M. Oakeshott 1947, *Rationalism in Politics*, RP, 10.
[235] K.R. Minogue 1980, pp. 38-9.
[236] Ibid., p. 34.

in the texts of those who were most critical of Oakeshott.[237]
Crick, whose conception of politics appears to be influenced
by Arendt and Oakeshott, writes in his *In Defence of Politics*
(1962) that:

> Political thinking is to be contrasted to ideological thinking. Poli-
> tics cannot furnish us with an ideology; an ideology means an end
> to politics, though ideologies may combat each other within a
> political system.[238]

Crick also claims that totalitarian ideology represents a clear
contrast to politics and that the academic theory of ideology
represents a false and even dangerous attempt to reduce all
political theory to sociological theory.[239] Many contemporary
'postmodern' writers also entertain a similar conception of the
relationship between ideology and politics. For example,
Zygmunt Bauman remarks that "the human costs of casting
society in ideological straight-jackets" are horrifying and
inherently opposed to politics."[240] Furthermore, the nature of
ideologies as projects is firmly established:

> An ideology without a project – some project which by being a
> project and a plan for action spells out a future different from the
> present – is an oxymoron, a contradiction in terms.[241]

I hope to stress the similarity between Oakeshott's earlier characterization of the doctrine of representative democracy and
what now seems to be his characterization of a 'proper' understanding of political activity:

> Politics I take to be the activity of attending to the general arrange-
> ments of a set of people whom chance or choice have brought
> together. In this sense, families, clubs and learned societies have
> their 'politics'. But the communities in which this manner of activ-
> ity is pre-eminent are the hereditary co-operative groups, many of
> them of ancient lineage, all of them aware of a past, a present, and
> a future, which we call 'states'. For most people, political activity
> is a secondary activity – that is to say, they have something else to
> do... With us it is, at one level or another, a universal activity.[242]

---

[237] This is not, of course, to claim that Oakeshott is the only one advocating this
conception, but surely he is among the most influential writers.
[238] B. Crick 1962, p. 55.
[239] Ibid., p. 47.
[240] Z. Bauman 1999, p. 131.
[241] Ibid., p. 125.
[242] M. Oakeshott 1951, *Political Education*, RP, 44-5.

A politics that cherishes plurality and focuses on taking care of general arrangements is in inherent contradiction to a politics based on one plan in a society.

In relation to ideology, it now seems that the doctrine of representative democracy, which was characterized earlier more as a tradition of ideas than a doctrine, is used in many respects to describe the 'universal' – and I take this to mean the Western – activity of politics. The features of the Continental doctrines seem to be condensed into a general concept of ideology, which can also be used to describe the rationalist style of politics in Great Britain.

Keeping this shift in mind, we may better understand Oakeshott's description of Hayek's *Road to Serfdom* and its "plan to resist all planning" as perhaps "better than its opposite," although still ideological and belonging to the rationalist style of politics:

> And only in a society already deeply infected with Rationalism will the conversion of the traditional resources of resistance to the tyranny of Rationalism into a self-conscious ideology be considered a strengthening of these resources.[243]

Thus, Oakeshott does not himself associate his thought with that of Hayek. And it is true that the distinction between Oakeshott's thought and Hayek's "political book"[244] is more visible in the essay *Rationalism in Politics* than in Oakeshott's 'libertarian' texts *Contemporary British Politics* (1949) and *The Political Economy of Freedom* (1949). In general, Hayek and Oakeshott both strongly criticized rationalism and defended the rule of law and the role of tradition. Yet Hayek's opposition to conservatism distinguishes him from Oakeshott, and Oakeshott, for his own part, did not advocate free market progress in Hayekian terms in his later accounts either.[245] As regards criticism of Hayek's book, it must thus be emphasized that at this point in time Oakeshott also saw British politics as having been infected by a rationalist style, particularly as a result of the war. One of the most disastrous ramifications of the war was the new customary application of its essentially rationalist vocabulary to politics.[246]

---

[243] Ibid., p. 26.
[244] F.A. Hayek 1944, p. v.
[245] J. Iivonen 1995, p. 250.
[246] M. Oakeshott 1947, *Rationalism in Politics*, RP, p. 34n.

In sum, ideological politics is the opposite of 'traditional' politics. It is rigid, fixed and a politics of destruction as opposed to a politics of repair. It is a distortion of both 'truth' and tradition. As a distortion of 'truth', a political ideology is not what it claims to be: it is supposed to be a product of intellectual premeditation that is capable of determining and guiding political activity. Upon closer inspection, this supposition turns out to be false:

> So far from a political ideology being the quasi-divine parent of political activity, it turns out to be its earthly stepchild... The pedigree of every political ideology shows it to be the creature, not of premeditation in advance of political activity, but of meditation upon a manner of politics. In short, political activity comes first and a political ideology follows after; and the understanding of politics we are investigating has the disadvantage of being, in the strict sense, preposterous.[247]

Thus, according to Oakeshott, parallel to this idea, a form of political education that concentrates merely on the study of ideologies – for example in the form of abstract ideas such as 'Freedom' – is mistaken. In addition, the traditions of ideas and habits of behaviour serve as the criterion of 'truth' in the study of political philosophy.[248] Therefore, Oakeshott's concept of ideology, which refers to a falsely regarded correspondence to some real state of affairs or to being independent of traditions, contains a specific epistemological claim which is naturally associated with a coherence theory of truth as opposed to a correspondence theory. Yet although the traditions and habits of behaviour are multiple and there is no *single* criterion for 'truth', a certain distinction of traditions as somehow more concrete than ideologies can be detected.

Oakeshott's conception of ideology does not cohere with Karl Mannheim's notion that our creeds are *wholly determined* by social facts.[249] Nor does it cohere with the idea that ideologies as 'myths' etc. stand in the way of political philosophy, in the sense of their being explained and justified in terms of motives and reasons, as Berlin seems to suggest.[250] The study of political ideologies may be acceptable, because "certainly the most useful of them (because they unquestionably have their use), are abstracts of the political traditions of some soci-

[247] M. Oakeshott 1951, *Political Education*, RP, p. 51.
[248] See ibid., p. 65.
[249] M. Oakeshott 1937, A Review of K. Mannheim: *Ideology and Utopia*, p. 329.
[250] I. Berlin 1962, p. 89.

ety."[251] But this is not to imply that political education or political philosophy could be said to somehow consist of the study of ideologies, or some fundamental political principles and their implications, as was often conceived in the political theory of the time.[252]

Another aspect of Oakeshott's use of ideology to be stressed here was its application as a means of distorting political traditions. This can be done either by abstracting an ideology from a sphere of activity other than political experience, such as war, religion or industry, or by first abstracting principles like 'democracy' from a concrete political tradition and then shipping this 'pack' abroad. In the former manner, ideology is not only abstract but also "inappropriate on account of the irrelevance of the activity from which it has been abstracted," the paradigm example of this being Marxist ideology.[253] It is to apply the 'scientific' model of a method to politics and to aim for certainty by absolutely distinguishing between knowledge and opinion in politics. Oakeshott also draws a specific distinction between a tradition of ideas and modern rationalism in politics:

> ...there is no question of ever winning true knowledge out of the 'childish notions we at first imbibed'. And this, it may be remarked, is what distinguishes both Platonic and Scholastic from modern Rationalism: Plato is a rationalist, but the dialectic is not a technique, and the method of Scholasticism always had before it a limited aim.[254]

The 'application' of scientific or philosophical 'methods', techniques or *technical knowledge* as a guideline of politics, which as a practical activity is inherently contingent, is to corrupt the conduct of politics itself. The second way of distorting traditions, by a 'packing and shipping' method, actually simplifies a given political ideology further, as it is no longer 'rooted' in its proper context. Thus, both of these rationalist operations are understood as potentially dangerous for understanding and conducting political activity, the latter point indicating a normative dimension in Oakeshott's political thought.

[251] M. Oakeshott 1951, *Political Education*, RP, p. 54.
[252] See, e.g., Salvador de Madariaga, a Spanish diplomat and a commentator of British political life, for whom Weldon's *The Vocabulary of Politics* simply brushed aside the importance of the present struggle over the axioms and principles. S. de Madariaga 1953/4, p. 69.
[253] M. Oakeshott 1951, *Political Education*, RP, p. 54.
[254] M. Oakeshott 1947, *Rationalism in Politics*, RP, p. 20.

One difference in relation to one of the most controversial issues of the discussion of political topics at the time, i.e. totalitarianism, becomes expressed in this point. Namely, Oakeshott's conception of ideology and rationalism makes it possible for him to speak about the phenomenon of totalitarianism without invoking mass psychological or reactionary explanations. Nor is totalitarianism a "denial of a universal moral law binding on all mankind and its replacement by a relativist view of morals."[255] Oakeshott also dismisses Morgenthau's identification of fascism as a reaction against the prevailing enterprise of rationalism and liberalism, "and for no better reasons than because this is what its prophets represented it as, and because of the anti-rational strain in its doctrines."[256] In Oakeshott's interpretation, totalitarianism 'is' conducting politics in a rationalist style; it is part of the 'continental' style of politics taken to its extreme.

Thus, I think the contemporary critique is misguided in its description of Oakeshott's figure of a rationalist as "a composite monster," which would also drive him to insist on conceiving the Nazis as rationalists.[257] Conversely, according to the critique, the correct interpretation would be that of stressing a conservative revulsion; "all the ancient ingredients of German romanticism – the appeal to intuition against reason, blood against intellect, communion with the people against personal judgement." Although Oakeshott does not share this view of conservatism or totalitarianism, he does not actually deny this interpretation in his critique of ideological or rationalist politics. A rationalist may well appeal to, for example, the notion of "blood against intellect" within such an ideological scheme. What he does see as dangerous, however, is the understanding of some possible final end of politics, which may be a consequence of an ideology and which depends first and foremost on forcing *one* overarching ideology upon a society.

[255] M. Ginsberg 1949, p. 26.
[256] M. Oakeshott 1947, *Scientific Politics*, RPML, p. 102.
[257] M. Postan 1947/1948, p. 397.

Traditional Politics

Of all the concepts in Oakeshott's postwar thought, it is arguably the concept of tradition that has elicited the most intense contemporary response, as well as the greatest number of posterior analyses and 'applications'. As to politics, there has been a rather solid duality in terms of its interpretation: the first course has been to emphasize the concept as embodying his conservative traditional*ism* with its inherent fear of "the democratic principles which challenge privilege and status."[258] In addition, political cynicism and the mystical qualities of tradition are also stressed.[259] The second course is to stress the fluid and unfixed character of traditions as exemplifying the possibilities for political action. For example, according to Mouffe, it is tradition that "allows us to think our own insertion into historicity."[260] In her view, the fact that the subjects are constructed through a series of existing discourses, i.e. tradition, is what indicates to us that "the world is given to us and all political action made possible."[261] Tradition has thus embodied both Oakeshott's "Anti-Politics" and his "looking down on politicians," as well as his 'Politics'.[262]

Yet it is surprising how little more recent Oakeshott literature has examined the concept of tradition and its use.[263] There may, however, be several reasons for this 'neglect' of tradition. Firstly, it is precisely this concept that Oakeshott himself explicitly rejects in his late theorizing as an inadequate means of expressing what he wants to convey.[264] In this sense, Nardin's brief comment that Oakeshott replaced tradition with "practice" due to his unsuccessful effort to turn the former concept, with its ideological connotations, into a philosophical term is correct.[265] Secondly, there is a real confusion of the actual contents and application of the concept, which is

---

[258] R.H.S. Crossman 1958, p. 137.
[259] See, e.g., G. Thomas 2000, p. 208.
[260] C. Mouffe 1993, p. 16.
[261] Ibid.
[262] Al Anon 1962, p. 2.
[263] See A. Farr 1998, S. Gerencser 2000, T. Nardin 2001. Efraim Podoksik's (2003a), Luke O'Sullivan's (2003) and Roy Tseng's (2003) books tackle the notion of tradition, however. Yet their perspective is not specifically political and thus my interpretation differs from theirs.
[264] M. Oakeshott 1976, *On Misunderstanding Human Conduct. A Reply To My Critics*, p. 364. As I have mentioned, the other 'rejected' concept was, of course, society.
[265] T. Nardin 2001, p. 76.

summed up quite well by Samuel Coleman, a sociologist and, at the time, lecturer at Columbia University:

> Professor Oakeshott slips from the employment of tradition to refer to the entire culture or the process of enculturation of a society to the meaning which refers to a single tradition of that society. Thus, '... a society's tradition of behaviour' refers to the 'body of tradition, the culture; similarly in '... a traditional manner of behaviour', the reference is to the manner of behaviour being enculturated. But '... existing traditions of behaviour' refers to traditions, organised collections of individual components of the society. That a society's political arrangements are related to its culture is descriptive, and can be formulated as an empirically verifiable position. That a society ought to adhere to a specific tradition – 'knowledge, as profound as we can make it, of our tradition of political behaviour' (*Rationalism in Politics*, pp. 123, 128-9) implicitly prescribes a specific tradition, and is something else again. Professor Oakeshott sometimes uses traditional to refer to the tiny bits and pieces of culture, or of learned dispositions to behave, such as individual components of words, or words themselves, and 'molecular actions' or 'actones'. At other times by 'traditional' he refers to the beliefs and practices composed of these bits and pieces.[266]

According to Coleman, in Oakeshott's use of the concept, tradition may refer either to the entire culture of a society or to a single tradition of that society. As regards politics, Coleman also acknowledges the occasional prescriptive nature of tradition. In addition, the term "traditional" may refer to learned dispositions of behaviour. In this connection, the concept of tradition becomes close to the later use of the concept of practice. In retrospect, then, it is possible to distinguish numerous aspects of Oakeshott's concept of tradition, from the theory of human behaviour to traditions, as appropriate contexts for reading, for example, philosophy. Tradition may well be highlighted as being an internally "contested concept" – to use W.B. Gallie's phrasing – in Oakeshott's thought, although this is not a very flattering observation about a thinker concerned with the "crookedness" in the usage of familiar concepts in our political vocabularies.[267]

This multifaceted concept and its critique have already appeared in several forms in the pages of this book and thus need not be repeated here. However, in order to better understand the development of both the important nuances in

---

[266] S. Coleman 1968, p. 249.
[267] M. Oakeshott 1951, *Political Education*, RP, p. 66.

Oakeshott's conception of politics and his relation to the linguistic turn in social sciences it is still necessary to return to some specific points related to the concept of tradition. Although it is not my intention here to 'rescue' the concept, it is possible to re-open some rather fixed conceptions and interpretations for discussion, especially by reading *Rationalism in Politics* (1962, 1991) as a collection of essays – which it is – rather than automatically lumping them all together.

It may well be that Oakeshott was seen by the generation of students who studied during the 1960s as a relic of the past, as someone who supported antirationalism and political conservatism with no relevance to the political theory of the day.[268] It may also be that Oakeshott's political philosophy should be clearly considered negligible in relation to his general philosophy.[269] My intention here, however, is to show that the examination of political tradition in relation to Oakeshott's 'master metaphor' of conversation (and the analogy of language), which was overlooked by the former party of interpreters and sublimated by the latter, requires the reassessment of both of these views.

The year 1939 once again offers a point of comparison in my examination, as it was at this particular point Oakeshott viewed the political system as lying on the surface of a society; it was the protection and occasional modification of a recognized legal and social order:

> It is not self-explanatory; its end and meaning lie beyond itself in the social whole to which it belongs, a social whole already determined by law and custom and tradition, none of which is the creation of political activity. Political activity may have given us Magna Carta and the Bill of Rights, but it did not give us the contents of these documents, which came from a stratum of social thought far too deep to be influenced by the actions of politicians.[270]

It is only on rare occasions, such as in times of war, that politics makes any remarkable impression on the life of a society; along with its main function as a protector of a society (or civilization), it only contributes to a "minor degree of merely

---

[268] See Q. Skinner in P. Koikkalainen and S. Syrjämäki 2002, p. 45, B. Barry 1965, p. 17.
[269] See, e.g., T. Nardin 2001.
[270] M. Oakeshott, *The Claims of Politics*, 1939, RPML, p. 93.

mechanical interpretation and expression."[271] What is important in a society, i.e. its values, is created and recreated by artists, poets and philosophers and not by the *politicians* whose
job is to guard them; a *social whole* represents the 'yardstick' of
all activity in the sense of organistic conservative thought and
parallel to the idealist, philosophical assumption of a totality
of experience.[272] Political activity does not make any significant contribution to the society or its traditions. As such, it is
no wonder Oakeshott saw it as representing "mental vulgar-
ity." Although Oakeshott says that political activity may often
result in valuable achievements, he is clear that they are never
"the most valuable things in the communal life of a society."[273]
Because the political system runs somewhat automatically, a
politician's activity involves an inseparable "limitation of
view," and the minds of politicians become "bogus from repe-
tition and lack of examination, unreal loyalties, delusive aims,
false significances."[274] Political activity involves the corruption of the deeper consciousness of society, which the politician is unable to reach. Although Oakeshott does not much use
the concept of tradition here, his implication seems to be that
artists and poets have a particularly significant effect on the
traditions that compose the society itself. He regards this kind
of 'enculturation' as far more important than political activity.

In the essay *Rationalism in Politics*, which in my reading
marks a moment of Oakeshott's deep pessimism as opposed to
his 'usual' skepticism, it is understood that political activity
may also alter the entire society to a significant degree in 'normal' times if the society is interpreted as being in a constant
state of crisis. And, as it is, the unfortunate situation in Great
Britain is that the prevailing *style* of "ideological" politics
coheres with rationalist notions. And much of the rationalist's
political activity consists in "bringing the social, political, legal
and institutional inheritance of his society before the tribunal
of his intellect; and the rest is rational administration, 'reason'

---

[271] Ibid.
[272] Christopher Dawson's account is exceedingly similar. For this Catholic historian and sociologist, the "highest spiritual resources of the community" are
not political but are found in the society as a whole. Dawson 1939, p. 27.
[273] M. Oakeshott, *The Claims of Politics*, 1939, RPML, p. 93.
[274] Ibid.

exercising an uncontrolled jurisdiction over the circumstances of the case."[275]

A rationalist does not value anything (traditions) for the sake of familiarity, but hopes to control everything by means of 'reason'. Rationalist politics may aspire to drive a society towards a uniform human condition by, for example, allowing only an exclusively rationalist form of education or by 'permanently' raising one political question over all others, such as the 'legend of mass employment' or the primary importance of 'social justice'. Rationalist politics goes hand in hand with the "morality of the Rationalist," i.e. the "morality of the self-made man and of the self-made society."[276]

Oakeshott's primary concern is to:

> …recover the lost sense of a society whose freedom and organization spring, not from a superimposed plan, but from the integrating power of a vast and subtle body of rights and duties enjoyed between individuals (whose individuality, in fact, comes into being by their enjoyment), not the gift of nature but the product of our own experience and inventiveness; and to recover also the perception of our law, not merely as an achieved body of rights and duties, the body of a freedom in which mere political rights have a comparatively insignificant place, but as a living method of social integration, the most civilized and the most effective method ever invented by mankind.[277]

'Proper' politics should thus rely on traditions as products of experience and inventiveness. However, politics plays a more important role in the life of a society than in the aforementioned account from 1939. It seems evident that in the intellectual and political atmosphere of Great Britain at that time, Oakeshott felt it was specifically *political* tradition that was under the most immediate threat; political tradition gains respect as a far more important part of a society than he had previously assumed. He notes here that the present surface of the tradition of political activity is also deeply rooted in the past, not only in other forms of 'social thought'.

In its immediate political context, this conception could be seen as contradictory to "the Labourite" reading of the political exigencies of the time and as a (classical) liberal interpretation of "British political tradition; institutions, categories of thought" and manners of behaviour as a compelling alterna-

[275] M. Oakeshott 1947, *Rationalism in Politics*, RP, p. 8.
[276] Ibid., p. 41.
[277] M. Oakeshott 1948, *Contemporary British Politics*, p. 490.

tive to a "democratic socialist perspective."[278] 'Traditional' politics cannot automatically be equated with the Conservative Party politics, but, in contrast to ideological politics, traditional politics consists of the art of participating in the concrete manner of tending to the arrangements of a society.

For the sake of brevity, I have chosen to organize my examination in the following sections on tradition around a few pivotal notions which, from my perspective, best illuminate the concept of tradition (and practices) in relation to political activity. My examination thus revolves around the understanding of parliamentary tradition; the figure of a politician, notions of change, continuity and contingency, and, albeit a bit separately, the analogy of language.

The Defence of Parliamentary Tradition

Summarizing one central aspect of the general atmosphere during the postwar years, Harold Laski restated his 1938 view that "the real alternative to the House of Commons is the concentration camp."[279] As the *locus* of Oakeshott's notion of 'proper' politics in Great Britain is Parliament, it is here that the views of the two holders of the LSE chair converge, although Oakeshott's emphasis is more on the art of parliamentary tradition than on parliament as an institution as such.

The fact that Laski argued in 1938 in favour of parliamentary institutions not as constituting the political area of life but more in terms of their being related to the societal class structure reveals quite a bit about the general discussion at that time. If a parliamentary government were to succeed, it would have to provide the promise of great results.[280] On the other hand, it was threatened by both counter-revolution if employed to radical ends and by the loss of the support of the masses if "it only maintained itself in being by doing nothing to alter the existing distribution of property."[281] Thus, Laski's view was predominantly critical, although he did not support the most radical socialist notions of even overthrowing Parliament. According to Barker's interpretation, during the inter-war years, Laski's account expressed a balance between the value of free politics, hostility towards despotism and a

[278] A. Botwinick 2001, pp. 130-1.
[279] H.J. Laski 1951, cited in Barker 1997, p. 179, see also H.J. Laski 1938, p. 155.
[280] R. Barker 1997, 173, see also H.J. Laski 1938, p. 35.
[281] R. Barker 1997, p. 173.

commitment to radical reform. The possibility that "a concern for substantive policies could tumble over into a pursuit of those policies with little regard for what would normally be thought of as politics" was seen as equal to the possibility that "adherence to calm and tolerant policies could equally tumble into a flight from radical policies lest they prove contentious."[282]

To a certain extent, the postwar years demonstrated the second of these possibilities, and the consensus of British politics in the 1950s was "about the general manner of government and politics" and "the one general aim of not having any general aims other than that of managing the existing system."[283] The "middle way" included the belief in the pragmatic politics of economic efficiency and the advancement of the overall standard of living; politics was presented as a "matter of housekeeping, of distributing the available goods and benefits and husbanding resources."[284] In Barker's interpretation, this consensus also aptly reflected the general observation made in 1955 by political scientist Thomas B. Peardon, for whom the generations before the mid-1940s dreamed of realizing Utopia, but the contemporary generation hoped to escape disaster either in the form of economic collapse or atomic destruction.[285]

According to Barker, the middle way appeared as lying between "ambitions and enthusiasms of all kinds and between socialism and unbridled capitalism" and was a reiteration of the "move from politics to administration," which was previously envisaged by the "Webbs, Wells and later Laski and by the whole broad oligarchic tradition."[286] There was a renewed belief in the reform of the machinery of government, which relied on the absence of major divisions of political strife. Yet not all of the arguments presented were in favour of de-politicization. For example, Bernard Crick argued in favour of the strengthening of the role of the opposition and the education of the public.[287]

It is to this both useful and insightful general view that Barker also connects Oakeshott's conception of politics as the

[282] Ibid., p. 178.
[283] Ibid., p. 180.
[284] Ibid.
[285] Ibid., p. 179.
[286] Ibid., p. 180.
[287] B. Crick 1964, pp. 193-8.

"enterprise to keep afloat on an even keel," pointing to the replacement of certainties and principles by qualified judgements.[288] He did not argue in favour of parliamentary reform, but joined the common consensus that "the one general aim" of government was "of not having any general aims other than that of managing the existing system."[289] At this point, however, the story serves as a general background in pointing out the *differentiae* in Oakeshott's conception and defence of the parliamentary tradition.

The most obvious and general points can now be listed. First, Oakeshott's diagnosis of the world situation differs from most of the views expressed by other contemporary political theorists. In *The Crisis in the University* (1949), which was written from a Christian standpoint, Sir Walter Moberly discussed the state and future of the university in a society. He argued:

> The crisis in the university reflects the crisis in the world and its pervading sense of insecurity. Two world-wars have culminated in the threat to civilization of the atom-bomb. The background of all that is planned or done in the years immediately ahead will be the imminent peril of world-wide disaster. We are living 'in the midst of uncertainties and on the edge of an abyss.'[290]

In his reply to Moberly's book, Oakeshott begins by taking a stand against the general analysis of the postwar situation in terms of its being an immediate political crisis and having a direct effect on other areas of life. He disagrees with Moberly's argument that the concentration of power in the Kremlin or the White House is already so great that the average person is aware that those in power have taken charge of his or her life, resulting in an overwhelming sense of hopeless insecurity.[291] Clearly, Oakeshott did not deny the existence of the atomic bomb or the possibility of some other catastrophe in the form of, for example, the complete exploitation of natural resources, but his reply to Moberly emphasized the primary importance of the variation that is inherent to interpretation and attitude:

---

[288] Similar analyses of postwar attitudes towards Parliament in the postwar years were presented as early as the 1960s. See, e.g., G. Marshall 1960.

[289] R. Barker 1997, pp. 179-180.

[290] W. Moberly 1949, p.15.

[291] M. Oakeshott 1949, *The Universities*, VLL, pp. 119-20. The essay was originally published in The Cambridge Journal, 2, 1949, pp. 515-42.

> But even on this wider view, the reading of the situation is, I think, at once too alarmist and too optimistic. The tone of this book is one of desperate urgency; it has the hysterical atmosphere of a revivalist meeting.[292]

On the other hand, Moberly could be described as having been overly optimistic, as there most probably could not be any revolution that would save us. On the other hand, there was far less to be alarmed about than he thought. The bomb should not be allowed to "unnerve us or we shall work ourselves into the state of mind which wishes that 'they would drop the damned thing and get it over'."[293] In 'world' or international politics, the "havoc wrought in Eastern Europe in the last few years is as bad as any atomic devastation; a powerful mass of deluded human beings is far more destructive than any bomb."[294] On the other hand, the degree of specifically physical security is a matter of custom and interpretation. In fact, no "man has ever been more worried about himself than Matthew Arnold in 1849, but few enjoyed greater 'security' than he did at that time."[295] Thus:

> In short, desperate urgency is something that belongs to a scale of events much smaller and less important than the scale Sir Walter has in mind: at bottom I find this a peculiarly faithless book.[296]

As such, although this may seem trivial, there was no aspect in Oakeshott's view of any kind of 'disillusionment' *in the form of turning away from utopias* in fear of a greater catastrophe, which would have resulted in a renewed respect for parliamentary government. In addition, Oakeshott emphasizes that even if there were a crisis situation, this situation is the least fruitful within which to carry out the rearrangement of a university or other political reforms.

Although Oakeshott did not participate in the analysis of the immediate crisis situation, he did, however, join the chorus of disillusioned thinkers, specifically with regard to political matters. Particularly in the essays written between 1947 and 1950s, politics was seen as infected by a rationalist style, particularly by the influence of the war, which forced the new customary application of its essentially rationalist vocabulary

---

[292] Ibid., p. 123.
[293] Ibid., p. 124.
[294] Ibid.
[295] Ibid., p. 123.
[296] Ibid.

onto politics. It can be plausibly argued that it is precisely in the essay *Rationalism in Politics* that Oakeshott actually considered the English political tradition as virtually *dead*: the 'automatic' system of politics was no longer functioning, but the rationalist disposition (and tradition) had managed to convert the informal manner of English politics into an ideology and to put "too high a value on political action and placing too high a hope in political achievement."[297] Although the knowledge that is necessary in order to participate in political activity is *both* practical and technical, the rationalist despises the former and, parallel to ideology, reduces the parliamentary tradition to a kind of political *machinery*.

In my reading, the strict justification of the critique against Oakeshott's notion of tradition in politics as 'inactivity' after the war is found only in this specific post-war essay. In John Pocock's analysis, for example, Oakeshott's notion reflects the institutionalization of politics, which goes hand-in-hand with an understanding of tradition as "pure usage."[298] This interpretation applies to the juxtaposition of a deliberate and conscious idea of political activity with the unconscious, habitual and customary nature of tradition, which was present in 1947, but not in *Political Education* in 1951, although some organistic and holistic assumptions still prevail.

It is essential to note, however, that it is not only the defence of parliament as an institution or a method that is central to Oakeshott's thought, which would also imply that he would have been quite content upon realizing that the institution is unlikely to fall. Instead, parliamentary tradition was seen as an inseparable aspect of a traditional society, and the 'correct' and 'English' understanding of political activity as secondary, limited and repairing.

Parliamentary government and rationalist politics do not belong to the same political tradition, although they may coexist within a society. Many writers, such as Morgenthau, misunderstood this point:

> Professor Morgenthau, in common with many American and almost all continental writers, believes erroneously that parliamentary institutions were the offspring of rationalistic politics. This is, perhaps, an excusable error, because in America and on the Continent of Europe parliamentary institutions were in fact

[297] M. Oakeshott 1947, *Rationalism in Politics*, RP, p. 26.
[298] J.G.A. Pocock 1968, pp. 215-7.

coeval with the full flood of rationalistic politics, and because the proper antidote to this error is acknowledgement of the only history that matters in this connection, the history of England. But the same illusion is entertained, less excusable, by Englishmen when they speak of 'democratic planning'; rationalist planning may, they think be 'democratic' because they believe (not from the history and experience of their own society but on the word of a set of ignorant foreigners) that 'democracy' and scientific politics sprang from the same root. The truth is, however, that the institutions of parliamentary government sprang from the least rationalistic period of our politics, from the Middle ages…[299]

Thus, I would emphasize that the main problem of British political life in the postwar context was the rationalist style of politics, which also had the potential to convert Parliament into a vehicle of the implementation of great plans within a society.

Due to Oakeshott's postwar opposition to the current style of politics, the tone of his defence of parliamentary tradition and the English manner of politics remains undeniably conservative.[300] Neil McInnes has observed that the contrast Oakeshott proposed had been stated by Benjamin Disraeli in 1872:

> In a progressive country change is constant and the great question is not whether you should resist change which is inevitable, but whether that change should be carried out in deference to the manners, the customs, the laws and the traditions of a people, or whether it should be carried out in deference to abstract principles, and arbitrary and general doctrines.[301]

Reliance on traditions instead of abstract principles is very much what Oakeshott recommends as the 'appropriate' form of politics in both his immediate postwar essays and in *Political Education*, although in the latter he seems also to have a growing appreciation for the 'consciousness' related to a reliance on tradition. His conception of politics thus emphasizes the 'English virtues' of political life, such as skepticism and moderation.

As regards his replacement of the concept of tradition, I would still like to provide one reminder as an example of the kind of critique that has likely fostered Oakeshott's rejection of

---

[299] M. Oakeshott 1947, *Scientific Politics*, RPML, p. 109.
[300] For a brief yet thorough discussion of the ideology of conservatism in the 20th century, see O'Sullivan 1976, 119-56.
[301] B. Disraeli 1872, cited in N. McInnes 2000, p. 84.

the concept. In a rather typical view, the Oxford scholar H.G. Nicholas accused Oakeshott's notion of political philosophy of "cerebral cannibalism" and of having a passive and negative effect on politics. In Nicholas's view, a politics that is conducted without the hope of arriving at a determined destination is inherently depressing.[302] Notably, in his response, Oakeshott explicitly denied "pursuit of intimations" as a circumlocution of inactivity, instead insisting that it was a mere misunderstanding.[303] Thus, one should not regard the concepts of tradition in 1947 and 1951 as identical.

It is important to note, however, that in the former essay, the main vice of a rationalist politician is the tendency to confuse politics with eternity, which actually belongs to the sphere of political philosophy, and thus to attempt to escape the "intricacy of the world of time and contingency."[304] Oakeshott's conception of tradition, and thus politics, has always included the notion of contingency, although with varying emphases, as I will argue later in this book.

In addition to this understanding of political activity as inevitably facing change and contingency, there is another aspect that rather paradoxically allies Oakeshott with 'old conservatism', but again turns out to be constitutive of the later-emphasized understanding of politics as linguistic action.

In 1957, Angus Maude (MP) presented a view in which he considered two philosophies of change and their supporters as central to British political life. Of course, Oakeshott can be distinguished from most *"reactionaries"* in terms of their belief in organic growth or original sin, but he is skeptical about the ability of men to solve all political problems by means of rational argumentation, and especially about the *"revolutionary"* belief in "virtually infinite" progress.[305] Of more relevance here, however, is Maude's view that for reactionaries there exists "a date of decline and fall" in British political life, which for "eminent men" may be the Reformation, the Renaissance or "the introduction of manhood suffrage," while for "less ambitious or less erudite" it may be "1914, 1939, or 1945." Generally speaking, Oakeshott can in this respect be considered to

---

[302] H.G. Nicholas 1951, pp. 538-9.
[303] M. Oakeshott 1951, *Political Education. A Reply to H.G. Nicholas*, p. 701.
[304] M. Oakeshott 1947, *Rationalism in Politics*, RP, p. 34.
[305] A. Maude 1957, p. 152.

be one of the "less ambitious men" with regard to the two last dates.[306]

However, there is another date of decline that appears in Oakeshott's postwar political thought: namely, the late 19th and early 20th century, i.e. the same period during which a certain *conversational* mode of politics in British parliamentarism is often seen to have 'declined'. This can be illustrated, for example, by the role of the oratory within Parliament as yielding in favour of public speeches, which were becoming an increasingly important element in the attainment of electoral victory. In addition, party leaders already began to perform as star actors after the 1867 Reform Act.[307]

The secondary literature on Oakeshott's thought has often neglected this other approximate date, although his politics is, of course, commonly characterized as the politics of conversation. This is not so surprising, since Oakeshott rarely explicitly commented on the matter.[308] In *Rationalism in Politics*, he says:

> Indeed, this is what contemporary politics are fast degenerating into: the political habit and tradition, which, not long ago, was the common possession of even extereme opponents in English politics, has been replaced by merely a common rationalist disposition of mind.[309]

Thus, not "long ago," i.e. in the 19th century, political habit and tradition played a primary role in English politics. In this manner, proper politics is an art to be "imparted":

> ... like the House of Commons or an old established business, it imparts something without having expressly to teach it; and what it imparts in this way is at least the manners of conversation.[310]

In a later account, Oakeshott states that politics "has always been three-quarters talk, and not to know to use the current vocabulary of politics is a serious hindrance to anyone who, either as an amateur or as a professional, wishes to participate

---

[306] And precisely in 1947 – although with some reservations – to "the eminent," as will also be argued in the analysis of the figure of the politician. Yet *suffrage* does not present as big a problem for Oakeshott as is often suggested by his critics.

[307] P. Langford 2000, 202, see, e.g. J.H. Grainger 1969.

[308] See also Oakeshott's correspondence with Popper cited above on p. 134.

[309] M. Oakeshott 1947, *Rationalism in Politics*, RP, p. 37.

[310] M. Oakeshott 1950, *The Idea of a University*, VLL, p. 99.

in the activity."[311] When these accounts are viewed alongside Oakeshott's notions of the importance of the role of the opposition in British politics, the analysis that "under a Labour Administration, Parliament is demoted to the position of an executive body for carrying out the items of a programme determined each year by an irresponsible body"[312] and the later account of the negative character of a demagogue or party leader, we are able to see the crucial link between the concept of tradition and the defence of the conversational, parliamentary mode of political action.[313] The politics of conversation is not only conversations between the past, present and future within a somewhat vaguely defined or even 'mystical' tradition, but it also includes the concrete model of parliamentary conversation.

Both of these aspects are present in the recently published essay *The Voice of Conversation in the Education of Mankind*, in which Oakeshott argues that politics is an activity which, more than any other, has "benefited from the civilising touch of conversation."[314] The approximation of politics to conversation is also the "gist and meaning of democracy."[315] Oakeshott dissociates this kind of "democratic politics" from "the rule of the people, the government of the majority, the propagation of a dogmatic faith and the pursuit of a manner of living to be imposed equally upon all men."[316] Oakeshott identifies politics as "a conversational art," which is a style of politics that alone recognizes "the evanescence of imperfection" as an illusion.[317] It is a politics with "mortal men in a world of mortal men" serving as its actors.

I will provide some fragmentary accounts here that should be reflected upon in light of the rest of this study. First, I do not claim that Oakeshott's account of tradition was already 'completely' linguistic in the late 1940s or early 1950s in the sense that is implied, for example, by his reference in *On Human Conduct* to moral practice as being an analogy of a vernacular language. However, its close relationship to the metaphor of

[311] M. Oakeshott 1962, *The Study of 'Politics' in a University*, RP, p. 206.
[312] M. Oakeshott 1948, *Contemporary British Politics*, pp. 479-80.
[313] M. Oakeshott 1961, *The Masses in Representative Democracy*, RP, p. 373.
[314] Oakeshott, M c.1948, *The Voice of Conversation in the Education of Mankind*, WH, p. 194.
[315] Ibid.
[316] Ibid.
[317] Ibid., p. 196.

conversation needs to be kept in mind. Oakeshott, of course, also characterized "civilization" and, for example, university education in terms of conversation, and Oakeshottian conversation can be interpreted as taking place between different "voices" or "modes" of experience, such as philosophy, history and politics, i.e. between the various practices by which civilization is comprised. It can also be said that the voices in Oakeshott's conversation of mankind are "modes, not persons, and their juxtaposition reveals no agreed truths, only necessary differences."[318] Yet I think we must not overlook the fact that it was Walter Bagehot who said that "the leading statesmen in a free country have great momentary power. They *settle the conversation of mankind*."[319] This connection would imply that the notion of political activity also plays a central role in Oakeshott's formulation of the metaphor of conversation.

Oakeshott's description of his understanding of politics as a conversation as opposed to an argument is simultaneously indicative of his defence of a view of parliamentary tradition that was shared, for example, by R.G. Collingwood, who is considered to be one of the pioneers of the linguistic turn:

> Contemptuous language about the 'talking-shop at Westminster', expressing not a desire for better talk, but a discontent with talk as such, are consciously or unconsciously dislike of dialectical politics and desire for its replacement by some kind of civil war.[320]

Those who support the 19th century conversational paradigm of politics tend to maintain the notion of the superiority of parliamentary practices and procedures over pure decision-making in political action. To emphasize this point, argumentation naturally belongs to the sphere of political conversation,[321] but the image or metaphor of conversation accentuates the proce-

[318] T. Nardin 2001, p. 233.
[319] W. Bagehot 1867, p.10, see J.H. Grainger 1969, p. 82, emphasis SS.
[320] R.G. Collingwood 1942, p. 213.
[321] One persistent debate in the sphere of British political thought concerns precisely this notion of the conversational or parliamentary mode of politics as *purely* 'aesthetic' or a 'club of gentlemen', with no mention of politics as 'demanding' results. Oakeshott's notion of politics has also been accused of both, although in my view usually mistakenly. His point is to defend the 'side' of political activity and its understanding that he sees as threatened in a given situation, although he does not deny the importance of the other side. The debate, however, has continued along rather similar lines for quite some time. For example, in 1931, J.L Hammond pointed out that parliamentary institutions were able to survive in the 1850s because parliamentary oratory offered

dure of discussion *in itself*, not only its possible result. As Bagehot had noted earlier, those who wish to act quickly see parliamentary government as their greatest enemy.[322] For him, the polity of discussion is a means of ensuring elaborate consideration and preventing hasty action, which is the defining characteristic of Oakeshott's ideal of 'traditional politics' and the politics of conversation. In other words, at the very least, Oakeshott's conception of tradition *entails* an understanding of politics as parliamentary conversation.

Furthermore, in his defence of and reply to the critique of both the concept of tradition in *Political Education* and his description of politics as "the pursuit of intimations," he importantly utilizes the game metaphor:

> I do not know why this expression should cause offence or incredulity. We are concerned with human activity, and to surmise the focal point from fragmentary glimpses of directions being followed, to perceive the order of a sum in advance of completing the process of addition, to guess from a few moves of a game the strategy being followed and the moves to come, are all common enough experiences; and I do not understand why they should be absent from politics or insignificant in political activity. Indeed, as I listened to a collection of party politicians discussing the possibility of the emergence within English politics of a new 'cause' which might give a new turn to political enterprise and a new alignment to political opinion, it did not seem so very far-fetched to describe their manner of thinking as the 'pursuit of intimations'.[323]

By applying the game metaphor, Oakeshott here clearly wishes to guide the interpretation of his understanding of politics as the "pursuit of intimations" towards the rather similar understanding of politics as a human activity in general; the

---

the people, who were rather ill supplied with theatres, music or other amusements, a "spectacle" of the "greatest actors and the greatest artists." J.L. Hammond 1931, p. 239. In the present "universal wireless" age, parliamentary institutions can only survive if proven efficient in a similar manner as trade unions. Ibid, p. 240. In 1961, Robert Skidelsky, favouring the revival of the notion of "national interest," accused politicians of overly enjoying "the game itself, the oratorical triumphs," which had no real chance of power, and saw the parliamentary tradition as being in a state of crisis. Skidelsky 1961, pp. 33-5. For Henry Fairlie "politics are primarily concerned with getting things done. Speech and debate are merely the instruments of action. The mark of the politician, as opposed to those who merely write about politics, is that (for a variety of motives) he actually wants to do things." H. Fairlie 1963b, p. 21.

[322] W. Bagehot 1872, p. 71.
[323] M. Oakeshott 1956, *Political Education*, 13n.

notion of tradition as the concept of a 'long period' of continuity thus begins to recede and its 'activity component' moves to the spotlight. This point was also accentuated in 1962, when Oakeshott denied the validity of any critique attributing "some mystical qualities" to tradition. Traditions of such different time-spans as "the Common Law of England, for example, the so-called British Constitution, the Christian religion, modern physics, the game of cricket, shipbuilding" are equated to one another.[324]

In the late 1950s and early 1960s, ordinary language philosophy had already experienced its heyday, and, as such, it does not sound all that unusual to speak of human activities or deeds in the context of traditions or, for example, forms of life. Nonetheless, the assumption that ordinary language philosophy simply *came* first, in conjunction with, for example, Wittgenstein's notion of "language games," and was only then followed by the linguistic turn in the social sciences, can be seen in rather a different light when examining the concepts of tradition and conversation and their relation to parliamentary politics. And this question arises even if they are viewed exclusively within the confines of Oakeshott's own thinking. For instance, it should be taken into account that the game metaphor was particularly popular in the British context of 19th century politics. Could this notion indicate that in some sense ordinary language philosophy extended the translation of the understanding that was already present in politics to include other activities, not the other way around?

Political Actors

It seems to me that in British discussions, it is perhaps the figure of a politician which serves as the most accurate 'indicator' of general attitudes towards political activity. Lists of the vices and virtues of a politician are particularly revealing; of course, there are some 'Machiavellians', but, generally speaking, if one is apt to think that private vices count as public virtues in the profession of politics, one might also be inclined to be more suspicious of politics in general and to favour, for example, administrative government. On the other hand, a respectful attitude towards politicians and their profession tends to go

---

[324] M. Oakeshott 1951/1962, *Political Education,* RP, p. 61n. This footnote was added to the 1962 *Rationalism in Politics* edition.

hand-in-hand with the praise of eminently political activities and procedures. Thus, generally speaking, we can maintain that a certain consensus regarding the importance of parliamentary procedures and accordingly (yet to a lesser extent) acting politicians prevails among political thinkers such as Berlin, Crick, Henry Fairlie and J.B.D. Miller, all of whom share the central notion of "the English ideology," i.e. that of *liberty*.[325] In this sense, all of these thinkers can be grouped together as 'liberal' writers. They all also share the view that conflict is essential to politics.

In the case of Oakeshott, who explicitly refrains from focussing too much attention on politicians, mentioning only a few by name, one may find it surprising that this indicator works both rather accurately and revealingly in relation to the development of his conception of political activity. Since Oakeshott has always supported "parliamentary government" and since his conception of the tasks of the politician in a society as "the gradual adjustment of human relationships" has actually largely remained unchanged, this has often been mistaken for permanent sameness in his conception of a politician.[326] However, in relation to, for example, tradition, it is precisely his increasing appreciation of political deliberation that is crucial, highlighting how his almost 'functionalist' view of politics shifts towards the emphasis of individual activity.

Yet the comparison of Oakeshott's thought to just one single classic text allows us to see some aspects of this change. In *The Profession and Vocation of Politics* (*Politik als Beruf*, 1919), Max Weber described the two deadly sins of a politician as "a lack of objectivity" (Sachlichkeit) and "a lack of responsibility."[327] "Vanity" is the main impetus leading the politician towards committing these sins. The demagogue is liable to become a play-actor who takes his responsibility too lightly, while on the other hand, a lack of objectivity tempts him to enjoy power for its own sake, without any substantive purpose.[328] For Oakeshott, in 1939, and in some of the late 1940s accounts, vanity and "sheer laziness" can, conversely, be counted amongst the 'virtues' of a politician; it is more tradition that masters political life than acting politicians, most of whom are rational-

[325] See, G. Watson 1973, pp.124-5.
[326] M. Oakeshott 1948, *Contemporary British Politics*, p. 489.
[327] M. Weber 1994, p. 354.
[328] Ibid.

ists by disposition. In 1956, with a parallel to Weber's definitions of the "ethics of responsibility" and the "ethics of
conviction," Oakeshott takes a stand for a conscious 'politician
of responsibility' as opposed to one who views government as
"an instrument of passion" and the art of politics as inflaming
and directing desire.[329] Whereas the earlier Oakeshott has
more faith in the smooth running of a system or tradition, his
later account emphasizes the current beliefs and activities of
political actors.[330] Oakeshott emphasizes that the laws and
rules should be modified regularly. A political actor is
required to *innovate* in order to ensure that the rules remain
appropriate as regards the activities they govern. The state of
sheer laziness, which would happily simply leave things as
they are or rely on the 'automatic' progression of things, no
longer suits a political actor's profile. In Oakeshott's later
account, the political actor is responsible for keeping subjects
at peace, and governing requires moderation, for example in
the form of the restraint and pacification of the – perhaps passionate – subjects.

In further contrast, it is important to recognize that
Oakeshott's early conception of a politician is not only negative in the common sense, but the politician is actually seen as a
potentially *harmful* figure in society by definition: "Indeed,
political activity involves a corruption of consciousness from
which a society has continuously to be saved."[331] The political
system lies on the surface of a society and must remain there;
its function is to provide protection and a "*minor degree of
merely mechanical interpretation and expression.*"[332] As I noted
earlier, social change and recreation come from other sources;
the poet, the artist and to a lesser extent also the philosopher:

> Societies, in fact, are led from behind, and for those capable of
> leadership to give themselves up to political activity is to break
> away from their true genius. And a society in which this becomes

---

[329] M. Oakeshott 1956, *On Being Conservative*, RP, pp. 426-33.
[330] For the sake of clarity, it must be noted that Oakeshott's paradigm conception
of a political actor is government or 'politicians in government' and is used
here accordingly. Cases of exception, like political parties, are singled out as
they appear. This view rather follows what seems to be the British paradigm
conception in which politics is "always connected with government." J.B.D.
Miller 1962, p. 19.
[331] M. Oakeshott 1939, *The Claims of Politics*, RPML, p. 95.
[332] Ibid., p. 93, emphasis SS.

common will, in a short while, be a society without leaders, a society ignorant of itself and without the power of recreating itself.[333]

These characters have access to the deeper sphere of a society's consciousness, which is determined by law, custom and tradition, whereas politicians are considered shallow:

> It is probably true that any man who can be strongly tempted to give himself up to political activity belongs to the world of politics, and he will not go wrong if he follows his genius. He will use his intelligence to reflect on questions of political importance; as a writer he will become a publicist. In action, if he is prudent and lucky, he may be successful. He will retain his fundamental views and opinions almost unchanged, being without time or inclination to examine them afresh; and he may take on the appearance of a leader.[334]

Read in retrospect, Oakeshott's understanding of virtually all politicians in 1939 is rather similar to the later account of a rationalist politician, whose fundamental views and opinions remain unchanged and who does not thus understand contingency, although he operates in its world. In the earlier account, all politicians seem to attempt to follow fixed principles in the manner of the rationalist politician of 1947. Still, in the earlier account, Oakeshott has faith in tradition and in the ability of a system to function. Political activity as the protection and occasional modification of a legal and social order is superficial and rests on a deeper stratum of social thought. Thus, politics can be left to people with a mind that is "fixed and callous to all subtle distinctions."[335] It is because so little can be achieved politically that spiritual callousness is involved in political action, entailing "the false simplification of human life implied in even the best of its purposes."[336]

It is against this background that I argue that the essay *Rationalism in Politics* marks a moment of distrust in the vigour of tradition as opposed to its appraisal, also in relation to the figure of a politician. The fact that a Rationalist represents a threat to a traditional kind of a society clearly indicates a certain fear that political activity has stepped away from its proper place and now threatens the 'deeper sphere' of a society. Here,

---

[333] Ibid., p. 96.
[334] Ibid., p. 94.
[335] Ibid., p. 93.
[336] Ibid.

Oakeshott's thinking seems to contain a rather difficult paradox: politicians *should* work by rather 'unconsciously' relying on traditions; however as this kind of understanding of politics no longer prevails, it is thus difficult to defend or revive, as doing so would certainly again require conscious action. Contemporary politicians and the political spectrum are characterized cuttingly:

> And it is for this reason that, among much else that is corrupt and unhealthy, we have a spectacle of a set of sanctimonious, rationalist politicians, preaching an ideology of unselfishness and social service to a population in which they and their predecessors have done their best to destroy the only living root of moral behaviour; and opposed by another set of politicians dabbling with the project of converting us from Rationalism under the inspiration of a fresh rationalisation of our political tradition.[337]

Here, Oakeshott also condemns conservative politics as an expression of the rationalist style of politics. Thus, the revival of a healthy political tradition seems unlikely or even impossible. On the other hand, by contrasting the politics of engineering or administration with a proper, traditional kind of politics, Oakeshott implies a growing appreciation of political activity as such in the fashion of 19th century British politics.

As has often been noted, it is not far-fetched to interpret some of Oakeshott's accounts as somewhat elitist; politics, for him, is a profession to be learned, but this "sharing of concrete knowledge" and "initiation into the moral and intellectual habits and achievements of his society, an entry into the partnership between present and past" takes "about two generations of practice."[338] Furthermore, it is the *ordinary* practical politics of European nations that is fixed in the vice of rationalism, and it is the "politics of the inexperienced." However, Oakeshott appears to want the politician to stay in his proper, rather insignificant place in a society, although in this text the profession would require that he both acquaint himself with the *nuances* that comprise the tradition and standard of behaviour of a politician as well as acquire an understanding of contingency. A proper politician – a somewhat lost character – would be able to recognize a change in the customary and traditional, but would would shy away from the rationalist

---

[337] M. Oakeshott 1947, *Rationalism in Politics*, RP, p. 41–2.
[338] Ibid., pp. 38-9.

notion of a "self-consciously induced change."[339] In fact, political life can be met from three differing positions: that of a political philosopher, exploring the relations between politics and eternity; that of a rationalist politician, erroneously identifying the promise of eternity in ideology, or taking mere technical knowledge as a guideline of behaviour;[340] and that of the proper politician. That is, whereas the philosopher seeks to reflect on political conduct in the language of explanation and avoids recommending any specific directions for it to take, the rationalist, ideological politician confuses the language of explanation with that of recommendation. Ideologies and abstract principles are seen as an escape from the intricacy of the contingent word in which the proper politician learns to operate.

The articles *Contemporary British Politics* and *The Political Economy of Freedom,* in which Oakeshott begins to place an increasing level of emphasis on the conscious politician, have already been examined quite thoroughly in this book. As such, I will only make a reminder that here the most important task of a politician is to oppose great concentrations of power and thus preserve freedom in a society. Oakeshott accuses the Labour Party of neglecting one of the requests of the Nineteen Propositions (1642), i.e. "that the great affairs of the kingdom may not be concluded or transacted by the advice of private men, or by any unknown or unsworn councillors."[341] The Labour Administration has a tendency to turn the House of Commons into a sort of syndicalist assembly that is under the influence of The Trade Union Congress, which is a constitutionally irresponsible body. Along similar lines, for example Leopold Amery, a conservative and a member of the Lloyd George government, argued that it is a misconception to view the British system of government as "based on the initiative of the voter and on delegation from below." Party politics represents a threat to parliamentary government, but an even greater threat is posed by the irresponsible power of an outside body, such as the TUC.[342]

Conservative party politics appears to be the lesser of two evils and the role of the opposition is emphasized:

---

[339] Ibid., p. 8.
[340] Ibid., p. 34.
[341] M. Oakeshott 1948, *Contemporary British Politics*, pp. 480-1.
[342] L.S. Amery 1947, p. 45.

> The truth is that parliamentary government as we know it depends for its continued existence more upon the Opposition than upon the party in power.[343]

Importantly, in contrast to the rationalist planner, the politician is characterized in positive terms. The limited activity of politics as unspectacular and unimpressive to the "mass of men and women brought up on melodramatic politics" demands "reasonableness, sincerity, patience, self-restraint, moderate foresight and a knowledge of the principles of integration and adjustment imbedded in the history of our society."[344] These requirements are emphatically human qualities for Oakeshott, and an MP might be expected to possess or be capable of acquiring these common qualities in "comparison with the godlike vision and superhuman mental grasp which the successful planner must have and which our planners certainly have not got."[345] Oakeshott thus takes a stand in favour of an understanding of a politician's qualities that is at least somewhat in line with the "myth" of the distinctiveness of English politics as moderation, skepticism and a certain degree of empiricism.[346]

Although similar types of view in various debates have long appeared in various contexts, with no probable ending in sight, it may still be illuminating to recall some contrary views, as Oakeshott's point is to emphasize precisely the 'ordinary' qualities of the politician. For instance, Frank Pakenham, who was better known as "Lord Pakenham" and who served, for example, as a junior minister in the Labour Government from 1946 to 1951, left the well-intentioned and ambitious young politician, "our young idealist," who supposedly wished to lead a Christian life, at the mercy of external resources such as money, connections etc.[347] Together with often antagonistic views and the coercion of the 'masses', the necessities of a politician's work, i.e. the persuasion of vast numbers of his fellow men of the superiority of his views and his own personality, leads to the suppression and distortion of one's own personality, which no other profession – like that of a soldier, a lawyer

---

[343] M. Oakeshott 1948, *Contemporary British Politics*, pp. 481.
[344] Ibid., p. 489.
[345] Ibid.
[346] J.H. Grainger 1969, p. 82.
[347] F. Pakenham 1942, p. 408.

or a businessman – calls for.[348] These descriptions also aptly apply to Oakeshott's notion of a politician as facing the current form of the rationalist style of politics, although he certainly does not agree with Pakenham's desire for more Christian ethics in politics and thus more 'good' men entering political life. Contrasting himself to Aldous Huxley, Pakenham believes that "it makes all the difference in the world whether or not we draw our rulers from among our wisest and best, the time is fully ripe for a codification of the long-suppressed truths of political morality."[349]

In contrast to Pakenham, Oakeshott joins those who oppose the figure of the philosopher king and his 'milder derivatives' – which are vividly redescribed in *On Human Conduct* as the theorist's return to a Platonic cave, along with his attempt to replace other languages with his philosophical one.[350] In the postwar years, however, it seems that the writers most committed to the "open society"[351] also opposed the attachment of some extraordinary faculties to the personalities of politicians, although in other respects their views of political activity may vary. For example, Fairlie cited Harold Macmillan's lucid statement:

> If people want a sense of purpose they should get it from their archbishops. They should not hope to receive it from their politicians.[352]

According to, for example, R.M. Hare, the philosopher of ethics and author of such works as *The Language of Morals* (1952), the idea is that if Plato's philosopher king were to make the laws we could be sure that by obeying them we would be leading absolutely morally blameless lives.[353] For Hare, however, the decision of ends, i.e. of choosing between policies,

---

[348] Ibid., pp. 409-10.
[349] Ibid., p. 413.
[350] OHC, p. 29.
[351] In this connection, however, we should note that Oakeshott disliked Popper's book. Here, Oakeshott is also criticizing 'the text-book approach' to the study and teaching of political thinking, much in the manner of the Cambridge school of history. Along with *The Open Society and its Enemies*, he lists Hobhouse's *Metaphysical Theory of the State* and Crossman's *Plato Today* as encouraging a reading of some notable books as 'political theory' containing a political 'ideal', programme or policy for today. M. Oakeshott 1962, *The Study of 'Politics' in a University*, RP, p. 208n.
[352] H. Macmillan cited in H. Fairlie 1963b, p. 20.
[353] R.M. Hare 1956, p. 594.

belongs to voters, which is actually quite a good example of the combination of a kind of 'engineering' view of politics with the critique of the figure of a 'superior' politician. Oakeshott, for his own part, already hinted at the end of the 1940s at the importance of the (parliamentary) responsibility of a politician, who must be careful in discovery and courageous in action.

In sum, with the exception of the essay *Rationalism in Politics*, Oakeshott's characterization of a good or proper politician in the late 1940s can best be described as a 'man of common sense' who is acquainted with the art of parliamentary politics. Illustratively, Oakeshott writes:

> ... he [Morgenthau, SS] says nothing about the art of statesmanship except that it involves 'a knowledge of a different and a higher order' than that which belongs to the social engineer, and the use of 'higher faculties of mind.' This comes pretty close to the higher nonsense, which we should avoid if we can. What, of course, the statesman requires is nothing higher than the ordinary 'faculties' and ordinary knowledge that everyone (even the convinced rationalist) uses everyday in the conduct of his life and in his relations with other men. The vice of the rationalist is not a denial of 'higher faculties', but a misapprehension about the quite ordinary faculties which he and the rest of mankind constantly call upon.[354]

However, in addition to the skills of conversation, the art of the politician is connected more obscurely to tradition:

> Such a policy is, indeed a kind of perennial politics, the form of all politics which make use of the past achievements of our society in enterprise and organization and which endeavours to add to those achievements."[355]

Thus, although the politician's situation is contingent in the sense that tradition never has a predetermined end or destination, Oakeshott still allows rather little room for deliberation. There is room for the differences of opinion and programme that constitute the *differentiae* of political parties, *but* this occurs in a situation that somehow appears ready-made to a politician; he consults "past achievements" and his art is of "knowing where to go next in the exploration of an already existing traditional kind of society."[356]

---

[354] M. Oakeshott 1947, *Scientific Politics*, RPML, p. 107.
[355] M. Oakeshott 1948, *Contemporary British Politics*, p. 489.
[356] M. Oakeshott 1949, *The Political Economy of Freedom*, RP, p. 406.

It is precisely this feature of Oakeshott's tradition which has been severely criticized; it appears as if tradition would somehow 'hint' at the right course for politics to follow, a notion that can also be found in the essay *Political Education*. In my view, the essay cannot be interpreted as 'innocent' of this accusation, although it can be fruitfully seen as presenting an optional logic of political judgement in the context of linguistic political philosophy, as was done by Greenleaf in 1966 and examined later in this book. Keeping the politician at the centre of our examination, however, one of the most revealing passages is:

> The arrangements which constitute a society capable of political activity, whether they are customs or institutions or laws or diplomatic decisions, are at once coherent and incoherent; they compose a pattern and at the same time they intimate a sympathy for what does not fully appear. Political activity is the exploration of that sympathy and consequently, relevant political reasoning will be the convincing exposure of a sympathy, present but not yet followed up, and the convincing demonstration that now is the appropriate moment for recognising it.[357]

The skill of the politician is thus mainly confined to the recognition of a given situation and the aim of increasing the coherency of legal arrangements in a society at precisely the right time.

Oakeshott's account of a politician begins to really take shape when compared with another eminent writer, Henry Fairlie, who has concentrated more specific attention on precisely this figure. In *The Life of Politics*, Fairlie also considered the readiness to "strike when the moment comes" as pivotal for a politician.[358] In relation to the 'readiness' of the situation and the moment of Oakeshott's inaugural lecture, it is interesting that he characterizes, for example, the Labour Government's reduction in physical planning between 1947 and 1950 as a situation in which the freedom of choice was not sufficiently "clear to allow us to talk confidently of decision."[359]

In international politics, where the actors are governments, the 'hands are tied' view is dominant. However, although it is often claimed that "at least in the legislative programme of a government," choices are available and decisions possible, Fairlie argues that this is not entirely clear either. For Fairlie,

---

[357] M. Oakeshott 1951, *Political Education*, pp. 56-7.
[358] H. Fairlie 1963a, 28.
[359] Ibid., p. 36.

too, a politician is a sort of "catalyst" and "free people," too, "must be patient enough to trust in the right instincts of the House of Commons; to believe that, in the long run, it will respond to common sense, justice and truths."[360] In J.B.D. Miller's view, the politician functions as "a point of contact with the public opinion," being not only a "receiver" but a "transmitter too."[361] Thus, both Fairlie's and Miller's views of the tasks of the politician come quite close to that of Oakeshott. Nor are their views on the practicing politician far from Oakeshott's account in this regard.

According to R.H.S. Crossman, both "being there at the right time" and "a sense of timing" are important to the statesman, although the notion of a politician as literally creating an occasion is fictional.[362] The statesman must know when "to capture public opinion by a bold, 'unpopular' decision and when to appease it by a calculated display of indecisiveness."[363] Although Crossman views the situation from the viewpoint of a politician's success, a similar account of the anticipation of the direction of change even before the general public is also present.

Despite the hint of the possibility of judging a political decision as 'right' from the hypothetical viewpoint of society as a whole – Oakeshott emphasizes that there is no mistake-proof manner by which to "elicit the intimation most worthwhile pursuing" from tradition; it is a matter of judgement.[364] Both Fairlie and Oakeshott recognize political activity as a learned art which requires both political education and a certain level of professionalism.[365]

In Fairlie's view, politics in the UK is still understood as a "human pursuit, fit to engage the whole life of a whole man, the supreme art of a highly civilised and polite society. It is the life that matters."[366] Fairlie criticizes Crick's suggestion of recruiting amateurs to Parliament as part of the parliamentary reform he advocates. Oakeshott, for his own part, speaks of the skill of political activity as the mixture of amateurism and pro-

---

[360] Ibid., p. 38.
[361] J.B.D. Miller 1958, p. 9.
[362] R.H.S. Crossman 1958, p. 36.
[363] Ibid.
[364] M. Oakeshott 1951, *Political Education*, RP, p. 57.
[365] See esp. Oakeshott, 1962, *The Study of Politics in a University*, RP, p. 207, compare with, e.g., Crick 1964.
[366] H. Fairlie 1963b, p. 18.

fessionalism "which political and administrative activity among us provokes" and also, rather regretfully, the "absence of settled professional standards."[367] He notes, however, that the establishment of a (somewhat unsuccessful) 'vocational' education of political activity stemmed from a situation in which "professional political skill ceased to be the exclusive business of Kings and hereditary ruling classes, when (in short) government ceased to be a mystery."[368]

In comparison to Fairlie, however, it is evident that Oakeshott still draws a sharp distinction between rationalist and 'rational' politicians. Whereas Fairlie seems to accept that a politician also has the role of persuading people in addition to participating in governmental or parliamentary discussions, Oakeshott 'legislates' about the proper form of argumentation for politics. His famous example of the "technical 'enfranchisement' of women" as remedying the incoherence of the arrangements of a society is defended as the sole valid argument in the situation at hand. In contrast, he deems, for example, arguments, which are "drawn from abstract natural right, from 'justice,' or from some general concept of feminine personality," as clumsy or irrelevant.[369] Additionally, in contrast to most liberal thinkers, Oakeshott denies the role of *interests* and the conflicts between them as fundamental to politics. Although for Fairlie, among others, politics is certainly public and limited – "too much a game of chance to be played by one's own rules" – Oakeshott is more severe in his account.[370]

Thus, for Oakeshott, an ideal politician would be a rather sensitive interpreter of the incoherencies in political tradition – someone who is educated in a certain style of argumentation within the conversation of politics, which has no 'foundation' other than an open-ended tradition of behaviour:

> The enterprise is to keep afloat on an even keel; the sea is both friend and enemy; and the seamanship consists in using the resources of a traditional manner of behaviour in order to make a friend of every hostile occasion.[371]

[367] M. Oakeshott, 1962, *The Study of Politics in a University*, RP, p. 207.
[368] Ibid.
[369] M. Oakeshott 1951, *Political Education*, RP, p.57.
[370] H. Fairlie 1963a, p.28.
[371] M. Oakeshott 1951, *Political Education*, RP, p. 60.

To recapitulate, limited strictly to the postwar context and the perspective of a politician, this metaphor can best be interpreted in light of an ideal politician in government, who is preferably a conservative. In a book review, he writes favourably:

> While others extol the virtues of the particular brand of Utopia they propose to create, the Conservative disbelieves them all, and, despite all temptations, offers in their place no Utopia at all but something quite modestly better than the present. He may, and should, have a programme. He certainly has a policy. But of catchwords, slogans, visions, ideal states of society, classless societies, new order, of all the tinsel and finery with which the modern political charlatans charm their jewels from the modern political savage, the Conservative has nothing to offer.[372]

However, in favouring a certain kind of situational argumentation as opposed to appealing to general principles, it can also be said that Oakeshott supports a contingent understanding of politics in which a practical politician cannot remain 'bound' to most of the general ideas or even promises made in conjunction with general elections, at least not in the strict sense of the word. Thus, compared to, for example, Hare's conception, it is politicians who must take responsibility for their actions in all cases.

In the inaugural lecture *Political Education* (1951), political activity is mostly described in positive terms. However, Oakeshott naturally continuously acknowledges that most contemporary politics involves the use of the language of interests and the pursuit of power. In fact, in the posthumously published *The Politics of Faith and the Politics of Skepticism*, Oakeshott himself advocates a view of politics as "a conversation between diverse interests, in which activities that circumstantially limit one another are saved from violent collision," thus becoming close to the common liberal conception of politics.[373] Here, in addition to viewing the ambiguity of modern political vocabulary as unavoidable, he also gives consideration to the motives of politicians. The Halifaxian "trimmer" represents the paradigm politician of the skeptical style of politics, who recognizes the partisans of power as his proper opponent.[374] However, the skeptic also recognizes that

---

[372] M. Oakeshott 1948, *Contemporary British Politics*, p. 486.
[373] PFPS, p. 130.
[374] Ibid., p. 128.

governing will always be "an activity for which human beings are not fully qualified: it demands a distinterdness which is always absent."[375] Thus, the skeptic also turns to the understanding of government in terms of the manner of "power shared conversationally between a multitude of interests, persons and offices, government appearing, for example, as a partnership between a cabinet and the members of a representative assembly, between a minister and a permanent official and perhaps between assemblies representative of different interests."[376] It is here that the conversational model of politics seems to also include competition over power and conflict of interest, as well as to occupy the middle region between the aesthetic politics of skepticism and 'play' and the politics of faith as the 'serious' pursuit of perfection.

Thus, Oakeshott is once again not far from contemporary political thinking. In the appendix of *Political Education*, he notes that his intention was "not a description of the motives of politicians nor of what they believe themselves to be doing, but of what they actually succeed in doing" in relation to tradition.[377] However, in the other account, in which competition etc. are seen as essential aspects of political activity *and* motive, politics is described as follows:

> Politics at any time are an unpleasing spectacle. The obscurity, the muddle, the excess, the compromise, the indelible appearance of dishonesty, the counterfeit piety, the moralism and the immorality, the corruption, the intrigue, the negligence, the meddlesomeness, the vanity, the self-deception, and finally the futility, like an old horse in a pound, offend most of our rational and all our artistic suspectibilities. For so far as political activity succeeds in modifying the reign of arbitrary violence in human affairs, there is clearly something to be said for it, and it may even be thought to be worth the cost. But, at the best of times, political activity seems to encourage many of the less agreeable traits in human character.[378]

Here, all politics is described in negative terms in relation to the qualities it encourages in politicians.

A contemporary economist reflected on the duality of political activity and actors as follows:

---

[375] Ibid., p. 37.
[376] Ibid., p. 89.
[377] Oakeshott 1962, *The Pursuit of Intimations. Appendix to Political Education*, RP, p. 67.
[378] PFPS, pp. 19-20.

> Politics is full of such contradictions. Take the contrast between politics in practice as a rather dirty game with politicians engaged in party intrigue and the pursuit of power, and politics as one of the highest forms of human activity with the ideal of statesmanship seeking to safeguard the public interest in a dispassionate and disinterested way. Is this not a dichotomy in our own behaviour?[379]

A similar dichotomy seems to lie in Oakeshott's accounts. On the one hand, skeptical politics requires dispassionateness and disinterestedness. On the other, the dominating pull of the politics of faith demonstrates the pursuit of power.

I suggest that viewing Oakeshott in the immediate postwar years and the early 1950s enables us to detect some indications of a change in attitude, particularly with regard to Oakeshott's comprehension of the relationship between tradition and political actors. The less a tradition is seen as automatic and guiding, the more emphasis is placed on the character and motives of a politician. This is not to say that Oakeshott would later become a supporter of the "higher faculties" view of a politician or statesman, but, in *On Human Conduct*, he supports the view that a politician must certainly be capable of fulfilling the special requirements of political, deliberative activity as something more than acquired or inherited conversational skills. One of his challenges in *On Human Conduct* is also to provide a satisfactory philosophical description of politics which "offers the most difficult of all 'literatures', the most difficult of all collections of 'texts', in connection with which to handle and manage the languages of explanation."[380]

On Being Conservative (1956) marks an important resting place in Oakeshott's intellectual voyage. Namely, it is in this essay that the *grip* of tradition on a political actor is decisively loosened in the sense of the earlier conception, which even implied the notion of a 'process-like' change. Whereas previously the job of a politician was to add to the past achievements and to stand between the past, present and future, he or she now primarily observes the current human circumstance, which most importantly denotes *individuality* – people's preference for making their own choices.[381]

Importantly, he reminds us of the Goetheian notion that:

[379] E. Devons 1956, p. 843.
[380] M. Oakeshott 1962, *The Study of Politics in a University*, RP, p. 218.
[381] M. Oakeshott 1956, *On Being Conservative*, RP, p. 427.

> Reflection may bring to light an appropriate gratefulness for what
> is available, and consequently the acknowledgement of a gift or
> an inheritance from the past; but there is no mere idolizing of
> what is past and gone. What is esteemed is the present; and it is
> esteemed not on account of its connections with a remote antiq-
> uity, nor because it is recognized to be more admirable than any
> possible alternative, but on account of its familiarity: not, *Verweile
> doch, du bist so schön*, but, *Stay with me because I am attached to
> you*.[382]

In my view, this kind of shift towards the Hobsbawmian
idea of "invented tradition" is more important than is often
recognized.[383] At this point, tradition does not 'automatically'
have a past in itself, but in practical politics this 'past' must be
and *is* invented, as is already implied in the 1948 review of K.B.
Smellie, *Why We Read History*, in which history was perverted
for our own purposes.

In 1956, Oakeshott 'translated' his multi-faceted concept of
tradition into the terms of "general rules of conduct," which he
emphasizes as being man-made and the result of human
choices; tools to be used in various enterprises.[384] There are
multiple rules in any given society, and since the conservative
regards government as resting upon the "acceptance of the
current activities and beliefs of its subjects," the appropriate
form of political activity is to make and enforce laws (as rules
of conduct) that "reflect, and never impose, a change in the
activities and beliefs of those who are subject to them."[385] As
the *reflected* 'tradition' or past no longer 'hints' at the course of
action, it is "enough" for a politician of conservative disposition only to reply "Why not"? to the question: "Why ought
governments to accept the current diversity of opinion and

---

[382] Ibid., p. 408.

[383] See Bauman 1999, p. 133.

[384] This shift is perhaps more important than is often recognized since it is
Oakeshott himself who, especially in both the 1956 footnotes to *Political Education* in *Philosophy, Politics and Society* and in the 1962 edition of RP, clearly
directs us along this course towards the 'right' interpretation of the concept of
tradition. It is notable, however, that in the texts *written* after 1956, Oakeshott
does not revert back to using tradition as a grand concept, but categorizes it
along with, e.g., idioms and languages. One question is, however, why
Oakeshott left the essay unaltered in the 1962 edition. In Julian Franklin's
words: "Why… does a serious philosopher find it needful to rely on terms that
so poorly represent his real intentions"? J. Franklin 1963, p. 814.

[385] M. Oakeshott 1956, *On Being Conservative*, RP, p. 431.

activity in preference to imposing upon their subjects a dream of their own"?[386]

In short, the paradigm politician is still governmental with a "conservative disposition" that allows him to think and behave in certain manners, to prefer certain kinds of conduct and certain conditions of human circumstances over others and thus to be disposed towards making certain kinds of choices – to preserving and respecting the rules and favouring the familiar over the unknown etc. In addition, he understands government as a limited activity, the business of which is to keep its subjects at peace with one another – to "inject into the activities of already too passionate men an ingredient of moderation; to restrain, to deflate, to pacify and to reconcile."[387] The politician is now an interpreter of the present situation, and politics is an activity "in which a valuable set of tools is renovated from time to time and kept in trim rather than as an opportunity for perpetual re-equipment."[388] As the task of the politician is to bring laws as compulsory rules of behaving into a closer relationship with current beliefs and activities, it can be called a 'politics of innovation' but not of invention.

Oakeshott's view of a proper politician is emphatically that he entertains a conservative disposition towards governing, which is seen as almost synonymous to politics. He recognizes the contingency of the situation as being a result of human choices and he sees the beliefs and activities of subjects as constantly changing, *but* the politician's task is in a way to work against change: "like the 'governor' which by controlling the speed at which its parts move, keeps an engine from racketing itself to pieces."[389] Here, the politician is required to remain "indifferent"; neither laziness nor sheer vanity alone are sufficient characteristics of a politician. With respect to the government, the politician acts as an "umpire," who governs the rules of the game but is not one of the players. His opposite is "a private enterprise politician," who mistakes governing for any

[386] Ibid., p. 427. As it seems, this might well also be Oakeshott's answer to the later questions of why *cives* should go on acknowledging the authority in *respublica* – 'governing' is no longer almost synonymous to politics but is translated into 'ruling', although the 'anti-foundational' emphasis remains similar. One need not believe in the general ideas of the absolute value of free human choice or natural rights, but must merely accept the contingent, historic situation.
[387] Ibid., p. 432.
[388] Ibid., p. 431.
[389] Ibid., p. 434.

other activity, for example making and selling a brand of soap or developing a housing estate, and sees governing as turning "a private dream into a public and compulsory manner of living."[390] A private enterprise politician – a character corresponding to a 'demagogue' or 'leader' in *The Masses in Representative Democracy* (1961)[391] – appeals to people with wants so vague that "they prefer the promise of a provided abundance to the opportunity of choice and activity on their own account."[392]

In light of our earlier reflection, it may seem that Oakeshott now emphasizes the view of politics in which it is seen as an activity that is 'only suitable for gentlemen' and disregards the conditions of modern politics, although with a renewed understanding of the contingency of tradition. However, this is not quite the case. In my view, his choice of exemplifying the concept of general rules is by no means casual:

> Consider the conduct of a public meeting, the rules of debate in the House of Commons or the procedure of a court of law. The chief virtue of these arrangements is that they are fixed and familiar; they establish and satisfy certain expectations, they allow to be said in a convenient order whatever is relevant, they prevent extraneous collisions and they conserve human energy. They are typical tools – instruments eligible for use in a variety of different but similar jobs. They are the product of reflection and choice, there is nothing sacrosanct about them, they are susceptible of change and improvement; but if our disposition in respect of them were not, generally speaking, conservative, if we were disposed to argue about them and change them on every occasion, they would rapidly lose their value. And while there may be rare occasions when it is useful to suspend them, it is pre-eminently appropriate that they should not be innovated upon or improved while they are in operation.[393]

Though a bit hidden in the text, in light of the earlier reflection we can now elicit Oakeshott's defence of procedural parliamentary politics, which also includes the notion of political activity as a 'dirty game'. Namely, the next example of general rules of conduct in the text directly concerns the rules of a game:

[390] Ibid., p. 426.
[391] The essay was first published as *Die Massen in der repräsentativen Demokratie*, in A. Hunold (eds.), *Masse und Demokratie*. Erlenbach-Zürich and Stuttgart: Rentsch, 1957, pp. 189-214.
[392] M. Oakeshott 1956, *On Being Conservative*, RP, p. 432.
[393] Ibid., p. 422.

Indeed, the more eager each side is to win, the more valuable is an inflexible set of rules. Players in the course of play may devise new tactics, they may improvise new methods of attack and defence, they may do anything they choose to defeat the expectations of their opponents, except invent new rules.[394]

Politicians refrain from changing the procedures and rules of their own activity during the game, thus entertaining a conservative disposition towards them. However, the politician's game is thus also one of winning and losing, and the politician is not naturally required to exhibit "indifference" in, for example, parliamentary debating, but only in relation to governing, which must always be seen as a limited activity. In this respect, the question of what kind of politician occupies a given office is important to Oakeshott, regardless of, for example, his party affiliation. In the *current* situation of a 'pluralist' society, the government must be such that it respects this plurality. Oakeshott's account is that this kind of government goes hand-in-hand with a broad diversity of self-chosen enterprises in a society, and he clearly also would like to see this situation preserved. Since, in comparison to his earlier texts, Oakeshott relies neither on tradition nor exclusively on the 'traditional way' of doing things, the ball is now even more in the politician's court. And, since we live in an electoral system, it is up to the voters to decide both what type of politicians they wish to see in parliament and what kind of rhetoric persuades them to elect them. A private enterprise politician, or the demagogue, promising to make choices on behalf of the people, may face a situation that:

...is not at all as plain sailing as it might appear: often a politician of this sort misjudges the situation; and then, briefly, even in democratic politics, we become aware to of what the camel thinks of the camel driver.[395]

A strong relationship between the beliefs of 'subjects' and politicians, both those in government and those heading for government, thus exists; Oakeshott's view implies that a human being who cherishes her/his individuality also tends to vote for a politician who shows respect for this condition. In this respect, it is quite evident that Oakeshott's politician acts

[394] Ibid.
[395] Ibid., p. 432.

as an interpreter of moralities in terms of his or her relation to the laws.

In conjunction with this mostly chronological examination, there is not so much to be said about the development of the notion of the political actor in Oakeshott's thought in the late 1950s and 1960s. It would, however, be useful to highlight a few specific points prior to turning towards the ideal type of politician in *On Human Conduct*.

First, in both the essay *The Masses in Representative Democracy* and the Harvard Lectures (1958) Oakeshott continues to connect certain types of politics, as styles of governing, to certain corresponding moralities of subjects, as well as to express the duality of modern political life in these terms. In the Harvard Lectures, he notably says that writers are not "apt to argue from morals to politics or from politics to morals; moral and political beliefs and sentiments usually develop in interaction with one another. Consequently, they may be used to elucidate one another as text and context."[396] In this sense, we have come a long way from understanding a politician as a mere "mechanical interpreter" who has no proper connection to the "deeper consciousness of a society." Politics also affects morality, not simply vice versa.

However, whereas in *The Masses in Representative Democracy* Oakeshott still considers the art of politics as 'ruling' (in quotation marks) and the new art of politics as leading, in the Harvard Lectures he separates political activity from governing as the exercise of "authority by the rulers over the ruled," which may be "that of the leader, of the judge or of the administrator."[397] Thus, the character of the "indifferent" ruler disappears from his characterization of political activity. Instead, political activity is seen as a question of determining the manner and matter of government and considering the composition and conduct of authority.

In *On Human Conduct*, as well as in other writings from the 1970s, governing is, of course, further distinguished from 'authority' in both the ideal character of *societas* and the vocabularies of the state.[398] In addition, it is possible to interpret that Oakeshott found a 'solution' to the difficulty of theorizing political activity, the idiom of which "is ever ready to impose

[396] PFPS, pp. 27-8.
[397] Ibid., p. 8.
[398] OHC, p. 189, Oakeshott 1975, *The Vocabulary of a Modern European State*, p. 210.

itself upon the manner in which it is studied,"[399] by shifting his focus to the theorization of civil association and the appropriate understanding of political activity and actors solely as its derivative. This is still the most accepted view to this day.[400] Yet I hope to have laid the groundwork for an emphatically complementary, not alternative, interpretation of how we can detect a connection between Oakeshott's independently growing esteem for political activity and actors and his most refined philosophical description of politics in civil association. For example, in a review of J.R. Lucas's *Principles of Politics*, Oakeshott says that the disappointments of the book are that it "has more to say about the conditions of a 'civil' than of a 'political' society, more about government than about politics, more about *jurisdictio* than about *gubernaculum*, and nothing about the considerations involved in conduct of a foreign policy."[401] In cases such as this, Oakeshott displays a specific interest in political activity over, for example, government.

It is hard to single out any general attitude towards politicians and political activity in the British discussions of the late 1950s and 1960s, but perhaps it can still be said that Oakeshott's attitude belongs to the side of those who defend the way of doing things politically. The change in his own attitude towards politicians seems to reflect an understanding that is similar to Fairlie's account, i.e. that people who have contempt for their governors have taken the first step towards rejecting free institutions.[402] There is not so much a fear of even the demise of parliamentary institutions as a heightened appreciation for parliamentary procedures among 'liberal' writers, a category to which as wide a range of writers as Crick, Crossman, Fairlie, Hayek (to some extent), Miller and Oakeshott can be included in this respect.

This is particularly true if we compare this view with two other 'moods' of writing on politics at the time, the first being certain socialist theories in which the "distinctiveness of England becomes mere provincialism and the continuity of England is merely 'centuries of staple constipation and sedimentary ancestor-worship'," as J.H. Grainger describes Tom Nairn

[399] M. Oakeshott 1962, *The Study of Politics in a University*, RP, p. 218.
[400] See Oakeshott 1976, *On Misunderstanding Human Conduct: A Reply To My Critics*.
[401] M. Oakeshott 1967, A Review of J.R. Lucas: *Principles of Politics*, p. 227.
[402] H. Fairlie 1963b, p. 20.

and Perry Anderson's view.[403] The other example is, of course, "political science" in its various manifestations. Oakeshott wrote on this approach already in 1949 that:

> If you want to be frightened, read this book; as a portent of the end of civilised life it is far more unnerving than the atomic bomb. After forty, one naturally prefers a holocaust to the ignominy of being buried alive under the indiscriminating volcanic ash of 'social reconstruction'.[404]

Equating political science with psychology, sociology or even the natural sciences also usually meant detraction from the specific nature of politics as an activity.

For 'liberal' writers, politics is mainly a means of channelling change in a diverse society, and it is contrasted with any ideas of the existence of 'scientific' or 'certain' ways of doing things. In Miller's words:

> Politics is a means of getting things done, often with a strong sense of moral urgency; but it does not provide this urgency from its own process.[405]

In my view, the fact that Oakeshott avoids using the concept of interests in his description of 'proper' political activity is related to his more emphatic separation of political activity from economical activity or the concept of social classes than many of his contemporaries. In comparison with writers like Berlin, Crick and Miller, who essentially define politics as arising out of conflict, this often seems to suggest Oakeshott's stricter denial of the existence of conflicts between any 'ready' ends in a given society. Thus, in comparison with, for example, precisely Miller's conception of politics as an activity that is "always connected with government" and that aims at guiding the government in a particular direction, my claim is that especially after the shift in the Harvard Lectures, Oakeshott's conception of politics is better prepared to face the situation of 'new political movements', although this aspect remains speculative in terms of the philosophical outlook of *On Human Conduct*.

Lena M. Jeger, a Labour MP, wrote an excellent 'overview' of this problem already in 1959. She does not speak in terms of

---

[403] J.H. Grainger 1969, p. 260.
[404] M. Oakeshott 1948, A Review of Harold D. Lasswell: *The Analysis of Political Behavior. An Empirical Approach*, p. 326.
[405] J.B.D. Miller 1962, p. 23.

'politicization,' but we can see her as referring to the redefinition of issues that are to be tackled politically. For her, issues like abortion and homosexuality are ones in which "many Labour Party members refuse to see the political reality of the non-political."[406] She goes on to say that:

> Yet if they would only take an initiative on matters which concern the well-being of so many individuals it would quickly be reflected in the sensitive mirror of Parliament. If it happened in all the parties represented, the change would come more quickly. Then the Private Member with the lucky ballot paper would no longer face Ellen Wilkinson's problem of a good day on a big issue or a successful Bill on a little one. Parliament would be strengthened by the knowledge that people expected their representatives to deal fearlessly, through the political machinery of government, with the erstwhile non-political, the difficult personal problems of morality. For though in the end they are for each man and woman to face, it is for the politician and those he represents to ensure that no archaic law, no lack of finance, no prejudice in Parliament, complicates or exacerbates the combat.[407]

Jeger advocates more sensitivity by politicians, which would allow Parliament to be better prepared to respond to changing situations and the moral conceptions of the people. This account clearly corresponds to Oakeshott's idea that any "want" may serve as a catalyst for change in *lex*.

In 1975, Oakeshott emphatically applied the concept of practices in place of tradition in the context of the discussion of civil association. Importantly, the vernacular language of moral practices is plural, although it lacks any other specific essence. Practices are expressions of human intelligence which are never 'applied' and can be used only by virtue of having been learned and understood:

> This acknowledgement does not reduce conduct to a process or impose upon it the character of a *mere* habit. Customs, principles, rules, etc. have no meaning except in relation to the choices and performances of agents; they are *used* in conduct and they can be used only in virtue of having been learned.[408]

The language of morals is also emphatically not a fixed stock of utterances but "a fund of considerations drawn upon and used in inventing utterances; a fund which may be used in virtue of having been learned and being understood, which is

---

[406] L.M. Jeger 1959, p. 378.
[407] Ibid.
[408] OHC, pp. 57-8.

learned only in being used, and which is continuously reconstituted in use."[409]

In a civil association, moralities are thus in a constant state of change. They are pointedly expressions of human intelligence, and, in a sense, it is the 'task' of political activity to transmit these changes to the *lex*, i.e. into a system of law, the recognition of which relates *cives* to one another as equals in *respublica*. Although the relationship is not direct, the changing morals have certain effects on the changing practice of civil intercourse, i.e. it is "a situation of continuous responses to circumstances in terms of rules" which presents itself to political deliberation.[410] Politics is concerned with determining "the desirable norms of civil conduct and with the approval or disapproval of civil rules."[411] However, laws are not moral sentiments, and a politician must recognize and interpret changing moralities (or other "wants") and translate them into the language of civil intercourse in order to make political proposals.[412] In my view, Oakeshott intends here to specifically avoid any hints of speaking in terms of processes or 'automatic' systems in relation to political activity – as with human conduct in general. He emphasizes law as a human responsibility and politics as essential to the duration of civil association:

> Nevertheless, where association is solely in terms of *lex*, a procedure in which response may be made to notable changes of belief or sentiment about the desirable conditions of civil conduct by deliberately altering these conditions is at least the emblem of *lex* as a human responsibility and it may be said to be a condition of the durability of this mode of association. And while the terms of this procedure may be any that commend themselves to the associates concerned, it is conditional upon their being recognized as authoritative. In other words, legislative procedure in civil association must be composed of rules and it must be recognized as itself a component of the system of *lex*.[413]

Politics is distinguished from the accurate *authority* of the procedure of enacting laws,[414] and "legislative opinion"

---

[409] OHC, p. 120.
[410] Ibid., p. 178.
[411] Ibid., p. 174.
[412] Ibid., p. 180.
[413] OHC, p. 138.
[414] Again, I wish to accentuate that these procedures can also be changed and political proposals directed towards the procedures, and there is no "'constitution' not subject to interpretation and immune from inquiry." Ibid, p. 151.

'shaped' by politics is characterized by "the necessary absence of a ready and indisputable criterion for determining the desirability of a legislative proposal," which, in turn, is concerned with "the desirable composition of a system of moral, not instrumental considerations."[415]

Furthermore, 'private' and 'public' refer here to relationships, not to persons or places: 'public' relationships, like those between a ruler and his subject and *cives* to one another, are constituted by *lex* and, as such, are distinguished from 'private' relationships, in which, for example, rulers seek satisfaction of certain imagined and desired needs and wants by their subjects.[416] There is no room in civil association for anything but a conditional distinction between so-called 'private' and 'public' law, and *all* wants may set off the process of changing *respublica*.[417] In other words, no 'issues' or 'spaces' are, for example, private by definition in the sense of Arendt's *oikos*, or even in the sense of the private sphere of liberalism. In this sense, Oakeshott's conception is much more open to the 'politicization' of different questions. It is only that a political utterance must loose its idiom of, for example, moral (or economical etc.) sentiment in order to become a political proposal, the result of which is an obligatory rule prescribing "conditions to be subscribed to by all alike in unspecifiable future performances."[418]

To reiterate this point, politics in a civil association is concerned with an imagined and wished-for condition of *respublica* as being more desirable than its present condition. Politics is thinking and speaking, a deliberative and argumentative engagement directed towards reaching conclusions by persuading others of their cogency and identified in respect to their focus of attention and *subject of discourse*; a civil rule.[419]

In *On Human Conduct*, Oakeshott reiterates that he is not concerned with "what may go on in the head of a politician," but with the ideal engagement of politics as considering the desirability of rules.[420] He also states that there is nothing in the view that suggests professionalism in politics. On the other

[415] Ibid., p. 140.
[416] Ibid., p. 144-5.
[417] Ibid., p. 151, p. 169.
[418] Ibid., p. 163.
[419] Ibid., p. 165.
[420] Ibid.

hand, he emphasizes that – like morals – political activity can be conducted more or less 'civilly', i.e. 'artfully'.[421] Efraim Podoksik aptly describes Oakeshott's conception of human freedom in terms of "recognized contingency," which combines the notions of a genuine choice of action and an agent's awareness of having such a choice.[422] As such, politics as a deliberative, reflective activity is the 'heightened' "recognized contingency" of the human choice and situation: an ideal type of politician (whether professional or 'occasional') recognizes a civil association as constituted in terms of rules, having no other 'back-up' than their continuing acknowledgement as rules or *lex*. He/she also realizes that his/her concern is with the desirability of these rules; political engagement involves "disciplined imagination," or the focus of one's attention upon civility and the practice of just conduct. In Oakeshott's lyrical language:

> It is to put by for another occasion the cloudy enchantments of *Schlaraffenland*, the earth flowing with milk and honey and the sea transmuted into ginger beer, it is to forswear the large consideration of human happiness and virtue, the mysteries of human destiny, the rift that lies between the aspirations of human beings and the conditions of a human life, and even the consideration of the most profitable or least burdensome manner of satisfying current wants.[423]

In this view, a politician also accepts responsibility for his actions in an 'extended' sense; he is dealing with 'justice', not in the sense of the promotion of a preconceived notion of justice, but, rather, in terms of its definition. This represents one crucial distinction between Oakeshott's antifoundational political thinking and, for example, John Rawls's and Bruce Ackerman's style of identifying *jus* as the "consideration of 'fairness' in the distribution of scarce resources'."[424] In Rawls's and Ackerman's scheme, the task of a politician is solely to consider *lex* in the sense of improving its instrumentality in terms of achieving a certain substantive state of affairs which suits the theoretically preconceived state of *jus* as 'fairness'. A politician would only apply the basis of the society, i.e. 'fairness', in any given situation. Oakeshott, for his part, does not

[421] Ibid., p. 180.
[422] E. Podoksik 2003b, p. 57.
[423] OHC, p. 164.
[424] OH, p. 156n.

support such preconceived notions of justice, but also takes into account the evident contingency of the changing morals in a society. These changing morals have the potential to *generate a political proposal* in terms of civil intercourse and may result in the establishment of a rule in *respublica*. However, the inherent justice of civil association is manifested in *respublica* as a system of laws, and it has no direct connection to the morals that may have initiated the change in any particular law or laws.

Oakeshott recruits his image of the exploration of "intimations" in this context, although he now emphasizes that what pushes any chance to the "surface" in *respublica* – in the sense of the subject of discussion – is political intelligence and a "lively political imagination may recognise them before they are half over the moral horizon."[425] As choosing is emphatically an inherent part of the contingent situation – "to choose what in this circumstantial flux should receive attention" – a politician also in a sense constructs the situation for him/herself. In this sense, political activity in civil association can be referred to as the politics of innovation and *limited inventing*; an art that, as I already cited in the beginning of this book, "calls for so exact a focus of attention and so uncommon a self-restraint that one is not astonished to find this mode of human relationship to be as rare as it is excellent."[426]

I will conclude this section by presenting some further fragmentary remarks. It is a well-known fact that Oakeshott employed the vocabulary of the Romans, *lex, respublica* etc., in preference to modern political vocabulary in order to emphasize the theoretical character of his ideal types. Thus, I wish to emphasize that no direct 'deductions' with regard to real life can be made, although *On Human Conduct* does indeed also offer us excellent tools for analyzing contemporary political situations. In addition, I claim that a certain independent development of Oakeshott's conception of political activity in relation to political actors can be identified in the manner described in this chapter.

Furthermore, I mentioned the figure of the 'occasional' politician above. Classically, this expression naturally refers to Weber's characterization of the citizen voter as an occasional politician during elections. Here, I think the figure is assigned

---

[425] OHC, p. 180.
[426] Ibid.

another meaning, i.e. that of a citizen as *acting politically* when addressing a political proposal to the law-enacting authority. There is nothing preventing laymen from participating in political activity and from learning judgement and the skill of presenting political proposals.[427] Keeping in mind that Oakeshott admired the Roman political experience above all others in European history because the Romans showed a 'real genius for politics', the republican tradition can also be connected to Oakeshott's thought in this context.

Coats contrasts the republican tendency – the willingness to live and intentionally nourish the tension between particular political goals and the concern for the general framework of authority – with the democratic tendency to reduce a constitution to a mechanism of the ministration of immediate needs, usually physical and material, and the exclusion and demotion of the concern for formality when it comes to fidelity to authoritative procedures: "in Platonic terms, democracy is the regime of the body and its needs, because democracy loves equality, and bodily existence is the one thing we all have in common."[428] Oakeshott's deep understanding of the contingency of current arrangements and *lex*, and the role of politics in changing them, thus also implies an understanding, or at least a possibility of the 'republican ideal' of citizenship. He obviously still does not wish to turn politics into any kind of universal duty, but, rather, citizens in a civil association understand that, as Skinner put it, "the key contention is that public service, paradoxically enough, constitutes our only means of ensuring and maximizing our own personal liberty."[429] Oakeshott's conception of political activity as a type of argumentation, deliberation and reflection of the law which should not conflict with the prevailing educated moral sensibility capable of distinguishing between the conditions of "virtue," moral association ("good conduct") and those which should be imposed by law ("justice") is certainly demanding for both 'occasional' and professional politicians. Yet perhaps this talent is ultimately the only one that is capable of protecting "our individual rights" from the corruption of politics and politicians in the form of their temptation to make decisions

---

[427] Ibid., p. 165.
[428] W. J. Coats 1992, p. 102.
[429] Q. Skinner 1992, p. 222.

that are in line with their own interests and those of powerful pressure-groups.[430]

Continuity, Contingency and Change

"The concept of tradition is paradoxical," writes Zygmunt Bauman, it "prompts us to believe that the past *binds* our present; it augurs, however (and triggers), our present and future efforts to *construe* a 'past' by which we need or wish to be bound."[431] Bauman continues by distinguishing the concept of tradition from custom and habit, although he says that they are often used quite confusingly as synonyms. For him, 'tradition' (in quotation marks) refers instead to a situation which is all about thinking, reasoning, justifying – and, first and foremost, *choice*.

In light of our earlier reflection, this kind of definition distinguishes the early nuances of Oakeshott's conception of tradition as habitual from the ever present possibility to choose and the contingency of the situation, which was increasingly emphasized after the 1951 inaugural lecture, *Political Education*. In my view, however, even the most 'refined' interpretation of the concept of tradition as a situation of choice and its various implications for the understanding of political activity, e.g. in the Mouffeian manner, is an inadequate means of describing Oakeshott's late conception of political activity as presented above; Oakeshott rejected the concept for a reason. Thus, to highlight and complement my earlier points, I will briefly examine the concept from the viewpoint of the specific aspects of continuity, contingency and change, my point being that Oakeshott's journey towards understanding political activity in relation to time can be described as the shift from an orientation towards the past through an emphasis on the present to a certain opening of future situations. These characterizations are naturally caricatures and do not accurately present Oakeshott's conception at any point, but, with reservations, they can be used as useful illustrations.[432]

---

[430] Ibid., p. 223.
[431] Z. Bauman 1999, p. 132.
[432] Also, it must be noted that my perspective is still directed towards Oakeshott's conception of conducting political activity, not towards his notions of the 'traditions of political philosophy' or the history of political thought, with regard to which Oakeshott does not unconditionally belong to the category of those thinkers who perpetuate the notion of the 'crisis' of tradition in the manner of

To repeat, in 1947, the concept of tradition included the notion of change but not the notion of self-consciously induced change. For the sake of clarification, it is, of course, true that a tradition of rationalist politics is no less of a tradition than its skeptic 'opponent', but its understanding of the self-made change as following premeditated principles is false. Rationalist politics operates in a world of continuous crisis, whereas in 'rational' political activity the intellect acts as a critic of political habit, which is an inherent part of the rhythm and continuity of a society. Tradition refers primarily to the unconscious continuity of political practices, denoting a somewhat Burkean partnership between *present* and *past*.[433] Contingency appears here to imply that the direction of tradition is unpredictable and that a politician is thus obligated to face changing situations without the luxury of permanent instructions.[434] However, it is equally clear that Oakeshott's conception does not emphasize the notion of contingency as both an essentially interpreted situation and a chance to open up different futures.

In *Political Education*, Oakeshott regards traditions of political behaviour as guiding the direction of change and as tools to be used by people capable of doing politics. In contrast, a society incapable of politics is, for example, "a society in which law was believed to be a divine gift."[435] Thus, the relationship between change and politics is accentuated, and Oakeshott's conception also presents a contrast to theories of 'social contract'; our institutions and arrangements are no more significant than the "footprints of thinkers and statesmen who knew

Arendt, Leo Strauss or Eric Voegelin. See J.G. Gunnell 1979; 1986. There are certainly similarities in their analyses, but one cannot describe Oakeshott's view as that of Western political society today facing a crisis that is both caused by and exemplified in the decadent state or restricted circumstances of political theory. J.G. Gunnell 1986, p. 97. Although Oakeshott definitely agrees with Arendt with regard to the critique of thinking about political activity "in terms of an analogy of fabrication," he criticizes her view for "an occasional note of exaggeration," which appears in the general level of Arendt's writing: "the peaks are apt to appear higher and the valleys deeper than they are; the differences between Greek and Roman and between ourselves as we are and ourselves as we were larger; and the degree to which a disposition has managed to impose itself greater, than it really is." M. Oakeshott 1962, A Review of Hannah Arendt: *Between Past and Future*, pp. 89-90. It is to be noted, of course, that he might well have been of a different opinion in 1947.

[433] M. Oakeshott 1947, *Rationalism in Politics*, RP, p. 28.
[434] Ibid., p. 34.
[435] M. Oakeshott 1951, *Political Education*, RP, 56.

which way to turn their feet without knowing anything about a final destination."[436]

In relation to tradition and contingency, this phase of Oakeshott's political thinking has also often been emphasized in various interpretations. For example, Pocock draws parallels with F.S. Oliver's understanding of politics as "the art of the possible" and as therefore contingent, "the endless adventure," and Oakeshott's "boundless and bottomless sea" as playing with the contingent, unexpected and unforeseen.[437] Burke's "prescriptive government," which "never was the work of any legislator," and Oakeshott's sea metaphor are compared to one another.[438]

Tradition, however, supplies the resources for 'salvation' during times of crisis, and the thorough understanding of one's own political tradition makes all of its resources more available to us.[439] In connection with a more 'conscious' understanding of political activity, the authority of tradition is now "diffused between past, present, and future; between the old,

---

[436] Ibid., p. 64.
[437] J. G. A. Pocock 1975, pp. 8-9, see also, K. Palonen 1998, p. 12. At this point, Oakeshott's conception of contingency relates to political activity in the manner of mainstream philosophical tradition, which accentuates the "philosophical unintelligibility" of contingency – the practical politician is forced to face the intricacy of the world, but a political philosopher deals with 'eternity' (in the meaning of idealist language and the study of concepts). See Palonen 1998, p. 13. However, in Oakeshott's case this does not naturally mean that he does not deal with contingency philosophically, i.e. by means of an explanatory language, but that he understands contingency as an important factor that separates political activity from political philosophy. Later, in *OHC*, I think he speaks more emphatically about the specific contingency of "theorizing." It is 'unconditional' only in the sense of its being an attempt to understand a 'fact' or a "going-on" in terms of its postulates, yet every understanding is recognized as both a new "not-yet-understood" understanding and an invitation to understand. OHC, p. 2. As such, theorizing is pointedly also an open-ended activity, its ever-changing points of departure lying in contingent human activities. One 'oscillation' between the *vita activa* and the *vita contemplativa* is already indicated in *The Voice of Poetry in the Conversation of Mankind*, in which Oakeshott points out in a footnote that in Athens, 'politics' was understood as a 'poetic' activity in which speaking was not mainly the persuasion but the composition of memorable verbal images and the means of achieving 'greatness'. M. Oakeshott 1959, *The Voice of Poetry in the Conversation of Mankind*, RP, p. 493. In fact then, political activity actually gained some aspects of *vita contemplativa* in *On Human Conduct*. There certainly is a connection, although not an exact similarity, between Oakeshott's reflections and Arendt's views and use of concepts in this manner.
[438] J. G. A. Pocock 1968, pp. 215-7.
[439] M. Oakeshott 1951, *Political Education*, RP, p. 66.

the new, and what is to come."[440] A certain dimension of the deliberation of the future is thus added to the contingent situation, but the continuity and coherence of tradition remains in a dominant position: we "are aware of a past and a future as soon as we are aware of a present."[441] Political reasoning is directed mostly towards the exploration of the "intimations of tradition" and the exposure of its sympathies; it reveals the past and present, but the future is "not yet followed up," and Oakeshott emphasizes the importance of continuity, particularly in relation to "identity," which rather vaguely denotes, for example, the identity of British political life or manners.[442] In other words, the principle of tradition is *continuity* and "the changes it undergoes are potential within it":

> Nothing that ever belonged to it is completely lost; we are always swerving back to recover and make something topical out of even its remotest moments: and nothing for long remains unmodified. Everything is temporary, but nothing is arbitrary. Everything figures by comparison, not with what stands next to it, but with the whole.[443]

Importantly, here Oakeshott differentiates between the knowledge of a tradition of behaviour and the distinction between essence and accident. The knowledge of a tradition is "unavoidably knowledge of its detail: to know only the gist is to know nothing."[444] Furthermore, what has to be learned is a concrete, coherent manner of living in all its intricacy. There is some uneasiness in Oakeshott's view here, which is sometimes quite difficult to interpret due to his use of metaphorical language. In general, however, I think it is still rather safe to assume that his thought is not free from the implication that, once learned properly in practice, tradition somehow takes care of the individual occasions of political deliberation or 'reasoning'.

In *On Being Conservative*, however, in which Oakeshott stresses enjoyment of the present as the main aspect of a conservative disposition, he also says that "change is a threat to identity, and every change is an emblem of extinction."[445] The

[440] Ibid., p. 61.
[441] Ibid., p. 62.
[442] Ibid., pp. 57-9.
[443] Ibid., p. 61.
[444] Ibid., pp. 61-2.
[445] M. Oakeshott 1956, *On Being Conservative*, RP, p. 410.

specific *fortuna* aspect of contingency is accentuated, as he refers here to the hostile force of change. Since a community's or a man's identity is nothing more than an unbroken rehearsal of contingencies, a man of conservative disposition is working against change in order to preserve his identity.

In other words, he prefers an innovation that resembles growth, which is intimated and not imposed upon the situation. And, as it seems, humans are liable to err in their choices; it is better to stick with small and limited innovations, because there is no way to know the right course of action in advance. The disposition of a conservative is thus:

> …warm and positive in respect of enjoyment, and correspondingly cool and critical in respect of change and innovation: these two inclinations support and elucidate one another. The man of conservative temperament believes that a known good is not lightly to be surrendered for an unknown better. He is not in love with what is dangerous and difficult; he is unadventorous; he has no impulse to sail uncharted seas; for him there is no magic in being lost, bewildered or shipwrecked.[446]

In my view, this means that the 'legitimation' of politics – mainly as preservation and small innovations – stems from the acknowledged contingency of a community (and a man) and the acceptance of the present situation. As such, a politician looks for guidance primarily from the past and the present, not the future. The connection between past and present denotes the familiarity of the situation, and reflection may bring out a fair appreciation of what is available without idolizing the past.[447] Yet, in comparison to earlier accounts, the emphasis is more on the reflection of the agent and no 'automatic' connection between the agent and the past is suggested.

With particular respect to reflection on the notions of continuity, contingency and change, it is actually in the essay *The Activity of Being an Historian* (1958) that Oakeshott's reflection is radicalized more clearly in relation to tradition and political activity. On the map of human activities, it is now emphatically *the historian* who, because of the *direction of his attention*, is concerned with the past.[448] In addition, the 'past' is stressed as something that is no longer present, although it is sought in the

---

[446] Ibid., p. 412.
[447] Ibid., p. 408.
[448] M. Oakeshott 1958, *The Activity of Being an Historian*, RP, p. 153.

present. Although Oakeshott has also previously warned us about perverting history for our own purposes, and although his understanding of history as such is not entirely 'new',[449] I still consider this essay to be extremely important in relation to the development of his thought.

Here, the past is considered entirely in terms of its being an 'interpreted' past as opposed to an 'intimated' one; the task of the historian is to create the 'past' by a process of translation from the present situation, which always comes to us in the form of a "practical idiom."[450] The emergence of an historical past requires a certain attitude of indifference. An historian's world is a world without the unity of feeling or a clear outline, and it is a world composed entirely of contingencies as intelligible occasions. Human activities as such are understood as an intelligible convergence of human choices and actions, none of which are "'accidental'," but none of which are "'necessary'" or "'inevitable'" either.[451]

Furthermore, any 'truth' about the past is also distinguished from the world of practice and thus of politics. The politician relates to the past from the present situation by *constructing* "a 'living past', which repeats with spurious authority the utterances put into its mouth."[452] Oakeshott emphasizes regretfully that, now more than ever, the past is viewed in light of our moral and political opinions, which represents an important shift in the appreciation of the direction of political judgement in relation to the orientation of time. In terms of political activity, the past is even more emphatically *used* and constructed in the present in comparison to Oakeshott's earlier essays. I think that he also warns very seriously against a blind belief in any political persuasion that attempts to convince us of some entirely 'correct' interpretations of the past and its 'hints' about the future:

> If he is a politician, he approves whatever in the past appears to support his political predilections and denounces whatever is hostile to them.[453]

It is not that a politician should not consult the past in his judgement, but, rather, Oakeshott emphasizes that the past

[449] See EM.
[450] M. Oakeshott 1958, *The Activity of Being an Historian*, RP, p. 180.
[451] Ibid., p. 172.
[452] Ibid., p. 181.
[453] Ibid., p, 169.

does not bind us and our choices in the present. In my view, it is also noticeable that in relation to the interpretation and understanding of the 'past', it is now politics that stands in the way of the appearance of the 'historical' past, whereas previously it was religion.[454] As regards Oakeshott's conception of proper political activity, the 'retrospective' reflection upon politics now really loses its authority in the sense of hinting at a 'right course' of action.

As indicated earlier, in the case of *On Human Conduct* we can speak of the heightened understanding of the contingency of human situations and associations that is required of a politician. Interestingly, an LSE sociologist, Donald G. Macrae, presented a rather similar understanding already in 1958. For him, it has haunted the minds of philosophers and poets that the world is or might be proven to be contingent "since the time of Hume."[455] In the present situation, however, a sense of the contingency of things is not only the concern of a few, but a constant constituent of all action and judgement. Contingency is not just an aspect of the public and external world, but also of the private and internal being of each of us. He criticizes David Riesman's typology of character; the "other-directed" and "inner-directed" persons represent a certain over-simplification since for "the former the inner world must always be contingent, but to the latter it might seem rather an area of will and decision which could be shaped to an approved and necessary pattern."[456] For him, the totally other-directed view devalues political action if visions such as Orwell's are taken too literally in the context of the conditions of the West, where freedom and choice can be seen as an essential part of the historical recognition of contingency. Macrae argues in favour of the revival of politics and presents the view that the awareness of contingency is seen as a possibility of private and public choice, as well as of bringing about some approximation between desire and reality through one's own efforts:

> In time we will probably learn to live in a largely contingent world without taking any refuge in conformity or merely private interest. When that happens politics in the old sense will become more

---

[454] Ibid., p. 182.
[455] D.G. Macrae 1958, p. 126.
[456] Ibid., p. 127.

possible and natural. There will be less talk of "rethinking" for there will be the possibility of new thinking.[457]

As regards Oakeshott, the view he presented of contingency in 1975 implies yet another change of emphasis in relation to political activity. This view does not imply that Oakeshott now thinks that ideas appear before practice or tradition, to use the older terminology, but, in a sense, the change political activity brings about is always rethinking; it resorts to already existing arrangements. However, since the emphasis is on contingency as opposed to continuity in the sense of the historical or theoretical explanation of human conduct or politics, all changing and changed situations or constellations of rules are in a sense 'new', as pointed out also by the future-directed time orientation of a politician's reflection.[458]

In 1950s, Oakeshott clearly distinguished between the "characters" of "'diurnal'" and "'secular'" activity.[459] The latter was to be considered "in respect of the new situations it opens up; every action being recognised as creating a new situation by modifying an old."[460] By the former he was referring to an activity to be considered in "respect of its internal structure."[461] He regarded politics as a conspicuously diurnal activity as regards its established *continuum* of dispositions and limited range of choices developed during the last four centuries.[462] In *On Human Conduct*, politics is distinguished from ruling, which is described as a diurnal engagement.[463] Still, politics, too, includes 'diurnal' considerations which must be taken into account as tools of deliberation. For example, projected innovations should be such that the *respublica* can accommodate them.[464] In a civil association, the value of "continuity and economy in political innovation" is recognized.[465] Oakeshott's conservative disposition is recognizable in the case of this consideration, and he (again) 'legislates' that a political argument in favour of a rule that does not "destroy

---

[457] Ibid., p. 131.
[458] OHC, pp. 176-8.
[459] M. Oakeshott 195?, *The Idea of 'Character' in the Interpretation of Modern Politics*, WH, p. 256.
[460] Ibid.
[461] Ibid.
[462] Ibid., pp. 261-2.
[463] OHC, p.166.
[464] Ibid., pp. 178-9.
[465] Ibid., p. 180.

the coherence of the practice" is superior to one which might result in "one good rule" that neglects this aspect.[466] He also states that the consideration must not be read as an unconditional principle. Although "etymological decencies and syntactical proprieties" are taken into account in "a vernacular language of civil intercourse," they may indirectly be "modified in the new expressions proposed for use."[467] In general, Oakeshott emphasizes that deliberate political innovations are made by exercising political intelligence without reference to "even plausibly unconditional principles."[468]

In this spirit, in the first essay in *On Human Conduct* we encounter a human being, the "agent" in Oakeshottian terms, who is *not* "in the position, for example, of a chess-player who has to choose between a fixed number of alternative moves."[469] The act of choosing is to be identified with deliberation. Reflection in the service of acting may be said to be a postulate of conduct:

> The alternative actions he has to consider are his own inventions, and deliberating is not merely reflecting in order to choose, it is also imagining alternatives between which to choose. No doubt (unless he is a lunatic) he will limit his deliberation to actions which he has both imagined and also believes himself capable of performing. But if to this circumstantial condition is added the qualification that (in order to address himself to his situation) he must deliberate only those actions which are plausibly responses to it, that is scarcely a limitation.[470]

Contingency is postulated in an agent's understanding of his situation; it is, but it could have been otherwise and remains alterable. Also noticeable is the idea that an agent's situation appears as he himself understands it. Practices, as stipulating the general conditions for choosing, which are less incidental than the choices themselves, endow human conduct with a formality in which "contingency is somewhat abated."[471] Yet practices are also in a continuous state of modification in action. For an agent, a practice is an instrument to be played, and it is a language in which he "discloses and enacts

[466] Ibid.
[467] Ibid.
[468] Ibid.
[469] Ibid., p. 43.
[470] Ibid.
[471] Ibid., p. 74.

himself and upon which his performances may leave a deep, but never indelible, impression."[472]

The theorist understands human action as a performance in terms of "the reflection of a practice it throws back," i.e. in terms of its "conventionality."[473] Contingency presents itself in theorizing in terms of its rationality and as a significant relationship. Oakeshott accentuates that expressions like 'ill fortune' may be useful in diagnosing situations in order to be able to respond to them, but they only have place in theoretical language if *fortuna* is itself identified as a process.[474] In other words:

> A contingent relationship in the full sense, however, is a sequential relationship of intelligent individual occurrences where what comes after is recognized to be conditional upon what went before, not merely because before and after cannot here be reversed, nor (of course) because what went before is recognized to be functionally related, but because they 'touch' and in touching identify themselves as belonging together and as composing an intelligible continuity of conditionally dependent occurrences.[475]

"Touching" here means the absence of both intervals and a mediator between occurrences in the sense of a 'law' or a 'function'. In this sense, contingency is the main principle of understanding human action theoretically. It implies that an "unbroken continuity of occurrences," each of which a unity of particularity and genericity, is a 'making' of a theorist – not how a situation necessarily appears itself to an agent.[476]

Oakeshott's notion of contingency in *On Human Conduct* seems to me to be a sophisticated version of his earlier thoughts from 1958. The concurrence with his philosophy of history continues in *On History*, in which he presents the concept of an historian as reconstructing contingent relationships, viewing them as clearly distinct from other, 'falsely' understood relationships, such as causal or functional relationships. Here, a contingent relationship is also one of 'touching', and the passage of antecedent events manifests itself to an historian as a construction that resembles a 'dry wall', which has no "glue of normality" or "cement of general causes" between its

[472] Ibid., p. 91.
[473] Ibid.
[474] Ibid., p. 102.
[475] Ibid., p. 104.
[476] Ibid.

stones.[477] Here, contingency represents a circumstantial relationship in terms of evidential contiguity, not, for example, based on family resemblance or mutuality.

In *On Human Conduct*, Oakeshott emphasizes that a theorist must have a "deep respect for the individual action" when theorizing the contingent relationships between agents, although he is not one of the parties to the transaction he is theorizing.[478] It is, in principle, an 'historical' understanding, and as such it is more closely related to the 'past' (in a very theoretical sense) than to individual action. In contrast, however, the action of a politician is not related to the 'past', as the deliberate and known result of his action is a rule which prescribes conditions to be subscribed to by one and all in unspecifiable *future* performances. Political activity does not work against change, because contingency and change are built-in aspects of the understanding of "civil freedom" in a civil association, in which *cives* are related to each other only in their acknowledgement of the authority of *respublica*. If politics were understood in any other manner than as a (deliberate and reflected) channel of change in *lex*, it would not respond to agents' continuous modification of the vernacular language of morals in their performances and (desired) self-understanding as contingent agents. To reiterate, in my view, this is quite importantly what Oakeshott means when he says that the deliberate alteration of conditions is the emblem of *lex* as a human responsibility and a condition of the durability of civil association.[479]

The Analogy of Language

Hitherto, I have to a certain degree acknowledged the criticism directed at Oakeshott's early notion of tradition in politics as including the implication that intuitive judgement is decisive in politics.[480] However, in my view, for example Brian Barry's (1965) classification of Oakeshott in these terms is long overdue when keeping in mind that the *Rationalism in Politics* collection, which included Oakeshott's addition and reply to the criticism of the essay *Political Education,* already appeared in

---

[477] OH, p. 94.
[478] OHC, p. 106.
[479] Ibid., p. 138.
[480] B. Barry 1965, p. 17.

1962, and the 'developments' of his thought are also visible in the other essays in that collection. At the very least, the interpretation that "instead of relying on discursive reasoning men should put their trust in intuitive judgement" falsely represents Oakeshott as a sort of enemy of the linguistic turn.[481]

It must be noted that Oakeshott's scheme of rationalism in politics as a 'false' understanding of political activity was constructed mainly in the postwar context, in which, for example, rational behaviour was sometimes represented as controlled entirely by reflective thought and determined by the consciousness of its purpose.[482] A bit later, for example Walter Lippman, in his *The Public Philosophy* (1955), put forth the idea that we cannot rely on the production of good government by institutions if the people do not accept certain over-riding principles of social behaviour. Oakeshott criticized Lippman's "public philosophy" as a doctrine of Natural Law, which includes a belief in the absolute, rationally achievable principles of good life which serve as the foundation of liberal-democratic society.[483] In Oakeshott's view, "general political ideas are not the 'cause' or the 'foundation' of conduct, they are conduct itself in another idiom."[484] As such, I would also like to emphasize that Oakeshott, in a 1951 reply to his critics, equated his conception of tradition with that of a language in terms of the *logical* priority that it assigns to grammar over chronology.[485] He stresses that he does not aim at erasing political principles entirely, but, rather, at distinguishing between their proper and improper use. Here, Oakeshott accentuates that political activity travels without predestined and specified destinations, as do other human activities, and he also presents another alternative explanation of political activity and judgement than the 'politics of principles' or reliance on mere 'intuitive judgement'.

Greenleaf's interpretation of the "idealist" Oakeshott as having much more in common with T.D. Weldon and "linguistic analysis" than tends to be acknowledged deserves to

---

[481] Ibid, p. 57.
[482] See M. Oakeshott 1948, A Review of Morris Ginsberg: *Reason and Unreason in Society*, p. 414.
[483] M. Oakeshott 1955, *The Customer is Never Wrong*, p. 301.
[484] Ibid., p. 302.
[485] M. Oakeshott 1951, *Political Education. A Reply to H.G. Nicholas*, p. 701.

be recalled here.[486] In his view, Oakeshott and Weldon initially cohere in their understanding of politics as an essentially practical activity, as well as in the view that theoretical or transcendental thinking is irrelevant and can be misleading in practical judgement.[487]

Oakeshott reviewed T.D. Weldon's *The Vocabulary of Politics* himself, describing it as a "light-hearted" book in a positive sense,[488] although Oakeshott's appreciation of more 'traditional' political philosophy separated him from Laslett's "death of political philosophy" thesis.[489] As John G. Gunnell aptly put it, Weldon argued "that the whole tradition of political theory rested on the mistaken belief that values could be objectively determined and rationally defended."[490] With logical positivism serving as his background, Weldon denied single meanings for words like 'justice' and 'freedom' and argued instead that they only have uses.[491] He rejected democratic, Hegelian and Marxist foundational theories equally. Referring to democratic theory, he writes: "It is natural to suppose therefore that we have here fundamental rules from which others can be deduced. If this were so 'foundations' would be a suitable word for describing them. But it is not so. Nothing follows from these high abstractions, or if you like anything does... as foundations they are useless. They do not and cannot do what they purport to do, that is, serve as axioms from which practical conclusions can be derived."[492]

As anti-foundationalists, we can regard Oakeshott and Weldon as playing for the same team. Oakeshott, however, did not go as far as Weldon in maintaining that traditional political philosophy is merely verbal confusion, which, when tidied up, becomes a question of empirical difficulties which can be dealt with by writers on political institutions and statesmen.[493] It should also be noted that Oakeshott and Weldon were often seen as opposites in the context of British postwar political thought; the former being a "new" conservative and a skeptic, the latter purely a linguistic theorist. On the other

[486] W. H. Greenleaf 1968, p. 95.
[487] Ibid., p. 97.
[488] M. Oakeshott 1953, A Review of T.D. Weldon: *The Vocabulary of Politics*, p. 405.
[489] P. Laslett 1956, p. vii.
[490] J.G. Gunnell 1979, p. 9.
[491] T.D. Weldon 1953, p. 19.
[492] Ibid., pp. 97-8.
[493] Ibid., p. 192.

hand, they were seen as connected in terms of their shift from universal to national values, the limits they place upon the possibilities of reason and, therefore, their characterization as supporting the status quo.[494]

Greenleaf, though acknowledging the important roles of, for example, Hare, H.L.A. Hart and the earlier British idealists, characterizes Weldon as representative of the dominant contemporary view as regards the linguistic turn and political philosophy. Namely, in his view, Weldon's work is the only general inquiry into the vocabulary of politics and the logic of its concepts based on the advancement of the linguistic understanding that constitutes the revolution in thought associated with modern philosophy. As Greenleaf also concentrates his examination on the specific comparison of the *political aspects* of Oakeshott's and Weldon's thinking, I still see his pioneering work as compelling and illuminating also with regard to the theme of this book.[495]

In sum, the constitutive element in both Oakeshott's and Weldon's work is argumentation against foundational thinking in politics, also in the form of the search for 'proof' of an a priori or scientific nature.[496] The central question, of course, now becomes: "If political activity is not properly to be seen as guided by foundations or ideologies, how is it to be made intelligible and in what terms are practical appraisals to be made?"[497]

In this respect, Greenleaf's interpretation can be seen almost as a direct reply to Barry's view, although he does not mention this connection himself. First of all, Greenleaf accentuates that the repudiation of ideological abstractions or foundations is not intended to leave the field clear for subjectivism. In addition, it is Oakeshott's view that to see politics in terms of individual caprice is unsatisfactory both because it renders the activity rationally unintelligible and because caprice is never absolute or complete.[498]

---

[494] T.B. Peardon 1955, p. 495.

[495] Another possibility for examining this line of interpretation would be to concentrate on Pitkin's *Wittgenstein and Justice* (1972), but I prefer to limit my examination to Greenleaf's text because of its brevity. For further reading, see also Greenleaf 1966.

[496] W.H. Greenleaf 1968, pp. 98-9.

[497] Ibid., p. 99.

[498] See M. Oakeshott 1950, *Rational Conduct*, RP, p. 126.

Weldon, for his part, denies the character of political appraisals as a matter of personal interest, impulse, preference or habit – as does Oakeshott, particularly after the 1951 *Political Education* criticisms. It is, however, Oakeshott whom Greenleaf sees as having been more successful than Weldon in answering the question of how a political judgement is achieved when it is not based on a theoretical foundation, mere habit or personal feeling.

The answer Greenleaf provides is "the logic of tradition," which Oakeshott considers in a more satisfactory manner, although Weldon's view is also dependent on it. In *The Vocabulary of Politics*, Weldon often refers to the empirical context in which practical appraisals are made, "to rules of behaviour which are 'generally regarded' in particular countries," although he "irritatingly skirmishes" around the main theme, i.e. the consideration of the nature of such traditions of conduct.[499] On other occasions, Weldon's indebtedness to the idealist view of traditions can, according to Greenleaf, be illustrated in a number of ways, and the only real and relevant context of political appraisal is "that of a traditional way of life, the implications of which are being followed" in the sense of 'pursuit of the intimations'.[500]

Oakeshott's account of these matters is that traditions are composed of institutions, customs and rules of behaviour, but not in a completely consistent fashion. In Greenleaf's interpretation, there may be conflicts and contrasting pressures in this world of "'what is'."[501] Therefore, there is an inherent implication of the existence of a more uniform and desirable world, namely the world of "'what ought to be'." In short:

> And the life of practice, of morals and politics, consists in the never-ending attempt to transform the one into the other. An existing tradition of behaviour intimates lines of development, how it might be improved or made more coherent. And these possible lines of improvement are derived neither from outside the tradition (by reference to some independently premeditated standard), nor from personal prejudice simply, but from the mode of behaviour, the way of life itself. Political action (political decision, for instance) involves neither following a superior or transcendental law nor doing what one likes or what one's mere conscience dictates: it is action in accord with not simply established

[499] W.H. Greenleaf 1968, p. 101.
[500] Ibid., p. 103.
[501] Ibid., p. 104.

rules (this would be reactionary or invite a state of *stasis*), but established rules and what they, and the inconsistencies they contain, imply.[502]

In Greenleaf's interpretation, politics is the activity of attending to the arrangements of society, the amendment of existing arrangements by "pursuing what is intimated in them," i.e. by following the implied developments. These intimations represent the discrepancy between the more coherent desirable world and the existing system of rules, which can be reasoned. These intimations thus provide the 'basis', although not the foundation, for political judgement.

Greenleaf also notices similarities between the outlook of many contemporary philosophers with regard to language games and ordinary language, as well as the idealist consideration of established or traditional modes of activity. That is, in these cases it is supposed that "there is immanent in the language or tradition a rationale which in a sense justifies its existence or present form" – rather in the manner of Hegel's concrete universal.[503] For example, J.L. Austin's famous concept of "performative utterance" necessarily presupposes a moral system. In his *Philosophical Papers* (1961), Austin stressed that language "develops in tune with the society of which it is the language," adding that, for example, "the social habits of the society may considerably affect the question of which performative verbs are evolved."[504] In other words, carrying out the act of saying "I promise" does not take place in a moral social vacuum, but the circumstances of the performative utterance have to be appropriate and must include "an accepted conventional procedure."[505]

In relation to both ordinary language philosophy and Weldon's linguistic analysis, one advantage of Oakeshott's concept of tradition in relation to even his own philosophical 'modes' or 'idioms' is a certain greater acknowledgement of the built-in model of traditional British liberalism.[506] For Greenleaf, this acknowledgement is also actually better equipped to protect Oakeshott's thought from accusations of its blindly favouring the status quo; paying close attention to

---

[502] Ibid.
[503] Ibid., p. 104-5.
[504] Ibid., p. 116.
[505] Ibid.
[506] Ibid., p. 122.

the insights of what this tradition has to offer could constitute a valuable change of direction, "not least in respect of the philosophical analysis of such practical thought and activity as politics."[507]

Thus, although I have thus far engaged in a predominantly 'conservative interpretation' of Oakeshott's concept of tradition, we can also suggest that Oakeshott was even 'ahead' of the linguistic turn, specifically its 'second phase', in terms of its application to the social sciences. Wittgenstein, among others, acknowledges that linguistic activity always implies a 'culture' and that language is founded on convention. Yet most ordinary language or linguistic philosophers appealed to a standard that was included in the ordinary language of the time but neglected its historicity and 'politicalness', particularly in their concentration on everyday examples.[508] In this sense, Skinner's concept of convention in relation to the explanation of social actions in *Social Meaning and the Explanation of Social Action* (1972) resembles Greenleaf's interpretation of Oakeshott's tradition. Skinner speaks about the conventions surrounding this type of performance and attempts to identify the *point* of an agent's argument (like Machiavelli's *Prince*) in its relevant context.[509] Thus, a certain affinity can be identified between Oakeshott and Skinner, although with regard to the concept of tradition Oakeshott is not concerned so much with an agent's intentions, but more with "languages" in the Pocockian sense of providing "resources for determining your own response."[510]

How Oakeshott himself understood the potentiality of his conception of tradition is not always clear. The least we can say of Greenleaf's interpretation is that it is plausible. Oakeshott abandoned the concept because of its numerous – also ideological – implications, but this does not diminish its value in the context of the 'linguistic turn'. Oakeshott already speaks in terms of texts and contexts in, for example, *The Politics of Faith and The Politics of Skepticism*, indicating a rather 'mature'

---

[507] Ibid., p. 124.
[508] Ibid., pp. 116-22. Compare with Benjamin Barber's notion of the "policity" as the judgmental criteria of the intelligibility of a theory. B. Barber 1988, pp. 174-5. Barber also speaks of a theorist's 'work' as also including the *political* selection of postulates of human conduct to be explained or interpreted in relation to Oakeshott's thought.
[509] Q. Skinner 1972, pp. 154-5.
[510] J. Pocock 1985, p. 19.

understanding of the constituting role of linguistic activity in politics in the early 1950s, although the text was actually published posthumously. Here, *practice* may "occasionally explain itself in terms of an abstract idea," but it is conditioned by more general habits of conduct and reflects changes in the habit of conduct in question.[511] However, this practice is the context through which we interpret and understand individual actions, its intelligibility being that of a pattern rather than an argument. However, in this particular book, "while practice and talk unfold themselves candidly and in continuous communication with one another," at the centre of his attention are those writings of political thought which are "occasional utterances, interruptions in the flow of talk and practice, bearing always the strong impress of an individuality."[512] Oakeshott is thus capable of moving in both directions of interpretation in relation to practices (or 'conventions', 'contexts', 'languages', or even 'traditions') and performances.

This is also what his understanding of an agent in terms of self-disclosure (in terms of participating in a moral practice) and self-enactment (in terms of an agent's motives as sentiments in performances) in *On Human Conduct* tells us, although it is possible that he is applying Austinian thought here. For example, in *A Plea for Excuses* (1956), Austin drew a distinction between a justification, which denies that the performed action was wrong, and an excuse, which denies that the agent was responsible for performing it.[513] The latter type of utterance is seen as setting limits with regard to the ascription of moral responsibility by stating explicitly how they differ from the more common cases.[514] As a point of comparison, Oakeshott's understanding of self-disclosure is "choosing satisfactions to pursue and pursuing them; its compunction is, in choosing and acting, to acknowledge and to subscribe to the conditions intimated or declared in a practice of moral intercourse."[515] Furthermore:

> To act is to be a 'free agent'; and these conditions articulate in relationships, customs, rules, duties, etc., considerations currently

---

[511] PFPS, p. 6.
[512] Ibid., p. 7.
[513] I. Kemerling 2003.
[514] Ibid.
[515] OHC, p. 76. Compare with Arendt's disclosure of the agent in speech and action. Arendt 1958, p. 176.

believed to be appropriate in the intercourse of 'free agents'. Subscription to them is unavoidably indeterminate, and moral association may as easily founder in censoriousness as in indifference. But notable failure to recognize these conditions is to be *guilty*.[516]

Self-enactment is, for its part, the choice of the sentiments with which to act, and its compunctions are conditions of the 'virtuous' self-enactment that is intimated in a language of moral conduct. An agent sets his own 'self-criteria', and the conduct of notably failing to observe this condition is considered *shameful*.[517] It must be emphasized, however, that Oakeshott is not referring to ordinary language here, but to how human conduct is theoretically understood. Oakeshott stresses that there is nothing 'merely subjective' in performances, as they always exist in a relationship with practices.[518] They are not, in an Austinian sense, used in justifying or excusing, but are an essential part of the performance.

Thus, refraining here from delving deeper into any kind of methodological reflection, I would merely suggest that Oakeshott's theoretical conception of human agency and action include innovations that could be utilized in analyzing the performance of political agents in their contexts.

Ideology and Tradition in Political Activity

There is some irony in the fact that as soon as mainstream political theory began proclaiming "the end of ideologies" in the 1960s, the value of ideology actually became enhanced by Oakeshott, who had previously been one of the fiercest critics of ideological politics. It must be noted emphatically that this naturally implies a change in his concept of ideology and its relation to political activity, not his metamorphosis into a supporter of any particular ideology or a political philosopher with 'great plans' of some sort. That is, in Oakeshott's later conception of politics ideologies appear *as vocabularies to be used* in political argumentation and reflection.

Oakeshott's interpretation of the discussion of the "end of ideology" also differs from the mainstream. He considers disappointment of the hope of achieving demonstrative political deliberation with the aid of an 'ideology' as one of the great

[516] OHC, p. 76.
[517] Ibid., pp. 76-7.
[518] Ibid., p. 75.

traumatic experiences of the early 20th century and detects a slackening of impulse in this style of politics.[519] However, in its "current form," this hope expresses itself in the search for information that is expected to provide the 'correct' diagnoses of political situations and lead to 'correct' political decisions.[520] To cite:

> This enterprise is pursued, now, by many different methods: in the so-called comparative study of social organizations, governments and instruments of government; in the elucidation of ideal types – 'democracies', 'police states', 'one-party governments', 'totalitarian regimes'– in the collection of statistics and in the calculation of probabilities. And this enterprise has come to describe itself as 'the end of ideologies'.[521]

Oakeshott's understanding of the end of ideologies is thus actually quite different from, for example, Daniel Bell's notion. Famously, the latter proclaimed that the end of ideologies does not necessarily mean the exhaustion of *utopia*. Utopia as opposed to ideology, as the "ladder to the City of Heaven," is an empirical notion: "a utopia has to specify *where* one wants to go, *how* to get there, the costs of the enterprise, and some realization of, and justification for the determination of *who* is to pay."[522] Thus, if one takes this understanding as a paradigm of the end of ideology, it is no wonder Oakeshott modified his own use of the concept of ideology. I would like only to remind my readers here of his horror of the Lasswellian view of 'politics'. Oakeshott's conception of the 'negative' side of 'political action' developed into the terms of enterprise association, with its strong economic emphasis.

It is indicative of Oakeshott's heightened appreciation of political activity that one of his kindred spirits in this respect is once again Bernard Crick, who views the discussion of "the decline of ideology" as the decline of the (silly or harsh) 'ideology' of any given party or group as quite nonsensical.[523] In Crick's view, most neo-Marxists or 'student Marxists' are actually, "if our nerves are strong enough to see, anti-ideological."[524] According to both thinkers, the most naive belief in

---

[519] M. Oakeshott 1991, *Political Discourse*, RP, p. 92.
[520] Ibid.
[521] Ibid., p. 93.
[522] D. Bell 1960, p. 405.
[523] B. Crick 1963a, p.14.
[524] Ibid.

"ideological politics" had already predominantly been updated. Yet ideological beliefs are *not* to be replaced with the equally naive belief in undermining political activity and equating it with fabricating activity.

The change in the attitude and understanding of ideologies is thus one visible aspect of the development of Oakeshott's conception of politics towards a pointedly deliberative and reflective activity. As regards the concept of tradition, however, I think it is important to stress that 'tradition', or practice, is also one *consideration* that can be conceptualized and used *in* political conduct. In 1965, Oakeshott described 'tradition' as providing us with a number of 'intimations' (both concepts in quotation marks) that point in multiple directions; there are many messages but no categorical injunctions:

> Indeed, what we receive may be described as a number of aids to reflection to be used in deciding upon and in justifying our responses to practical situations. Our task is never that of judging conduct or a proposal by referring it to a unique and undeniable norm; it is always that of determining the relative importance, in the given circumstances, of the numerous, competing normative and prudential considerations which compose our 'tradition'.[525]

What is sought in political activity is a decision which promises "the most acceptable balance between competing goods; and what we expect in justification of a choice is argument to persuade us that what has been sought has been achieved."[526] In other words, for example ideologies in the form of our "current beliefs" are part of 'traditions' that can be invoked in political argumentation.[527] With regard to this view, we can understand that the vocabulary related to the understanding of the state as *societas* would offer a 'tradition' of political discourse that Oakeshott prefers in contrast to the *universitas* vocabulary, as examined in the chapter entitled *Talking Politics*.

One important aspect of the concept of ideology is thus Oakeshott's distinctive understanding of political theory, which he approximates with ideologies, also in his earlier production. In his review of Laslett's edition of Locke's *Two Treatises of Government*, 'political theory' appears as the ques-

---

[525] M. Oakeshott 1965, *Rationalism in Politics: A Reply to Professor Raphael*, p. 91.
[526] Ibid.
[527] Ibid., p. 92.

tionable enterprise of recommending a political position in the idiom of general ideas, and it is to be distinguished from political philosophy.[528] In *Political Discourse*, however, this kind of 'task' is *properly* limited to the sphere of ideologies. As such, here, we find yet another connection to Skinner's understanding of political theories as tools for the legitimation of politics, although Skinner's approach is of course much more 'approving' than Oakeshott's. Yet, despite their difference in attitude, their understanding of the specific expression 'political theory' is much more similar than in its more common comprehensions in Anglophone discussions.[529]

In the essay *Political Discourse*, the father of demonstrative political discourse is Plato, for whom the political situation was constituted by its 'injustice' and a political decision was seen as the recognition of this injustice.[530] Oakeshott is not, of course, anachronistically criticizing Plato for his philosophical understanding, but rather other writers who have understood that demonstrative discourse can be 'applied' to any concrete situation; it should be noted that "as soon as argument concerns itself with any contingent emergent situation (with what to do about a subject city in revolt, for example) it must relapse from proof into undemonstrative argument."[531] The search for demonstrative argument, whether in the form of the search for information in political theory or 'ideological' discourse in the 'old' and 'Marxist' sense, can at best "provide a vocabulary of beliefs in terms of which some marginally more reliable maxims might be formulated. These are not at all to be despised: they are what every politician has sought ever since the emergence of political activity. But maxims are not axioms, nor are they categorically informative propositions about human conduct."[532]

---

[528] M. Oakeshott 1962, A Review of P. Laslett (eds.): *Locke's Two Treatises of Government*, p. 100. In a later account, Oakeshott modifies his description of political theory, as will be elaborated in the last chapter of this book.

[529] In a review of Skinner's *The Foundations of Modern Political Thought*, Oakeshott says that Skinner has gone too far in suggesting that reflection on political theory as ideological permeates the entire genre of 'political thought', leaving out both instrumental reflection in service to administrative invention and philosophical reflection. M. Oakeshott 1980, A Review of Quentin Skinner: *The Foundations of Modern Political Thought*, p. 450.

[530] M. Oakeshott 1991, *Political Discourse*, RP, pp. 82-3.

[531] Ibid.

[532] Ibid., p. 94.

Thus, properly understood, political ideologies are an essential part of political activity and "vocabularies of beliefs, which invite political discourse."[533] This should be the understanding of the "logical design" of ideological discourse, as distinguished from demonstrative reasoning on the basis of 'axioms'. Proper political argumentation is concerned with contingencies, not necessities, and is reasoning designed to persuade in cases of decision and action in which the propositions in the proposal can neither be proven nor disproven.[534] Here, Oakeshott naturally invokes Aristotle's *Rhetoric* as a classic position from which to view the subject: reasoning may (but not necessarily) take a syllogistic form as *enthytheme*, and thus, a maxim is a general statement regarding what is usually to be expected in human conduct or normally considered desirable.[535] In short, as with all political discourse, although it lacks the ability to prove, this kind of 'ideological' discourse is used to persuade in a contingent situation in which there are possible alternative actions.

All political discourse, even the most informal, utilizes general abstract ideas, usually reverting back to some general ideas about notions of human conduct (compare with the use of 'justice' *in* political discourse and its use in 'explaining' political activity in political philosophy). However, how special vocabularies of 'ideologies' deviate from the common general vocabulary of political discourse (with words like 'public', 'private', 'revolutionary', 'Afro-Asian', 'war' etc.) is that they are comprised of a certain selection of words and thus compose a special vocabulary. This vocabulary is then used in the identification of political situations, as well as in the formulation, recommendation and defence of responses to them. This specialization often also imposes a particular and exclusive meaning upon some of the words included in the vocabulary. Oakeshott thus also views 'ideologies' in another respect than in terms of the logical design of their arguments, i.e. he sees the beliefs as comprising a vocabulary of political discourse with respect to their content: they are idioms of deliberation and

---

[533] Ibid., p. 77.
[534] Ibid., p. 80.
[535] Ibid., p. 78-9.

discourse in virtue of which, for example, 'liberalism' can be differentiated from 'syndicalism'.[536]

In Oakeshott's view, the variety of vocabulary among different 'ideologies' is not as great as it might appear, and the differences between them are often only marginal. They usually overlap each other, but nothing forbids "commerce between them."[537] Very importantly, however:

> Few of them are incapable of change; it is often possible to translate the terms of one into the terms of another, but, generally speaking, it is impossible to deliberate on political situations or to participate in political discourse without having some command over one of the special political vocabularies current in contemporary Europe. And these vocabularies have, of course, now spread themselves about the whole world.[538]

Ideologies are thus an inseparable part of political activity. In the 1960s, Oakeshott sees the 'old enemy' of political activity – as the belief in ideologies in the sense of their being 'projects of salvation' or representations of a single 'reality' of the *whole* human condition[539] – as having basically receded, at least in the Western, plural states. However, he does not join the chorus of those who support the 'end of ideologies', since it is actually "nothing of the sort" but instead indicates a more topical 'threat' to our *being* as historical agents. The understanding of 'political activity' has been condensed into the sole emphasis on economically oriented policy-making as related to 'politics' as making 'correct' decisions.

Thus, in Oakeshott's later conception of political activity, ideological vocabularies are tools to be used in contingent political situations. They can be used more or less skilfully, more or less flexibly and with a varying degree of 'conviction', but using ideological vocabularies does not imply any removal of the responsibility of an agent. That is, *whether or not*

---

[536] Political discourse can basically be approximated to 'tradition' here.

[537] Ibid., p. 76.

[538] Ibid.

[539] This kind of political deliberation is capable of generating a closed real–imaginary world of political situation which corresponds to itself, but which also *breaks if the insulation breaks down*. M. Oakeshott 1964, *Political Laws and Captive Audiences*, p. 298. In (Stalin's) Russia, the government rested not upon the truth of alleged 'laws' of social change, but upon the belief of its subjects' that they are true and effective. Although this view may also be a bit naive, at least in retrospect, it is important that Oakeshott here accentuates that this kind of understanding 'releases' the rulers, "the adviser of a ruler or whoever it might be, of any responsibility for his actions or recommendations." Ibid.

the political agent understands it, "prescription always entails judgement about what is better or worse, and these are always *doxai*, for they always relate to contingent situations."[540] A craving for demonstrative political argument may corrupt us by "suggesting that we have not got to make choices, sometimes on little more than the courage of our convictions, or by suggesting that we can pass off the responsibility for making these choices upon some axiom or 'law' for which, in turn, we have no responsibility."[541] In the essay *Political Discourse*, Oakeshott thus also explicitly hopes that this kind of thinking will not discourage the "only sort of intellectual effort capable of improving the quality of our political discourse."[542] By this, Oakeshott means the effort to understand our 'principles' and our 'admitted goods' in such a way as to recognize each as a choice we have made for ourselves regarding our own moral responsibility so that each 'principle' or 'admitted good' is given its due and none becomes tyrannical per se.[543] Oakeshott thus acknowledges the importance of both political activity and taking responsibility as regards the essential contingency of human life, and also expresses a means of improving political activity and political discourse as its inherent 'tool' in the direction of the conscious approval of such contingency.

We have come a long way with Oakeshott's changing conceptions of ideology and tradition and their relation to political activity from the late 1930s to the late 1960s and 1970s. However, the picture is still not complete and certainly does not sufficiently describe Oakeshott's scope as an historian, a philosopher or even a political thinker, especially in relation to the complex concept of tradition, which in all its nuances is sometimes connected to a view put forth by Edward Shils. Like Oakeshott, Shils also contrasts traditions with "rationalisation," sees the "tacit knowledge" of traditions as essential aspects of human knowledge and regards change and tradition as mutually dependent.[544]

My point, however, has been to illustrate how tradition has lost all its implications of being an 'automatic instructor' in relation to political actors, as well as how practices are point-

[540] M. Oakeshott 1991, *Political Discourse*, p. 93.
[541] Ibid., p. 95.
[542] Ibid.
[543] Ibid.
[544] E. Shils 1981.

edly considerations that are both used in reflected action and continuously modified in their use. Yet if "political discourse" is understood in terms of political 'tradition', we are naturally 'born into it' as historic beings just as we are born into other spheres of contemporary language. However, as the expression the "common stock" of vocabulary illustrates,[545] Oakeshott's paradigm politics is no longer distinctively British, but, rather, the inherently 'European' perspective of *On Human Conduct* should be taken into consideration when examining his work. The contrast to, for example, the view presented in 1949 is clear. Namely, then, English parliamentary politics did not centre around the promotion of a rationalist society but, rather, around the limitation of the exercise of political power and opposition to tyranny in any and all forms and the skepticism towards the perfectibility of a society or man.[546] The inherent danger in terms of the political education of citizens was that they would learn from 'ignorant foreigners' instead of their own political tradition. On the other hand, in the later account, the notion of ideology no longer represents a caricature of rationalist politics in Oakeshott's dual understanding of political activity, but is a vocabulary to be invoked in choosing within all political situations in our present conditions of modern politics.

4: Conclusion

We have now gained a window into the development of Oakeshott's conception of political activity by examining the concept pairs of power/authority and ideology/tradition. My aim has been to illustrate how Oakeshott's attitude towards politics has changed along with internal changes in his very conception or description of political activity. I have also examined the relationship of these changes to their contemporary context and observed both its distinctive and conventional aspects in this respect. For the sake of clarity, I will briefly reiterate my main points.

I began by arguing that the concept of power as used by the postwar Oakeshott was closely connected to the contemporary context. His negative treatment of power reflected the general atmosphere of postwar Britain, in which many politi-

---

[545] M. Oakeshott 1991, *Political Discourse*, RP, p. 73.
[546] M. Oakeshott 1949, *The Political Economy of Freedom*, RP, p. 388.

cal thinkers, such as Hayek, presented the concentration of power as perhaps the greatest fear in the British political situation. Oakeshott's postwar essays did not show any specific originality in this respect: power was rather conventionally equated with might and property. Yet in relation to his notion of rationalist politics, this kind of conceptualization of power also served as an instrument of critique. In Oakeshott's view, the attempt to assimilate politics with economic activity seriously corrupts politics. We must note, however, that Oakeshott also objected to other kinds of concentrations of power. His view of proper politics is that it is a limited activity, which he opposes to all kinds of 'politics of one plan'. In this sense, we can conclude that his postwar thought coheres with British liberal thought, as represented, for example, by Berlin.

In the 1950s, as well as in *On Human Conduct*, Oakeshott linked power especially to the concept of the 'anti-individual'. Similarly to Foucault's notion of ideas regarding subjects, power is seen as present in the formation of 'anti-individuals' via techniques of control and manipulation. Oakeshott's notion of the 'anti-individual' refers to a disposition that exists in all of us, which becomes actualized under certain conditions. One such condition is modern (rationalist) politics, which relies on the power of numbers as regards the election of leaders. 'Mass men' endow governments with unforseen power and bring about the amalgamation of authority or authorization to power. The consideration of authority as the right to make choices on behalf of others by referring, for example, to some substantive states, such as economic security, as an unconditional right, is a fetter to freedom. This is one of the central aspects of Oakeshott's critique of rationalist politics.

Authority, when clearly distinguished from power, is connected by Oakeshott to the positive side of politics or 'proper' politics. However, his style of closely associating authority with the ambiguous concept of tradition in the late 1940s and 1950s is problematic as regards the understanding of political freedom. This connection entails the implication that the governing authority always has the support of tradition, and that this support is understood as the 'right' way of doing things. This implication seems to be due in part to Oakeshott's paradigm understanding of politics as specifically British. For him, British parliamentarism is clearly authoritative in both the sociological and legal sense of the word; it is both voluntarily accepted by habit and entails the legal status of authority. I have attempted to emphasize, however, that, as regards traditions, Oakeshott never advocates a completely conformist view of human behaviour. Instead, individual caprice and, in his later conceptualization, variety in performances are always present. Accordingly, although the authenticity of law-making procedures in *On Human Conduct* cannot entirely be questioned without dissolving civil association, he emphasizes that procedures, such as constitutions, can also be changed through a political process. In *On Human Conduct*, it is notable that authority actually facilitates politics. It also enables civil freedom, since it does not appeal to expert knowledge or the approval of the content of laws. In civil association, citizens need only to acknowledge the authority of laws as adverbial considerations of their actions. Laws are not commands that demand a particular action, as is the case in an enterprise association.

Thus, Oakeshott most clearly distinguishes between concepts of authority and power when discussing them as categorically different vocabularies in European political discourse, which is always connected to the characteristics of modern states. Continuing his earlier criticism of rationalist politics and the 'power politics' of mass men, he emphasizes that power does not endow a person or an office with authority. The office of authority refers to the way that states are constituted as associations in terms of the acknowledgement of the authority of rules. Politics is related to authority because it involves what might be characterized as a kind of bargaining with the office of authority in order to prescribe laws. It is the process of deliberation over the desirability of laws and the promotion or withstanding of changes to them. Proper politics in the Oakeshottian sense would be impossible to achieve in a modern state without authority. In the context of the modern state, power refers to an apparatus of power that is linked with the office of authority. The mobilization of power is legitimate only if a subject fails to fill an obligation ascribed in *lex*. This is the only case in which a specific agent can be demanded to carry out a specific performance in a state that is constituted in terms of civil association. Laws are instrumental in an enterprise association and can be equated to commands. Oakeshott does not see this type of association as suitable to a modern state, this clearly representing one of the normative aspects of his theorizing. The preservation and reverence of individuality represents one of the central and continuing themes of his political thought.

The concept of ideology occupies a central place in Oakeshott's view of rationalist politics. He is famous for his critique of ideological politics, especially in the essays *Rationalism in Politics* and *Political Education*. His presentation of a pursuit of ideals as a misapprehension of the nature of political activity has also generated fierce criticism of his being both a conservative and even the ultimate skeptic.

In the British context, the understanding of political activity as ideological posed the threat of approximating British politics to Continental politics, with its more superficial parliamentary traditions. On the other hand, in his pessimistic mood during the late 1940s, Oakeshott saw British politics as already having surrendered to this kind of false understanding of political activity. Similarly to his critique of concentrations of power, he especially warns against those styles of politics which present either a ready-made, final end or one great plan for the organization and activities of an entire society. Keeping in mind the undertakings of the Attlee government, Oakeshott's critique of ideologies in politics can be seen as a topical commentary on the situation. Accordingly, some flashovers in his conception are perhaps now easier to comprehend. In connection with the concept of tradition, however, his description of ideological politics presents the clearest dichotomy with regard to his understanding of proper politics in its immediate postwar, conservative form. Oakeshott's description of rationalist politics reveals that he does not yet emphasize the role of individual deliberative activity in politics, but prefers instead to rely on 'unconscious' change within political tradition.

The substratum of this dichotomy was his earlier negative comprehension of political activity as a whole, not only its corrupted version. In 1939, he had argued that political activity has nothing significant to contribute to a society's traditions, but, rather, that their regeneration relies particularly on artists and poets. Political systems were seen as superficial, relying on deeper traditions of thought. In the immediate postwar accounts, however, *political* tradition was seen as the pinnacle of proper politics. It was comprised of the habit and conduct of

British politics and supplied the resources of politics itself. I argued that this versatile concept had a specific relationship to British parliamentary tradition. Oakeshott's characterization of politics as conversation acquires a more precise content as we understand that the 'habits' a politician must acquire in order to participate in politics importantly entail the art of participating in parliamentary discussions. Oakeshott's view of good political conduct thus involves the defence of the parliamentary style of politics in opposition to "democratic politics," which is understood as, for example, the government of the majority.

Thus, deviating from earlier interpretations of Oakeshott's conception of politics, I have examined the notion of the political actor and the figure of the politician at length. Although this figure is by no means central in Oakeshott's work, its development in terms of the attributes attached to it quite accurately illustrates the development of Oakeshott's attitude towards politics from an almost entirely negative conception into a positive one. Namely, in 1939, Oakeshott saw a politician as a potentially injurious figure in a society. His view was that the less a politician tries to do consciously, the better. The deeper spheres of a society and tradition would take care of the smooth running of a society. In 1947, when he expressed his distrust towards the existence of a healthy political tradition in Britain, it was still the role of a proper politician to act rather subconsciously by relying on tradition, despite the difficulty or even impossibility of doing so in that particular situation. On the other hand, the rationalist politician attempts to escape from the world of contingency to the world of (permanent) ideologies, mistaking the language of explanation and eternity for that of recommendation. It is notable, however, that in contrast to his earlier account, his negative attitude towards politics starts to be argued in terms of rationalist, corrupted politics, whereas politics as such begins to take on positive attributes. In the late 1940s, he contrasts the proper, traditional kind of politics with false understandings of political activity as similar to engineering or administration. A moderate, reasonable and skeptical politician is contrasted with a rationalist planner. A good politician possesses the skills of parliamentary conversation, although his activity is also more obscurely connected to tradition. His deliberation is directed more towards the past and present than the future, and he seems to rely on intuitive judgement in relation to the intimations of tradition. On the other hand, his account, particularly in *Political Education,* is also reminiscent of, for example, Fairlie's, Miller's and Crossman's later accounts of the political art of striking at precisely the right moment and thus cannot easily be dismissed as 'obscure conservatism', as was often done by his contemporary critics. Oakeshott's dismissal of argumentation in terms of unconditional principles is part of his defence of politics as an anti-foundational activity. In contrast to the ideas of mimetic representative democracy, Oakeshott's preference for situational argumentation emphasizes the politician's responsibility in all situations.

In 1956, Oakeshott sets even higher demands for a politician (in government); as the idea of tradition begins to lose ground in his concept of politics, laziness is no longer seen as an acceptable characteristic, as the politician is required to carry out increasingly 'conscious' activity. He is now the interpreter of a current situation and his task is to bring laws closer to current beliefs. A politician begins to take on the character of an innovator.

Then, in *On Human Conduct,* politics in civil association is presented as a deliberative, reflective activity, which I have characterized as a heightened recognized contingency. On the one hand, he sets strict requirements for a politician, while on the other hand he commends him and his activity. As opposed to a 'politician' in an enterprise association, a proper politician has no long-lasting, 'rational' end in sight that structures his actions. Instead, his action is structured solely by its object as a desirability of laws. In a contingent civil association, he has no other 'foundation' for his activity than this direction of reflection. I have named this phase of Oakeshott's theorization of political activity in relation to political actors and politicians as the politics of innovation and limited inventing. The earlier rather traditional conservative turned the time-orientation in his conception of politics away from deliberation towards the past and present to a deliberation between the present and future.

As a partly alternative interpretation to my earlier reflections, I presented Greenleaf's idealist interpretation of Oakeshott's concept of tradition. He compared Weldon and Oakeshott as anti-foundationalists who are both seeking an answer to the question of how a political judgement is arrived at without basing it on a theoretical foundation, mere habit or individual caprice. According to Greenleaf, Oakeshott was more successful in presenting the logic of tradition as an answer to this question. The political judgement is formed by considering the discrepancy between the more coherent world of 'what ought to be' and the existing system of rules. This is the meaning of the intimations of tradition. In comparison with Weldon, Oakeshott's understanding of tradition more clearly highlights the background assumptions of the inherent model of British liberalism in relation to the making of political judgements. This is also the benefit of Oakeshott's view in comparison to contemporary ordinary language philosophy as presented, for example, by Austin. Oakeshott's concept of tradition can easily be compared with both Pocock's notion of political languages as serving as resources for political action and Skinner's conception of conventions as an interpretative context of political action.

This linguistic potentiality of the concept of tradition seemed to be actualized in the 1960s both in the posthumously published essay *Political Discourse* and in some correspondences between Oakeshott and his critics. From 1958 onwards, Oakeshott substituted the concept of tradition with practices and used 'tradition' in quotation marks. He emphasized the role of politics as a rhetorical activity, and the concept of 'tradition' appears as one consideration which can be conceptualized and used in political argumentation. Accordingly, he also emphasized that he does not shy away from the use of principles in argumentation, although they must not be seen as unconditional truths, but rather as instruments of political discourse. Ideologies no longer belong exclusively to the sphere of rationalist politics, but they are understood as specific vocabularies of political discourse, without which European politics would be impossible in the present situation. In Oakeshott's late theorizing, ideologies are seen as tools of argumentation which can be utilized in contingent political situations. They may aid our political reflection, but must be recognized as contingent as 'traditions', practices, modern states and human life in general.

CHAPTER IV

Rationalism in Politics/Rational Politics

"Nobody's perfect," as the saying goes. This saying provides a partial answer to my question of how Oakeshott should be characterized as a political philosopher, particularly with regard to his conception of political activity in the context of British postwar political thought. More aptly, it characterizes the perspectivist picture I have drawn in this book. But, as for Oakeshott, this characterization is by no means pejorative: Oakeshott consciously avoided the notion of the possibility of attaining perfection, even in philosophy, adding that any endeavour to do so in human life would be both inherently impossible and a sign of stagnation. This description suggests that we should view Oakeshott as an extraordinarily profound and versatile thinker who meets the 'demands' of real life contexts in his thinking without being absorbed by them.

Thus, one of my main arguments in this study has been that Oakeshott continually 'updated' and manipulated his own political thinking in response to criticism, contemporary political life, the continuous reading of other schools of political thought – both old and new – and simply by following the many 'intimations' of his own texts over the period of the five decades followed here. His re-descriptions were not always linear or consistent, but the single pervading thought of the endeavour to *understand* was sustained. Oakeshott may be a conservative in many respects, but in this connection the word 'conservative' also needs to be reassessed, at least in its most common political sense.

I hope that by concentrating on his shifting conceptions of political activity, I have been able to at least dissolve certain 'frozen' yet influential images of Oakeshott's thought, such as that expressed by Ernest Gellner in the following quotation:

> What does Oakeshott stand for? A certain romantic conservatism, a sense of historic continuity, an anti-intellectualism in politics which considers politics to be the rightful sphere of an instinctual or half-conscious wisdom, born of experience rather than conscious thought. This anti-intellectualism has a certain affinity with populism, but there is a crucial difference: the wisdom is credited not to a *Volk*, *Narod* or peasantry, but to a ruling class with roots and continuity. The pursuit of ideals, the implementation of abstract theories, all this is lumped together by him under the term *Rationalism*, which in his language is pejorative and is to be eschewed, and is indeed a symptom of political inexperience and immaturity… It is not the job of government to implement ideals, but to keep the community going in an inherently and permanently imperfect world. The doctrine rather vacillates between seeing *tradition*, in the keeping of those long habituated to the exercise of political power, as a kind of very cunning and effective but gentle automatic pilot – the English water-colour version of Hegel's *List der Vernunft* – and the merely negative, pessimistic doctrine that no active theory- or ideal-inspired interference can do any good, and is bound to do harm, so that traditional, instinctive management, though not in any way guaranteed fool-proof is at any rate the least of evils.[1]

In addition, Oakeshott's legacy lives on in a positive manner in the thought of many others writers, both 'friends' and 'foes', although perhaps sometimes a bit one-sidedly. One example is provided by the conservative Ferdinand Mount, who describes politics as a practical mode of experience; "its task is to reconcile habits, not to intensify and explore sensation. The politician has to make friend not only of occasions but of individuals and groups to whom his heart may be hostile or indifferent."[2] It is not my intention to tell anyone how Oakeshott's conceptions of politics should be 'properly' used. Instead, we can see many of Oakeshott's metaphors on politics as conceptual innovations or reformulations which have been utilized in various ways in political thought.

However, my central aim in this book has been specifically to interpret his thought in a way that often does an injustice to

---

[1]   E. Gellner 1980, p. 12.
[2]   F. Mount 1972, p. 9.

the 'private language' of this marvellous stylist, having instead attempted to relate it to other lines of contemporary thought, or to translate his often concise descriptions into 'other words'. As such, prior to reflecting more on Oakeshott's legacy with regard to the theorization of political activity, I will take a brief glance back at some of his most famous metaphors and descriptions of political activity, thus reviewing some of my main points. For the sake of brevity, this chapter also represents a mere snapshot of my own analysis, but hopefully it will illustrate my main point that Oakeshott's conception of political activity really *did* change during the postwar period.

I still wish to stress that the *ambiguity* of Oakeshott's conceptions need mostly be understood as an interpretative and sometimes rhetorical device that he uses in order to bring his point to a head. Oakeshott thus rather coheres with Gallie's (1956) thesis of the essential contestability of concepts. However, as for the later Gallie, Oakeshott perhaps belongs to the category of those "political theorists" who have recently called attention to and been irritated by the ambiguity of the politics of words; this point is something that must still be accentuated.[3] Oakeshott's degree of annoyance varies, and for various reasons, as I hope to have illustrated here. Yet his understanding that "the patient analysis of the general ideas which have come to be connected with political activity – in so far as it succeeds in removing some of the crookedness from our thinking and leads to a more economical use of concepts, is an activity neither to be overrated nor despised" does not mean that he thinks *politics* should be 'organized' in an unambiguous manner.[4] Thus, Oakeshott's very basic observation of the diversity of the human character remains steadfast throughout his career if we think 'in terms of reality', but in order to describe this variation philosophically, we must view it in terms of extremes – whether in terms of "characters," "political dispositions," "styles of activity" or "vocabularies."

The first quotation derives from the essay *Rationalism in Politics*:

---

[3]   W. B. Gallie 1973, p. 442.
[4]   M. Oakeshott 1951, *Political Education*, RP, pp. 65-6.

> That all contemporary politics are deeply infected with Rational-
> ism will be denied only by those who choose to give the infection
> another name. Not only are our political vices rationalistic, but so
> also are our political virtues. Our projects are, in the main, ratio-
> nalist in purpose and character; but what is more significant, our
> whole attitude of mind in politics is similarly determined. And
> those traditional elements, particularly in English politics, which
> might have been expected to continue some resistance to the pres-
> sure of Rationalism, have now almost completely conformed to
> the prevailing intellectual temper, and even represent this confor-
> mity to be a sign of their vitality, their ability to move with the
> times. Rationalism has ceased to be merely one style in politics
> and has become the stylistic criterion of all respectable politics.[5]

First, both this essay and *Rational Conduct* (1950) are examples of Oakeshott's participation in both the 'old' and the contemporary discussion of the meaning of the notions of human
reason, irrationalism and rationality.[6] He dislikes the *vulgar*
Baconian and Descartian thinking with regard to the understanding of any human activities. In politics, rationalism can
be seen as an umbrella concept for various attempts to reduce
'politics' to administration, a scientistic understanding or economic fabrication. This is not at all as trivial as it may perhaps
seem today, as, for example sincere notions that 'fundamental
problems of government' are treatable by exact biological
methods occurred regularly in discussions on politics. Rational activity in relation to politics as well as to other activities is
both a deliberately laudable definition of the quality of that
activity and also stands for the advisable understanding of the
very word itself. We should also keep in mind that the period
immediately after the war was also a time of serious introspec-
tion for many political philosophers with regard to the causes
of the war and totalitarianism.

"Continental influences" represented a present threat to the
British way of life, the custodian of which should be politics.
The war itself, at the very least, imposed its rationalist vocabu-
lary upon politics and provided its 'executors' with full plan-

---

[5]   M. Oakeshott 1947, *Rationalism in Politics*, RP, pp. 25-6.
[6]   See, e.g., A. Koestler 1953, *A Guide to Political Neuroses*, pp. 25-32, L. Woolf
       1953, *Reason in Politics*, pp. 54-6.

ning mentality. Oakeshott understands contingency as belonging to the sphere of political life, but the typical contemporary prototype politician aimed at imposing rationalist, total plans upon a society. British parliamentary institutions offer no real 'protection' from rationalist politics as they can also be converted into devices of rationalist politics. The intellect in politics has ceased to inhabit its role as a critic of political habit, and there is no longer a partnership between the present and the past as the proper political tradition is actually dead: the British way of life as the 'enjoyment of rights and duties' is under threat of extinction. As the role of proper political activity in Oakeshott's understanding is to work rather instinctively in relation to a living tradition, there seems not to be much hope for the survival of the accustomed way of life.

In *On Being Conservative* (1956), the gloomy tone of desperation has receded. It is possible to consciously entertain a conservative disposition in politics, which also indicates a certain 'revived' trust in the parliamentary tradition. An historic condition of human individuality and diversity in society is possible to sustain without the support of a strong tradition:

> For most there is what Conrad called the 'shadow line' which, when we pass it, discloses a solid world of things, each with its fixed shape, each with its own point of balance, each with its price; a world of fact, not poetic image, in which what we have spent on one thing we cannot spend on another; a world inhabited by others besides ourselves who cannot be reduced to mere reflections of our own emotions. And coming to be at home in this commonplace world qualifies us (as no knowledge of 'political science' can ever qualify us), if we are so inclined and have nothing better to think about, to engage in what the man of conservative disposition understands to be political activity.[7]

Here then, a politician of a conservative disposition, an impartial ruler, understands that *everything* in human life is contingent and that the legitimation of political activity cannot be sought from any other realm than the present condition of things. For the most part, Oakeshott's view in this essay is very 'liberal' in its emphasis on the pacifying role of politics in a society of many projects, and in this respect his view was similar to other prominent British thinkers at the time – Berlin,

---

[7]   M. Oakeshott 1956, *On Being Conservative*, RP, pp. 436-7.

Fairlie and Miller were among those mentioned in this connection. In addition, the fear of tyranny of any sort, whether in the form of a group of people or one activity over another, is ever present – as it is in most postwar British liberal thought.

All in all, the endeavour of a conservative politician to "be at home" in the world is not only a very 'Continental' expression, but also an understanding that contingent situations need to be properly understood before they can be dealt with. Yet in spite of the demanding qualifications that a politician of a conservative disposition is expected to fill in this essay, the excerpt illustrates the fact that he only enters politics if he has nothing better to do, and Oakeshott's view is condensed in the conception that it is desirable to be radical in every other respect in human life, but not in politics.

However, it is my contention that Oakeshott himself is most radical in his understanding of political activity in his late work, *On Human Conduct* :

> Thus, the situation which presents itself to political deliberation, a practice of civil intercourse in use, is neither quiescent nor agitated; it is a situation of continuous responses to circumstance in terms of rules. And it is this situation which provides not only the subject of political deliberation but also the intellectual equipment available to be employed when critical attention fastens upon some small or large part of it and deliberate innovation is canvassed. There are some general ideas ready to be invoked, although they do not all pull in the same direction, but criterion of approval or disapproval untouched by contingency is necessarily absent. The desirability or otherwise of every proposed innovation must be argued in terms of the alleged defects of what is found wanting and the alleged virtues of what, on the occasion, it is proposed to leave unchanged. The anchorage of this deliberation and argument is a sea-anchor. Demonstrative conclusions are necessarily impossible; final solutions and alternative ideal systems of *lex* are persuasive subterfuges or corrupting delusions.[8]

Oakeshott's description of the "rare" and "excellent" intelligence which is required in political activity bears no connotations at all of his previous near disdain for politics. Here, of course, he is referring emphatically to the 'ideal character' of civil association as representing the context of political activity, but indications of a kind of 'self-correction' of his conception are clearly visible. The politician is no longer a

---

[8]   OHC, p. 178.

rationalist planner or solely interested in his own self-interest – the benevolent 'ruler' and the manager of enterprise association have largely acquired these characteristics. The aforementioned quotation summarizes Oakeshott's understanding of political activity as a deliberate response to contingent situations, which appears also as the agent's own reflected understanding of the situation. The aim of political activity is to bring about change in *lex*. Political activity is carried out by taking full responsibility for one's own actions and with the knowledge that one has no more solid support for making judgements than the formal practices, some 'political ideas' in discourse, and focus of attention. Contingency encompasses all aspects of political situations, but most importantly, although *lex* appears to a certain extent to abate contingency in civil association, for a politician, contingency is first and foremost a chance to change situations and open up different futures.

Thus, Oakeshott's conception of political activity is ultimately even more emphatically *anti*-foundationalist, historical and situational than it was, for example, in the 1950s. This aspect has of course been noted and examined by scores of other writers, and, as such, I will not delve any further into this discussion here, as my point lies elsewhere. Still, I would like to re-mention that Richard Rorty deserves to be recognized as perhaps the most important figure in the celebration of these features in Oakeshott's political thinking. In addition to the other interpreters already mentioned in this book, David R. Mapel also deserves to be singled out in this connection. He also points out how the uncritical appeal to 'our' traditions as the tendency to replace epistemic foundationalism with social foundationalism renders the overly intimate association of Rorty with Oakeshott suspicious.[9]

Perhaps it would still be illuminating to provide one more example of Oakeshott's 'living' legacy in today's political thinking. One self-confessed postmodernist describes the situation of the postmodern political agent as follows:

> The focus must be now on agency; more correctly, on the *habitat* in which agency operates and which it produces in the course of operation… Unlike the system-like totalities of modern social theory, habitat neither determines the conduct of the agents nor defines its meaning; it is no more (but no less either) than the set-

---

[9]   D. R. Mapel 1990, p. 403.

ting in which both action and meaning assignment are *possible*.[10]

Bauman's rather typical postmodern understanding of agency closely resembles Oakeshott's account in *On Human Conduct*. Here, however, it merely highlights that Oakeshott's thought is also relevant for philosophy and political theory after two decades.

Last, but not least, in light of the journey presented in this study, Oakeshott's master metaphor of political activity as a "boundless and bottomless sea" does not lose any of its glamour. With regard to its importance in the context of British postwar political thought, I think the following passage speaks for itself:

> The more profound our understanding of political activity, the less we shall be at mercy of plausible but mistaken analogy, the less we shall be tempted by a false or irrelevant model. And the more thoroughly we understand our own political tradition, the more readily its whole resources are available to us, the less likely we shall be to embrace the illusions which wait for the ignorant and the unwary: the illusion that in politics we can get on without a tradition of behaviour, the illusion that in politics there is anywhere a safe harbour, a destination to be reached or even a detectable strand of progress. 'The world is the best of all possible worlds, and *everything* in it is a necessary evil'.[11]

[10] Z. Bauman 1992, pp. 190-1.
[11] M. Oakeshott 1951, *Political Education*, RP, p. 66. The quote derives from the *Preface* to F.H. Bradley's *Appearance and Reality*. See T. Fuller, RP, 66, an editor's footnote.

CHAPTER V

The Voyage of Theorizing Political Activity

Is it mere coincidence that a philosopher of such subtlety and distinction as Oakeshott preferred to describe the activity of *theorizing* as opposed to philosophizing in the book that he must have regarded as his main legacy, or does it indicate the invention of a private linguistic style? We have seen earlier how the political theorist, with John Locke as a prime example, was a figure who was considered somewhat inferior to a philosopher. The political theorist's ambition to influence practical politics distinguished him from a philosopher. What does it tell us that in *On Human Conduct,* if read carefully enough, we are able to see that Oakeshott uses concepts of philosophical reflection and theorizing almost synonymously?

In my view, this shift in *On Human Conduct* marks another station pole in Oakeshott's understanding of human conduct and politics and most probably also posits a response to the earlier reception of his own *oeuvre.* It is simultaneously a conscious divergence from the ambiguous and muddled contemporary language that occurs through his reference to Greek terminology, his rethinking of the terminology in a more contemporary context and his suggestion of a more apt understanding of the theorization of human conduct in the English language.

Previously, in the *Introduction to Leviathan* (1946), it was the human predicament that was the main source of inspiration for the political philosopher, always appearing as some form of mischief, whereas a philosopher searches for the remedy in the universal. A political philosopher oscillated between the call of the eternity and *some* notion of perfection and the more profound acceptance of the contingency of human conduct and association, as well as the ultimate imperfectibility also in philosophy. As such, although I see him as having entertained the latter position for most of his career, it is in *On Human Conduct* that he wishes to clarify his position.

In *On Human Conduct*, *theorizing* is described as an activity which has no finality but only temporary "platforms" – *theorems* – which can be reached and resolved into a new not-yet-understood by another theorist.[1] Oakeshott emphasizes that philosophical reflection has a course to follow but no ultimate destination.[2] Theorizing, which remains constantly unconditional because all postulates are identities waiting to be understood, constitutes the calling of a 'philosopher'.[3] All that constitutes the unconditionality of the theorist's perpetual voyage is the continuous recognition of the conditionality of conditions, and thus a *theorist* may drop conditional anchors here and there without denying his engagement to be continuously *en voyage*.[4] The attempt to understand the postulates of human conduct, and thus to theorize human conduct and civil association, is a conditional engagement which is capable of having its own conditional 'truth'. In the theorization of human conduct the anchor dropped is the recognition of the ideal characters of human conduct as exhibitions of reflective intelligence. An agent is a reflective consciousness whose actions are the outcomes of what he understands his situation to be and in whose situation contingency is postulated.[5]

In my interpretation, an agent as a reflective consciousness may well apply the knowledge of a theorist in the formation of an understanding of his situation, although the theorization of moral conduct should not be confused with knowing how to subscribe to a moral practice.[6] Oakeshott does not deny that the conditional achievements of a theorist may be 'used' in the world of contingency, for example by broadening the horizon of one's self-understanding, but this is still not to be confused with offering guidelines to be followed. Oakeshott is only resentful towards the 'theoretician', as he does not recognize the contingent character of human conduct but seeks a definite

---

[1]   OHC, p. 2.
[2]   Ibid., p. vii.
[3]   Ibid., pp. 10-1.
[4]   Ibid., p. 11.
[5]   Ibid., p. 38; p. 41.
[6]   Ibid., p. 26.

understanding with which to *replace* the understanding of the agents themselves.[7]

As regards political activity, my suggestion is that, in keeping with his theorization of human conduct, Oakeshott's increased appreciation of the reflective character of political activity also suggests that an ideal type of a politician is now capable of engaging in a discussion with the theorist on rather equal terms, although the 'modes' or languages of explanation and practical conduct are still distinct as such. Just as a "cave-dweller" and a theorist may converse with one another,[8] the former perhaps, although not necessarily, having the chance to broaden the horizons of his imagination, I see that a *political actor* may consult a political theorist, whose theorization of activity is conditioned and qualified "by the word 'politics'."[9]

There are many ways of understanding this shift as regards the theory/practice relationship, if we even consider it as accepted. Robert Devigne has raised the question of whether the late Oakeshott could have been concerned with "creating, and not solely understanding, being-in-the-world"?[10] He wonders whether Oakeshott felt that the philosopher contributes to "the change of values posthumously, suggesting that his arguments for a separation of philosophy and politics were meant in the more narrow, prosaic sense"?[11] In Devigne's view, Oakeshott hints at the answer to this question in the prewar essay *The Claims of Politics*, in which he suggests that societies are led from behind by the artist, poet and philosopher. This view seems rather misleading, however, in its neglect of Oakeshott's increased appreciation of precisely political activity – it is not that a philosopher or a poet leads politics *from behind*, but that political activity and political theorizing are ideally conceived as relating 'playfully' to each other; the political concepts and ideal characters that a political theorist examines are also contingent; they change in political activity,

---

[7]   Ibid., pp. 29-30.
[8]   Ibid., p. 30.
[9]   M. Oakeshott 1973, *What is Political Theory*, WH, p. 401.
[10] R. Devigne 1999, p. 6.
[11] Ibid.

and one aspect of a theorized identity or character is always contemporary.[12]

Thus, Greenleaf actually 'discerned' these shifts already on the occasion of Oakeshott's retirement from the chair of the LSE. In his view, both Oakeshott and T.D. Weldon overlooked "something essential about the relationship between philosophy and practical activity."[13] In his view, at the very least this indicates that "when the philosopher himself turns from his professional preoccupation to political activity (in the wide sense of dealing with political problems) then he cannot, being the same person simply forget what his philosophy has taught him; he does not change when he changes his hat or alter simply because he turns and faces another way."[14]

In conclusion, my suggestion is that Oakeshott's late description of political activity as a deliberative engagement also implies his hope that political activity may to some extent utilize and learn from other activities as well as relate to them conversationally, without attempting to dominate them. Earlier, in Oakeshott's view, the poet, the scientist and the philosopher were not: "*Homo Sapiens* and *Homo Laborans*, the clever users of the resources of the world, but *Homo Ludens*, the one engaged in the activities of 'play'," i.e. "the civilized man."[15] In the essay *Talking Politics* – as is also indicated in *On Human Conduct* – Oakeshott also puts his trust in this 'civilized man' with regard to political activity,[16] although there is always also a 'serious' component in politics. He holds out a glimmer of hope that caring for conditions specifically in terms of civil association will be more common in the future. In terms of both the theorization and even the practice of politics, it is precisely this idea that I see as representing an important aspect of the legacy of this great political philosopher, who has broadened our understanding of the nature of political activity.

---

[12] See M. Oakeshott 1959, *The Voice of Poetry in the Conversation of Mankind*, RP, pp. 492-3.

[13] W. H. Greenleaf 1968, p.109.

[14] Ibid.

[15] M. Oakeshott c. 1960, *Work and Play*, WH, p. 313.

[16] M. Oakeshott 1975, *Talking Politics*, RP, p. 460.

Bibliography

Oakeshott References

Oakeshott, M. 1930. A Review of G.E.G. Catlin: The Principles of Politics. *Cambridge Review*, 51, p. 400.

Oakeshott, M. 1933. *Experience and Its Modes*. Cambridge: Cambridge University Press, 1985.

Oakeshott, M. 1937. A Review of K. Mannheim: Ideology and Utopia. *Cambridge Review*, 58, p. 329.

Oakeshott, M. 1939. *The Social and Political Doctrines of Contemporary Europe*. Cambridge: Cambridge University Press,1950.

Oakeshott, M. 1947. A Review of Professor William Aylott Orton: The Liberal Tradition: A study of the Social and Spiritual Conditions of Freedom. *English Historical Review*, 62, p. 262.

M. Oakeshott 1947. A Review of R.G. Collingwood: *The Idea of History*, English Historical Review, 62, pp. 84-86.

Oakeshott, M. 1947. Scientific Politics. A Review of Hans Morgenthau: Scientific Man Versus Power Politics. *Cambridge Journal*, 1, pp. 347-358.

Oakeshott, M. 1948. Contemporary British Politics. *Cambridge Journal*, Vol.1, No. 8, pp. 474-490.

Oakeshott, M. 1948: A letter to Karl Popper, January 28. In: www.michael_oakeshott_association.org/lifeworkspopper.pdf. Accessed in October 2003.

Oakeshott, M. 1949. A Review of Harold D. Lasswell: The Analysis of Political Behaviour. *Cambridge Journal*, 1, 1948, pp. 326-327.

Oakeshott, M. 1948. A Review of K.B. Smellie: Why We Read History. *Cambridge Journal*, 1, pp. 766-767.

Oakeshott, M. 1948. A Review of Morris Ginsberg: Reason and Unreason in Society. *English Historical Review*, 63, p. 414.

Oakeshott, M. 1949. A Review of G.C. Field: Principles and Ideals in Politics. L.T. Hobhouse Memorial Trust Lecture, *Cambridge Journal*, 2, pp. 444-445.

Oakeshott, M. 1949. A Review of Howard Selsam: Socialism and Ethics. *Cambridge Journal*, 2, pp. 692-694.

Oakeshott, M. 1949. A Review of J.D. Mabbot: The State and the Citizen. *Mind*, 58, pp. 378-389.

Oakeshott, M. 1950/1. A Review of R. H. Barrow: Introduction to St. Augustine. *Cambridge Journal*, 4, pp. 567-8, 570, 572.

Oakeshott, M. 1951. Political Education. A Reply to H.G. Nicholas. *Fortnightly*, 170, pp. 701-702.

Oakeshott, M. 1951. A Review of Thomas Wilson: Modern Capitalism and Economic Progress. *Cambridge Journal*, 4, pp. 504-506.

Oakeshott, M. 1953. A Review of T.D. Weldon: The Vocabulary of Politics. *Spectator*, 191, pp. 405-406.

Oakeshott, M. 1955. The Customer is Never Wrong. *Listener*, 54, pp. 301-302.

Oakeshott, M. 1956. Areas of Order. A Review of 'Minos of Minotaur' by John Bowle. *Spectator*, July 6, pp. 31-32.

Oakeshott, M. 1956. Political Education. In Laslett, Peter (ed.), *Philosophy, Politics and Society*. Oxford: Basil Blackwell, 1963, pp. 1-21.

Oakeshott, M. 1956. A Review of John Brooks: The Chatham Administration. *Spectator*, November 23, p. 746.

Oakeshott, M. 1957. A Review of Bertrand de Jouvenel: Sovereignty. *Crossbow*, 1, pp. 43-44.

Oakeshott, M. 1962. A Review of Hannah Arendt: Between Past and Future. *Political Science Quarterly*, Vol. 77, No. 1, pp. 88-90.

Oakeshott, M. 1962. A Review of Peter Laslett: Locke's Two Treatises of Government. *Historical Journal*, 5, pp. 97-100.

Oakeshott, M. 1964. Political Laws and Captive Audiences. In Urban G.R. (ed.), *Talking to Eastern Europe*. London: Eyre and Spottiswoode, pp. 291-301. (Oakeshott's talk in the series given originally in December 1963.)

Oakeshott, M. 1965. A Review of Peter Laslett & W.G. Runciman (eds.), Philosophy, Politics and Society. *Philosophical Quarterly*, 15, pp. 281-282.

Oakeshott, M. 1965. Rationalism in Politics: A Reply to Professor Raphael. *Political Studies*, 13, pp. 89-92.

Oakeshott, M. 1965. A Review of The Conservative Opportunity: 15 Bow Group essays on tomorrow's Toryism. *New Society*, 15 July, pp. 26-27.

Oakeshott, M. 1967. A Review of J.R. Lucas: The Principles of Politics. *Political Studies*, 15, pp. 224-227.

Oakeshott, M. 1975. *On Human Conduct*. Oxford: Clarendon Press, 1996.

Oakeshott, M. 1975. The Vocabulary of a Modern European State. *Political Studies*, 23, pp. 319-341, 409-414.

Oakeshott, M. 1976. On Misunderstanding Human Conduct. A Reply To My Critics. *Political Theory*, Vol. 4, No. 3, pp. 353-367.

Oakeshott, M. 1980. A Review of Quentin Skinner: The Foundations of Modern Political Thought. *The Historical Journal*, Vol. 23, No.2, 1980, pp. 449-453.

Oakeshott, M 1983. *On History and Other Essays*. Oxford: Basil Blackwell.

Oakeshott, M. 1989. *The Voice of Liberal Learning*. Fuller, T. (ed.), originally published: New Haven and London: Yale University Press. Indianapolis: Liberty Fund, 2001.

Oakeshott, M. 1991. *Rationalism in Politics, and Other Essays*. New and expanded edition. Fuller, Timothy (ed.), Indianapolis: Liberty Press.

Oakeshott, M.1993. *Morality and Politics in Modern Europe. The Harvard Lectures*. Letwin, S. (ed.), New Haven and London: Yale University Press.

Oakeshott, M. 1993. *Religion, Politics and The Moral Life*. Fuller, T. (ed.), New Haven and London: Yale University Press.

Oakeshott, M. 1996. *The Politics of Faith and The Politics of Scepticism*. Fuller, T. (ed.), New Haven and London: Yale University Press.

Oakeshott, M. 2004. *What is History? and Other Essays*. O'Sullivan L. (ed.), Exeter: Imprint Academic.

Other References

Al Anon 1951. Tradition in Politics. *Times Literary Supplement*, June 1, p. 341.

Al Anon 1962. Political Realities. *Times Literary Supplement*, September 28, pp. 1-2.

Amery, L.S. 1947. *Thoughts on the Constitution*, London: Oxford University Press, Third edition, 1949.

Annan, N. 1998. Foreword to Berlin, I. 1998. *The Proper Study of Mankind. An Anthology of Essays*. Hardy, H. and Hausheer R. (ed.), London: Pimlico, pp. ix-xv.

Arendt, H. 1958. *The Human Condition*. Chicago: The University of Chicago Press, Paperback edition, 1989.

Arendt, H. 1961. *Between Past and Future*. London: Penguin Books.

Austin, J.L. 1961. *Philosophical Papers*. Urmson, J.O. and Warnock, G. J. (ed.), Oxford: Oxford University Press, 1990.

Austin, J.L. 1962. *How to Do Things with Words*. Urmson, J.O. and Sbisá, Marina (ed.), Oxford: Oxford University Press, 1980.

Bagehot, W. 1872. *Physics and Politics*. In:
http://www.ibiblo.org/gutenberg/etext03/phypl10.txt
Accessed in October 2003.

Bagehot, W. 1867: *The English Constitution*. In:
http://www.ibiblo.org/gutenberg/etext03/thngl10.txt
Accessed in October 2003.

Ball, T. 1988. *Transforming Political Discourse*. Oxford: Basil Blackwell.

Ball, T. 2002. Confessions of a Conceptual Historian. *Finnish Yearbook of Political Theory* 2002, vol. 6, University of Jyväskylä: SoPhi, pp. 11-31.

Barber, B. 1988. *The Conquest of Politics. Liberal Philosophy in Democratic Times*. New Jersey: Princeton University Press.

Barker, R. 1997. *Political Ideas in Modern Britain. In and After the 20th Century*. London: Routledge. Second edition, first published 1978.

Barry, B. 1965. *Political Argument*. London: Routledge.

Bauman, Z. 1992. *Intimations of Postmodernity*. London: Routledge.

Bauman, Z. 1999. *In Search of Politics*. Cambridge: Polity Press.

Bell, D. 1960. *The End of Ideology. On the Exhaustion of Political Ideas in the Fifties.* New York: The Free Press. Revised edition, 1962.

Berlin, I. 1958: Two Concepts of Liberty. In Berlin, I. 1998. *The Proper Study of Mankind. An Anthology of Essays.* Hardy, H. and Hausheer, R. (ed.), London: Pimlico, pp. 191-242.

Berlin, I. 1962. Does Political Theory Still Exist? In Berlin, I. 1998. *The Proper Study of Mankind. An Anthology of Essays.* Hardy, H. and Hausheer, R. (ed.), London: Pimlico, pp. 59-90.

Berlin, I. 1988. The Pursuit of the Ideal. In Berlin, I. 1998, *The Proper Study of Mankind. An Anthology of Essays.* Hardy, H. and Hausheer, R. (ed.), London: Pimlico, pp. 1-16.

Botwinick, A. 2001. Wolin and Oakeshott. Similarity in Difference. In Botwinick, A. and Connolly, W.E. (ed.), *Democracy and Vision. Sheldon Wolin and The Vicissitudes of the Political.* Princeton: Princeton University Press, pp. 118-137.

Brecht, A. 1959. Political Theory. *The Foundations of Twentieth-Century Political Thought.* Princeton: Princeton University Press.

Burke, E. 1774. Members of Parliament and their Constituents. A Speech at Bristol on being Elected to Parliament of the City. In Hughes, A.M.D. (ed.), *Edmund Burke. Selections.* Oxford: Clarendon Press. Reprinted in 1921, 63-65.

Coats, W. J. 1985. Michael Oakeshott as Liberal theorist. *Canadian Journal of Political Science*, Vol. 18, No. 4, pp. 773-787.

Coats, W. J. 1992. Some correspondence between Oakeshott's "Civil Condition" and the Republican Tradition. *Political Science Reviewer*, 21, pp. 99-115.

Coats, W. J. 2000. *Oakeshott and His Contemporaries.* Pennsylvania: Susquehanna University Press.

Coleman, S. 1968. Is There Reason in Tradition? In King, P. and Parekh, B. C. (ed.), *Politics and Experience.* Cambridge: Cambridge University Press, pp. 239-282.

Collingwood, R.G. 1942. *The New Leviathan: or Man, Society, Civilization and Barbarism.* Boucher, David (ed.), Oxford: Clarendon Press, Revised edition, 1992.

Covell, C. 1986. *The Redefinition of Conservatism; Politics and Doctrine.* London: Macmillan.

Cranston, M. 1967. Michael Oakeshott's Politics. A Conservative Skeptic. *Encounter*, 28, January, pp. 82-86.

de Crespigny, A. 1968. Power and Its Forms. *Political Studies*, Vol. 16, No. 2, pp. 192-205.

Crick, B. 1962. *In Defence of Politics.* London: Penquin Books. Pelican Edition, 1964. Reprinted in 1983.

Crick, B. 1963a: *Political Theory and Practice.* London: The Penguin Press, 1971.

Crick, B. 1963b. The World of Michael Oakeshott. Or the Lonely Nihilist. *Encounter*, Vol. 20, No. 6, pp. 65-74.

Crick, B 1964. *The Reform of Parliament. The Crisis of British Government since 1960s.* London: Weidenfeld and Nicolson.

Crick, B 1991. The Ambiguity of Michael Oakeshott. *Cambridge Review*, 112, pp. 120-124.

Crosland, C.A.R. 1952. The Transition from Capitalism. In Crossman, R.H.S. (ed.), *New Fabian Essays*. London: Turnstile Press, 1953, pp. 33-68.

Crossman, R.H.S. 1952/53. On Political Neuroses. *Encounter*, 1, pp. 65-67.

Crossman, R.H.S. 1958. *The Charm of Politics*. London: Hamish Hamilton.

Dahrendorf, R. 1995. *LSE. A History of the London School of Economics and Political Science, 1985-1995*. Oxford: Oxford University Press.

Dawson, C. 1939. *Beyond Politics*. London: Sheed and Ward.

Day, J. 1963. Authority. *Political Studies*, 11, pp. 257-271.

Devigne, R. 1994. *Recasting Conservatism. Oakeshott, Strauss and the Response to Postmodernism.* New Haven: Yale University Press.

Devigne, R. 1999. The Legacy of Michael Oakeshott. *Political Theory*, Vol. 27, No. 1, February 1999, pp. 131-140.

Devons, E. 1956. The Role of the Myth in Politics. *Listener*, 21 June, pp. 843-844.

Dowse, R.E. 1961/2. Representation, General Elections and Democracy. *Parliamentary Affairs*, 15, pp. 331-346.

Fairlie, H. 1963a: The Life of Politics. Politicians, Statesmen, and Leaders. *Encounter*, 20, January, pp. 25-38.

Fairlie, H. 1963b : The Lives of Politicians. Ordinary and Extraordinary. *Encounter*, 21, August 1963, pp. 18-37.

Farr, A. 1998. *Sartre's Radicalism and Oakeshott's Conservatism. The Duplicity of Freedom.* London: MacMillan Press.

Foucault, M. 1979. *Discipline and Punish. The Birth of the Prison.* New York: Vintage Books.

Franco, P.1990a. Michael Oakeshott as Liberal Theorist. *Political Theory*, Vol. 18, No.3, pp. 411-436.

Franco, P. 1990b. *The Political Philosophy of Michael Oakeshott.* New Haven and London: Yale University Press.

Franklin, J.H. 1963. A Review of Michael Oakeshott: Rationalism in Politics, and Other Essays. *Journal of Philosophy*, vol. 60, No. 26, pp. 811-820.

Fuller, T. 1991 : Remembrances of Michael Oakeshott. *Political Theory*, Vol. 19, No.3, pp. 326-333.

Gallie, W.B. 1956. Essentially Contested Concepts. In Gallie W.B. (ed.), *Philosophy and the Historical Understanding.* London: Chatto & Windus, 1964.

Gallie, W.B. 1973. An Ambiguity in The Idea of Politics and Its Implications. *Political Studies*, Vol. 21, No. 4, pp. 442-452.

Gellner, E. 1957. Contemporary Thought and Politics. *Philosophy*, 32, pp. 336-357.

Gellner, E. 1980. The LSE – Contested Academy. *Times Higher Education Supplement*, 7th November, pp. 12-13.

Gerencser, S. 2000.*The Skeptic's Oakeshott.* New York: St Martin's Press.

Ginsberg, Morris. 1949. The Moral Basis of Political Conflicts. *Scrutiny*, 16, pp. 23-35.

Grainger, J.H. 1969. *Character and Style in English Politics*. Cambridge: Cambridge University Press.

Grant, R. 1990. *Oakeshott*. London: The Claridge Press

Gray, J. 1993 *Post-Liberalism*. New York and London: Routledge.

Gray, J. 1995. *Berlin*. London: Fontana Press.

Gray, J. 1997. *Endgames. Questions in Late Modern Political Thought*. Cambridge: Polity Press.

Greenleaf, W.H. 1966. *Oakeshott's Philosophical Politics*. London: Longmans.

Greenleaf, W.H. 1968. Idealism, Modern Philosophy and Politics. In King, Preston and Parekh, Bikhu C. (ed.), *Politics and Experience*. Cambridge: Cambridge University Press, pp. 93-124.

Gunnell, J.G. 1979. *Tradition and Interpretation*. University Press of America, 1987.

Gunnell, J.G. 1986. *Between Philosophy and Politics. The Alienation of Political Theory*. Amherst, Massachusetts: The University of Massachusetts Press.

Hammond, J.L. 1931. The Romance of the Nineteenth Century Politics. *Political Quarterly*, 2, pp. 224-240.

Hampshire, S. 1953. Human Nature in Politics. *Listener*, 3 Dec, pp. 947-948.

Hare, R.M. 1956. Can I Be Blamed for Obeying Orders? *Listener*, 13 October, pp. 593-594.

Harisalo, R. and Miettinen E. 1997. *Klassinen liberalismi*. Tampere: Tampere University Press.

Hayek, F.A. 1944. *The Road to Serfdom*. London and Henley: Routledge and Kegan Paul, 1979.

Hindess, B. 1996. *Discourses of Power. From Hobbes to Foucault*. Oxford: Blackwell Publishers, 2001.

Iivonen, J. 1995. Bibliografinen huomautus. In F.A. Hayek. 1995. *Tie orjuuteen*, Helsinki: Gaudeamus.

Jahanbegloo, R. 1992. *Conversations with Isaiah Berlin*. London: Phoenix Press.

Jeger, L. M. 1959. The Politics of the Non-Political. *Political Quarterly*, 10, pp. 367-378.

de Jouvenel, B. 1953. The Nature of Politics. *Cambridge Journal*, 7, pp. 451-465.

Kemerling G. 2003. J.L. Austin. In: http://www.philosophypages.com/ph/aust.htm. Accessed in September 2003.

King, P. 1968. An Ideological Fallacy. In King, Preston and Parekh, Bikhu C. (ed.), *Politics and Experience. Essays presented to Professor Michael Oakeshott on the Occasion of His Retirement*. Cambridge: Cambridge University Press, pp. 341-394.

Kocis, R.A. 1980. Reason, Development, and the Conflicts of Human Ends: Sir Isaiah Berlin's Vision of Politics. *American Political Science Reviewer*, 74, pp. 38-52.

Koestler, A. 1953. A Guide to Political Neurosis. *Encounter*, 1, pp. 25-32.

Koikkalainen P. & Syrjämäki S. 2002. Quentin Skinner on Encountering the Past. An Interview with Quentin Skinner, 4th October 2001. In *Finnish Yearbook of Political Thought* 2002, Vol. 6, University of Jyväskylä: SoPhi, pp. 34-63.

Langford, P. 2000. *Englishness Identified. Manners and Character 1650-1850.* Oxford: Oxford University Press.

Laski, H.J. 1938. *Parliamentary Government in England.* London: George Allen and Unwin Ltd, 1959.

Laslett, P. 1956. Introduction. In *Philosophy, Politics and Society.* First series. Oxford: Basil Blackwell, 1963, pp. vii-xv.

Lippman, W. 1955. *The Public Philosophy.* New York: Mentor, 1956.

Mabbot, J.D. 1948. *The State and the Citizen.* London: Hutchinson University Library, 1970.

MacCallum J.H. 1955/6. The Public Philosophy. *Parliamentary Affairs*, 9, pp. 195-202.

Macrae, D.G. 1958. Politics: Necessary and Contingent. *Political Quarterly*, 29, pp. 124-132.

de Madariaga, S. 1953/54. Where Do We Go from Nowhere? *Encounter*, 2, pp. 65-69.

Mapel, D.R. 1990. Civil Association and the Idea of Contingency. *Political Theory*, Vol 18, No. 3, August, pp. 392-410.

Marshall, G. 1960. Anglo-Saxon Platitudes. *Listener*, September 15, pp. 403-404, 423.

Maude, A. 1957. Political Tension and Social Reform. *Listener*, August 1, pp. 151-153.

McInnes, N. 2000. A Skeptical Conservative. *National Interest*, No. 61, Fall, pp. 82-88.

Miller, J.B.D. 1958. *Politicians.* Leicester: Leicester University Press.

Miller, J.B.D. 1962. *The Nature of Politics.* London: Gerald Duckworth and Co. Ltd.

Minogue, K.R. 1976. The Boundless Sea of Politics. In de Crespigny, A. and Minogue, K.R. (ed.), *Contemporary Political Philosophers.* London: Methuen, pp. 120-146.

Minogue, K.R. 1980. On Identifying Ideology. In Cranston, M. and Mair, P. (ed.), *Ideology and Politics.* Firenze: Badia Fiesolana, pp. 27-42.

Minogue K.R. 1991. Oakeshott and the History of Political Thought Seminar. *Cambridge Review*, October, pp. 114-117.

Moberly, W. 1949. The Crisis in the Universities. London: SCM Press.

Modood,T. 1980. Oakeshott's Conceptions of Philosophy. *History of Political Thought*. Vol. 1, No. 2, pp. 316-322.

Morgenthau, H. 1946. *Scientific Man vs. Power Politics.* Chicago: The University of Chicago Press.

Mouffe, C. 1993. *The Return of the Political.* London and New York: Verso.

Mount, F. 1972. The Literary Spirit in Politics. *Encounter*, 38, January, pp. 3-9.

Mure, G.R.G. 1949/50. International Socialism as Political Theory. *Cambridge Journal*, 3, pp. 541-549.

Nardin, T. 2001. *The Philosophy of Michael Oakeshott*. Pennsylvania: The Pennsylvania State University Press.

Nicholas, H.G. 1951. Political Education. *Fortnightly*, 170, pp. 535-539.

Nisbet, R. 1986. *Conservatism*. Milton Keynes: Open University Press.

Orwell, G. 1949. *Nineteen Eighty-four*. New York: Harcourt, Brace & World, Inc.

O'Sullivan, L. 2003. *Oakeshott on History*. Exeter: Imprint Academic.

O'Sullivan, N. 1976. *Conservatism*. London: Dent.

Pakenham, F. 1942. 'Grey Eminence' and Political Morality. *Political Quarterly*, 13, pp. 407-412.

Palonen, K. 1998. Das 'Webersche Moment'. *Zur Kontingenz des Politischen*. Opladen/Wiesbaden: Westdeutscher Verlag.

Palonen, K. 2003a. Four Times of Politics: Policy, Polity, Politicking and Politicization. *Alternatives*, Vol. 28, No. 2, 2003, pp. 171-186.

Palonen K. 2003b. *Quentin Skinner. History, Politics, Rhetoric*. Cambridge: Polity Press.

Palonen, K. 2003c. Translation, Politics and Conceptual Change. In *Finnish Yearbook of Political Thought* 2003, vol. 7, University of Jyväskylä: SoPhi, pp. 15-35.

Parekh, B. 1982. *Contemporary Political Thinkers*. Oxford: Martin Robertson.

Parekh, B. 1995. Oakeshott's Theory of Civil Association. *Ethics*, 106, pp. 158-186.

Peardon, T.B. 1955. Two Currents in Contemporary English Political Theory. *American Political Science Review*, 49, pp. 487-495.

Pettit, P. 1997. *Republicanism*. Oxford: Clarendon Press.

Pitkin, H. 1973. The Roots of Conservatism. In Coser, L.A. and Howe, I. (ed.), *The New Conservatism. A Critique from the Left*. New York and Scarborough Ontario: New American Library, 1974, pp. 243-288.

Pitkin, H. 1972. *Wittgenstein and Justice*. Berkeley: University of California Press, 1993.

Pitkin, H. 1976. Inhuman Conduct and Unpolitical Theory. Michael Oakeshott's On Human Conduct. *Political Theory*, Vol. 4, No. 3, pp. 301-320.

Pitkin, H. 1998. *The Attack of the Blob. Hannah Arendt's Concept of the Social*. Chicago and London: The University of Chicago Press.

Pocock, J.G.A. 1968. Time, Institutions and Action: An Essay on Traditions and Their Understanding. In King, P. and Parekh B.C. (ed.), *Politics and Experience* Cambridge: Cambridge University Press, 1968, pp. 209-237.

Pocock, J.G.A. 1975. *The Machiavellian Moment*. Princeton: Princeton University Press.

Pocock, J.G.A. 1985. *Virtue, Commerce and History. Essays on Political Thought and History, Chiefly in the Eighteenth Century*. Cambridge: Cambridge University Press.

Podoksik, E. 2003a. *In Defence of Modernity. Vision and Philosophy in Michael Oakeshott*. Exeter: Imprint Academic.

Podoksik, E. 2003b. Oakeshott's Theory of Freedom as Recognized Contingency. *European Journal of Political Theory*, Vol. 2, No. 1, January, pp. 57-77.

Popper, K. 1945. *The Open Society and Its Enemies*. London: Routledge and Kegan Paul, Fifth revised edition, 1969.

Karl, Popper. 1948. A letter to Michael Oakeshott, January 31st. In http://www.michael_oakeshott_association.org/pdfs/mo_lette rs_popper.pdf. Accessed in October 27, 2003.

Postan, M. 1947/8. The Revulsion from Thought. *Cambridge Journal*, 1, pp. 395-408.

Powell, E. 1969. *Freedom and Reality*. Kingswood, Surrey: Elliot Right Way Books.

Pulkkinen, T. 1996. *The Postmodern and Political Agency*. Helsinki: Hakapaino Oy.

Rayner, J. 1985. The Legend of Oakeshott's Conservatism. Skeptical Philosophy and Limited Politics. *Canadian Journal of Political Science*, Vol. 9, No. 2, pp. 313-332.

Raz, J. 1986. *The Morality of Freedom*. Oxford: Clarendon Press.

Riley, J. 2001. Interpreting Berlin's Liberalism. *American Political Science Review*, Vol. 95, No. 2, June, pp. 283-295.

Rorty, R. 1983. Postmodernist Bourgeois Liberalism. *Journal of Philosophy*, Vol. LXXX, No. 10, pp. 583-589.

Rorty, R. 1989. *Contingency, Irony and Solidarity*. Cambridge: Cambridge University Press.

Scruton, R. 1983. *A Dictionary of Political Thought*. London: Pan, in association with Macmillan.

Shils, E. 1981. *Tradition*. London: Faber and Faber.

Skidelsky, R. 1969. Politics is not Enough. On the "Dying Metaphor" of National Interest. *Encounter*, 32, January, pp. 25-33.

Skinner, Q. 1989. Meaning and Understanding in the History of Ideas. In Tully, J. (ed.), *Meaning and Context: Quentin Skinner and his Critics*. Princeton: Princeton University Press, 1989, pp. 29-67.

Skinner, Q. 1972. 'Social Meaning' and the Explanation of Social Action. In Laslett, P., Runciman, W.G., Skinner, Q. (ed.), *Philosophy, Politics and Society*. Fourth series. Oxford: Blackwell, 1972, pp. 136-157.

Skinner, Q. 1978. *The Foundations of Modern Political Thought I-II*. Cambridge: Cambridge University Press.

Skinner, Q. 1985. Introduction. In Skinner Q. (ed.), *The Return of Grand Theory in Human Sciences*. Cambridge: Cambridge University Press, 1985, pp. 3-20.

Skinner, Q. 1989. A Reply to My Critics. In Tully, J. (ed.), *Meaning and Context*. Princeton and New Jersey: Princeton University Press, pp. 231-288.

Skinner, Q. 1992. On Justice, The Common Good and the Priority of Liberty. In Mouffe, Chantal (ed.), *Dimensions of Radical Democracy*.

Pluralism, Citizenship, Community. London and New York: Verso, pp. 211-224.

Skinner, Q. 2002a. A Third Concept of Liberty. *London Review of Books*, April 4, pp. 16-18.

Skinner, Q. 2002b. *Visions of Politics. Vol 1: Regarding Method.* Cambridge: Cambridge University Press.

Spitz D. 1976. A Rationalist *Malgré lui.* The Perplexities of Being Michael Oakeshott. *Political Theory*, Vol. 4, No. 3, pp. 335-352.

Soltau, R. 1948. The Study of Political Science. *Political Science Quarterly*, 19, pp. 348-356.

Sparkes, A.W. 1994. *Talking Politics. A Wordbook.* London and New York: Routledge.

Strachey, J. 1956. *Contemporary Capitalism.* New York: Random House.

Subra, L. 1997. *A Portrait of the Political Agent in Jean-Paul Sartre. Views on Playing, Acting, Temporality and Subjectivity.* Jyväskylä: University of Jyväskylä.

Thomas, G. 2000. *Introduction to Political Philosophy.* London: Duckworth.

Tseng, R. 2003. *The Sceptical Idealist. Michael Oakeshott as a Critic of the Enlightenment.* Exeter: Imprint Academic.

Watkins, J.W.N. 1952. Political Tradition and Political Theory. *Philosophical Quarterly*, Vol. 2, No. 9, pp. 325-337.

Watson, G. 1973. *The English Ideology. Studies in the Language of Victorian Politics.* London: Allen Lane.

Weber, E. 1953/4. Political Language and Political Realities. *Cambridge Journal*, 7, pp. 408-423.

Weber, M. 1994. The Profession and Vocation of Politics. In Lassman, P. and Speirs, R. (ed.), *Weber: Political Writings.* Cambridge Texts in the History of Political Thought, Cambridge: Cambridge University Press, pp. 309-369.

Weldon, T.D. 1953. *The Vocabulary of Politics.* London: Penguin Books, 1955.

Winch, P. 1958. *The Idea of a Social Science and Its Relation to Philosophy.* London: Routledge and Kegan Paul. Eleventh impression, 1986.

Wolin, S. 1960. *Politics and Vision. Continuity and Innovation in Western Political Thought.* Boston: Little, Brown and Company.

Woolf, L. 1953. Reason in Politics. *Encounter*, 2, pp. 54-56.

Index

A

Ackerman, Bruce, 184

action (human), 7, 9, 25, 27, 34, 35, 39, 40, 47, 59, 65, 69, 73, 80, 87, 102, 114, 117, 124, 136, 138, 145, 162-3, 167, 174, 184, 191-7, 203-4, 204n., 205, 209, 210n., 212, 214-5, 225-6, 228
   government(al), 31, 34, 97
   linguistic, 11, 154
   political, 1, 17, 26, 30, 32, 35, 37, 67, 88, 101-2, 122, 134, 136, 143, 145, 152, 156-8, 158n., 162, 167, 171, 174, 184, 193, 201, 206, 217-8
   state, 45

agency, 16, 22-3, 25, 39, 45, 45n., 46, 46n., 49- 51, 65, 78, 114, 124, 205, 225-6

Amery, Leopold, 164

Anderson, Perry, 180

Annan, Noel, 44

Aquinas, Thomas, 127

Arendt, Hannah, 15, 21, 131, 138, 183, 188n., 189n., 204n.

Aristotle, 8n., 21, 126, 209

association, 7, 21-3, 29, 35, 51n., 68, 88, 98, 98n., 113, 119, 121-2, 124, 182, 186, 193, 205, 214, 228
   civil, 24, 29-30, 33-6, 39, 46, 50, 52, 54, 65, 67-9, 77-8, 80, 98n., 104-6, 110, 113-7, 122-4, 131, 136, 179, 181-6, 194, 197, 214, 217, 224-5, 228, 230
   enterprise, 35, 68, 73, 98n., 106, 114, 116, 121-3, 206, 214, 217, 225

Attlee, Clement, 62, 101, 215

Augustine, 8n.

Austin, John, 106

Austin, J. L., 202, 204-5, 218

authority, 9, 14, 33, 35, 40-2, 45, 50, 50n., 51, 54-6, 66-9, 71-5, 77, 80, 83, 85, 87-91, 94, 96, 98n., 100-25, 175n., 178, 182, 186, 189, 192-3, 197, 212-4

autonomy, 23, 25-8, 30, 33-5, 49, 135

B

Bacon, Francis, 96, 111, 222

Bagehot, Walter, 157-8

Ball, Terence, 25-6

Barker, Ernest, 127

Barker, Rodney, 148-9

Barry, Brian, 197, 200

Bauman, Zygmunt, 187, 226

Bell, Daniel, 19n., 206

Beloff, Max, 101

Berlin, Isaiah, 13, 18, 23, 36-42, 42n., 42-6, 49, 51-2, 78, 86, 93, 101, 136n., 140, 160, 180, 213, 223

Beveridge, William, 90

Bill of Rights, 67, 145

Bosanquet, Bernard, 72

Bradley, R. H., 6, 226n.

Brezezinski, Z. K., 141

Burke, Edmund, 21, 53-5, 60, 64, 188-9

C

capitalism, 68, 95, 149

Catholicism, 127-8, 130

Experience and Its Modes, 6, 70-1, 71n., 76, 82
Introduction to Leviathan, 74, 76, 112, 124, 227
The Masses in Representative Democracy, 176, 178
The Moral Life in the Writings of Thomas Hobbes, 77
On Being Conserative, 115, 173, 190, 223
On History, 6-7, 196
On Human Conduct, 6-7, 12, 21, 39, 46, 65, 69, 80, 82, 87-8, 92, 99, 105-6, 112-3, 117-8, 166, 173, 178, 180, 183, 185, 189n., 194-7, 204, 212-4, 217, 224, 226-8, 230
Political Discourse, 208, 211, 218
The Political Economy of Freedom, 4, 24, 62, 90-1, 94, 139, 164
Political Education, 6, 127, 152-3, 158, 168, 171-2, 174n., 187-8, 197, 201, 215, 217
Political Philosophy, 9n., 17, 71-2
The Politics of Faith and the Politics of Scepticism, 41, 112, 171, 203
Rational Conduct, 124, 222
Rationalism in Politics (collection), 5-6, 61, 63, 80, 144-5, 197
Rationalism in Politics (essay), 55, 82, 84, 86, 127, 132, 139, 146, 152, 155, 162, 167, 215, 221
Religion, Politics and Moral Life, 71
The Rule of Law, 105
The Social and Political Doctrines of Contemporary Europe, 127
Talking Politics, 118-9, 207, 230
Thomas Hobbes, 74
The Voice of Conversation in the Education of Mankind, 156
The Voice of Poetry in the Conversation of Mankind, 70-1, 76, 189n.
Oliver, F. S., 189
opposition, 55, 90, 149, 156, 164-5
Ortega y Gasset, José, 100
Orwell, George, 38, 86, 193

P

Pakenham, Frank, 165-6
Palonen, Kari, 83, 189n.
Parekh, Bikhu, 54, 116
Parker, John, 133
parliament, 31, 55, 100, 102, 148, 152, 177,
Parliament, 50n., 148, 150n., 153, 155-6, 169, 181
Peardon, Thomas B., 136, 149
philosophy, 5-8, 11, 15-9, 38, 46, 47n., 57, 59, 71, 71n., 72, 75, 77, 79, 81-3, 92, 126-7, 134, 144-5, 157, 196, 198, 200, 226, 228-30
linguistic (ordinary language), 126, 159, 168, 202, 218-9
political, 5, 7, 9, 9n., 10-11, 13, 18-21, 23-5, 37, 51, 53, 59, 66, 69-74, 77, 79-84, 87, 90, 103-4, 113, 126, 132n., 134, 137, 140, 145, 154, 168, 187n., 189n., 199-200, 208-9
Pitkin, Hanna, 62, 65, 88, 200n.
Plato, 9, 21, 126, 141, 166, 208
Podoksik, Efraim, 10n., 12n., 20n., 143n., 184
policy, 8, 14, 34, 52, 55-6, 60, 66, 86, 123, 166n., 167, 171, 179, 210
political activity, 2-3, 7, 9, 12-4, 16, 23, 37, 54, 58, 61, 63-4, 71-2, 79-83, 85, 102, 104-5, 109, 112, 122-5, 129, 133-8, 140-1, 145-8, 152, 154, 157, 157n., 158-63, 166, 168-72, 174, 176, 178-80, 182, 184-7, 187n., 188, 188n., 189, 189n., 191-4, 197-8, 200, 205-12, 215-7, 219-21, 223-6, 229-30
politician, 12, 19, 55, 58, 64, 83, 93, 97, 101, 103, 117, 143, 145-6, 148, 154, 155n., 158, 158n., 159-61, 161n., 162-79, 181-6, 188, 189n., 191-4, 197, 208, 216-7, 220, 223-5, 229
politics,
ideological, 131, 133, 135-7, 139, 146, 148, 205, 207, 215
parliamentary, 20, 159, 167, 176, 212
party, 102-3, 123, 133, 148, 164